MW01640149

First Edition

ISBN: 1-893619-32-X
Library of Congress Card Catalog Number: 2003102315

Historic Louisiana: An Illustrated History

author: William D. Reeves
photography editor: Carolyn Kolb
contributing writers for "Sharing the Heritage": Marie Beth Jones
Carolyn Kolb

Historical Publishing Network

president: Ron Lammert
vice president: Barry Black
project managers: Joe Neely
Robin Neely
Robert Steidle
director of operations: Charles A. Newton III
administration: Angela Lake
Donna M. Mata
book sales: Dee Steidle
graphic production: Colin Hart
Mike Reaves
John Barr

PRINTED IN SINGAPORE

The dress of Creole women of color in 1800s often infuriated the Anglo upper class, which believed that gay attire was their province.

COURTESY OF THE LOUISIANA STATE MUSEUM.

Contents

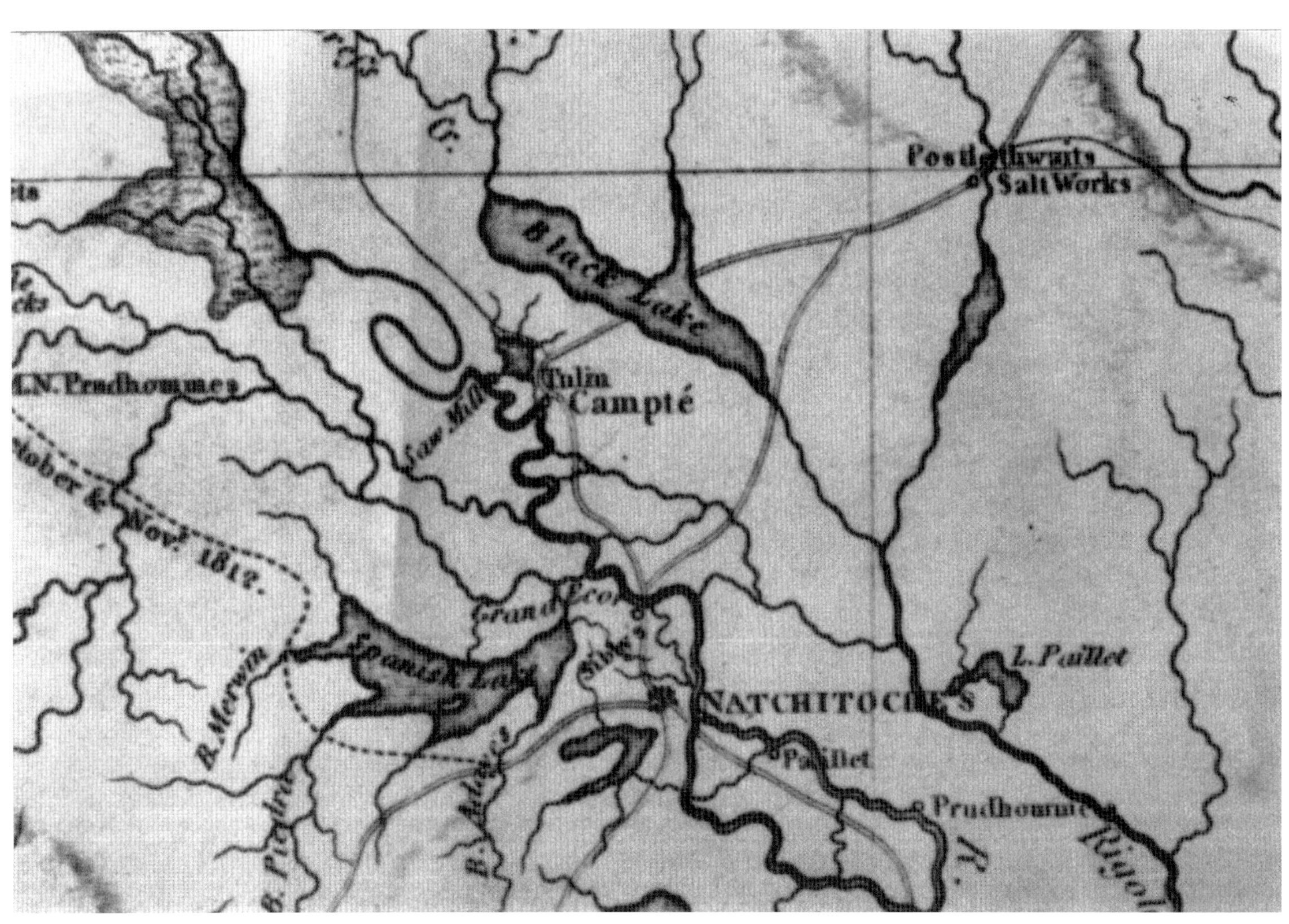
Salt Works
Black Lake
Tulin
Campté
Saw Mill
N. Prudhommes
Nov. 1812
Grand Ecore
Spanish Lake
B. Merwin
NATCHITOCHES
L. Paillet
Paillet
Prudhomme
R.

Chapter I

FOUNDATIONS OF LOUISIANA

Native Americans, Frenchmen, Africans, Acadians, Germans, and Spanish Isleños founded Louisiana in the eighteenth century. The frontier where they settled gradually dissolved their distinctiveness. The frontier operated with peculiar efficacy because isolation and opportunity led to generations of mixed heritage. Though European laws sought to preserve old world class and ethnic distinctions, in Louisiana's frontier environment they were a notable failure.

Louis XIV reigned in France when Europeans first settled Louisiana. Until then Louisiana had been just the uninhabited northern shore of the Gulf of Mexico along which convoys of silver from Mexico passed on their way to Havana and Seville. Spain had long ago claimed Florida, but settled only St. Augustine on Florida's Atlantic coast. As the seventeenth century wound down, England, France and Spain simultaneously realized that opportunity knocked. All three powers outfitted expeditions to colonize that northern shore, and all arrived in the first half of the year 1699. Spain headed for the best harbor nearest to Florida—Pensacola. France trained her sights on the mouth of the Mississippi River which Robert Cavelier de La Salle had explored two decades earlier, but contented herself with occupying Biloxi, just east of the river.

England hesitated initially. France's enterprising leaders Pierre Le Moyne d'Iberville and his younger brother Jean-Baptiste Le Moyne de Bienville made contact with the Native Americans. With their help they explored the natural connection between the Gulf Coast and the Mississippi via the lakes and bayous of present-day Orleans, Jefferson, St. Charles, and St. John the Baptist Parishes. In August 1699, Bienville penetrated Bayou St. John to the Mississippi River, where he embarked in Native American pirogues to explore downstream. There, just twelve miles below New Orleans, he met the first English explorers on their ship and convinced them that the French had already settled the area. The English ship turned around and departed. This turn has remained a memorable moment and place in Louisiana history. This double bend of the Mississippi River requires that a sailing ship ascending the river to anchor and wait for the wind to change at least once in order to get around all the bends.

✧

A map of the state of Louisiana with part of the Mississippi Territory from an actual survey by William Darby, 1816. This detail shows Natchihotches, with Grand Ecore to the north, then Tulin and Campté. Roads cross the Red River and head northeast. To the southeast the road crosses Isle Brevelle past Paillet and Prudhomme.

The sudden burst of interest in the Gulf of Mexico's northern shore is a characteristic of natural and human history. Change does not occur in steady predictable stages. Life and nature seem to remain motionless for long periods, until suddenly a dramatic change occurs. Change comes in a series of jagged breaks, with long stretches of peaceful rest between.

Louisiana's geology exemplifies this paradigm. The dominant factor in Louisiana geology is the Mississippi River and its delta. Six Mississippi River outlets formed during the past seventy-five hundred years remain identifiable in the geologic strata. They show that the river followed a certain path for a thousand years, while hidden forces prepared for a change. The bottom of the channel gradually rose while surrounding lands compacted and settled. Suddenly in a flood year the river burst through its banks to form a new channel to the Gulf. All the settlements of Deltaic Louisiana are located on banks of former branches of the Mississippi. There is no cultivatable land that was not once a river bank. Between the various historic branches of the Mississippi is the fabled Louisiana wetlands. It makes up forty percent of all the wetlands in the United States. Louisiana's pattern of land formation is quite different from land formation in the Midwest. There native grasses growing for millennia created vast fields of topsoil hundreds of miles in extent.

The former branches of the Mississippi have created a variety of natural features in southern Louisiana. One of the ancient streambeds, Bayou Teche, was part of the third Mississippi River meander belt from 6,200 to 3,800 years ago. More recently, deposits from the St. Bernard outlet closed in a former bay and created Lakes Maurepas, Pontchartrain, and Borgne. The older deltaic plain of western Louisiana has been shaped by other forces. Long thin lines of higher ground

✧

Above: Pierre Le Moyne d'Iberville was the most acccomplished of the Le Moyne brothers, but also the first to die. He led the expedition from France in late 1698 that first settled French Louisiana the following year. He planted the first forts at Biloxi and the lower Mississippi. He arranged for the settlement of Mobile and dispatched the largest group of early colonists. The European War of the Spanish Succession drew him into a naval war in the Caribbean where he died of yellow fever at the age of forty-five.

COURTESY OF THE HISTORIC NEW ORLEANS COLLECTION, 1991.34.3.

covered with oak trees running east to west define its coastline. North of this chenier plain are the Sabine, Calcasieu, Grand, and White Lakes.

The geologic structure of northern Louisiana consists of rocky layers that slope toward and under the deltaic plain. Time and weather wore down the softer rock into valleys. The harder rock formed higher land or hills. The further north in Louisiana, the older the geology. The Kisatchie Hills have ridge crests exceeding four hundred feet. Fragments of the Kisatchie Hills are the chalk hills, named for a fine white chalky rock, actually volcanic ash. Sicily Island was once the eastern end of the Kisatchie Hills. The Ouachita River created the "island" when it cut a gap through the Catahoula sandstone of Kisatchie and isolated it. The highest points in the state, Driskill Mountain, with an elevation of 535 feet, and Grand Encore Bluff, with an elevation of 150 feet, are parts of the Nacogdoches Hills. The Macon Ridge and Bastrop Hills consist of Early Wisconsin-age (20,000 B.C.) glacial deposits formed when the Mississippi River was just a braided series of smaller streams.

Native Americans flowed into the developing Louisiana as the Mississippi River gradually pushed soil southward, extending the coastline. The Poverty Point Native American site near Monroe, Louisiana, dates back twenty-five hundred years to when the Mississippi was oscillating in a wide bed between the Macon Hills and the cliffs of Natchez. By 1700, when the Europeans came to settle, the Native Americans had broken into numerous distinct groups. Chitimachas were south of Lake Pontchartrain and the Mississippi River; Muskhogeans were north of the lake. Their most famous tribe was the Houma, who spoke a Choctaw dialect. Bayougoula clustered at a single village on the site of modern Bayou Goula. Atakapas occupied southwest Louisiana. The Natchez were astride the Mississippi. The western group were the Avoyel people, near Marksville, known as traders or middlemen. Tunicas were further north, and Caddos were in the northwest. Numerous additional groups moved into Louisiana during the course of the eighteenth century. The Spanish invited Choctaw settlers from the east to occupy Bayou Rapides and the Ouachita River. In the nineteenth century mixtures of Native Americans expelled from the Atlantic coast and African Americans settled in western Louisiana along the Sabine where they acquired the name "Red Bones."[1]

The Native American presence facilitated European settlement. Native Americans explored the best lands to form villages. They knew the good waterways. Since they used fire extensively, they had cleared land for fields adjacent to their favored sites. When their fires had gotten out of control, large areas burned. Future loggers in Louisiana appreciated the high-quality fire-tolerant longleaf pine that replaced the earlier forests. The Native Americans introduced slash and burn techniques to prepare land for farming. The resultant ashes helped decrease soil acidity. Native Americans introduced new foods that became a staple of the European diet, foods such as maize, beans, squash, pumpkins, filé (pounded sassafras leaves), and wild rice.

Native Americans chose most of the important Louisiana settlements. The Europeans moved onto their camps, fields, and paths. Of course, the qualities of a site that attracted Native Americans also attracted the Europeans. They both knew that water

Right: Poverty Point (1700 to 700 B.C.) was a commercial and communal success story. The Native Americans traded with peoples as far away as the Ohio River Valley, northern Georgia, and Minnesota. The site contains remains of great concentric circles upon which houses stood, creating a very large town for the era. To the west was a mound seven hundred feet high constructed in the form of a bird.

COURTESY OF THE LOUISIANA OFFICE OF TOURISM.

connections were essential to move goods and people. Proximity to a crossing bayou or river determined a settlement's exact spot on the river. Thus portages played an important role in early Louisiana history.

But Native American villages were not compact. Houses were normally very far apart, and villages stretched out for miles. Riverine settlements resembled long strings. French settlements, except at forts, seemed to duplicate the earlier Native Americans patterns. Native American government ranged from the authoritarian Natchez to the relaxed volunteerism of the Choctaws. Disobedience was not punished. The only crimes were murder and quarreling. The Caddo government was somewhat in the middle. The Chickasaws were more warlike and had a king called Mindo, but rule was hereditary in the female line. Cultivation was the domain of women. Their crops included two kinds of corn, various beans, sweet potatoes, strawberries, and orchards of peaches, apricots, and plums. Native Americans had game laws or rules. Each band chief had to report to the head chief how much his hunters killed each month. For environmental reasons during the last of February and March, they would no more kill a rabbit than they would a horse. Native Americans generally practiced the moral code of an eye for an eye. Native American warfare was characterized by cunning, not bravery, a mode of fighting that also characterized the Americans when they later fought the British.

Above: Le Page du Pratz was in Louisiana from 1718 until 1734, an experience he chronicled in his later writings. These writings were published in English in 1774 as Histoire de la Louisiane. *His detailed description of Louisiana Native Americans, flora, and fauna provided the earliest thorough account of the original natural society. He is especially remembered for his descriptions of the life of the Natchez Indians.*

COURTESY OF THE HISTORIC NEW ORLEANS COLLECTION, 1980.205.32.

Left: Contemporary Houma Indians building a palmetto house using native materials. Louisiana tribes and groups may be found at the following website sponsored by Northwestern State University at Natchihotches: http://alpha.nsula.edu/department/folklife/cultures/.

COURTESY OF THE LOUISIANA OFFICE OF TOURISM.

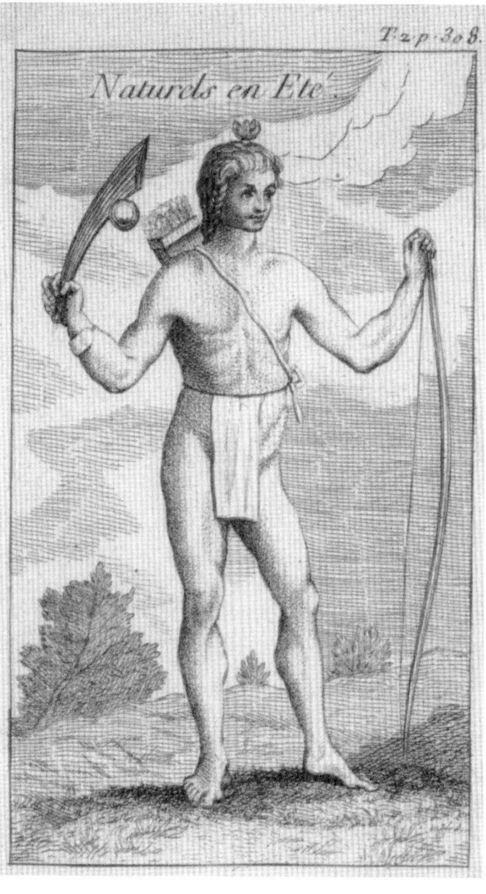

✧

Left: An illustration of a Natchez Indian in summer dress by Le Page du Pratz.
COURTESY OF THE HISTORIC NEW ORLEANS COLLECTION, 1980.205.30.

Right: An illustration of a Natchez Indian in winter dress by Le Page du Pratz.
COURTESY OF THE HISTORIC NEW ORLEANS COLLECTION, 1980.205.31.

Though the Native Americans brought many advantages to the Europeans, it is hard to find a reciprocal benefit for the Native Americans. The meeting of the Europeans and Native Americans in the eighteenth century was an unmitigated disaster for the Native Americans. Disease, slavery, and warfare decimated the tribes.

While most transportation in lower Louisiana was by water, in northern Louisiana paths or roads existed in the eighteenth century. William Darby's map of 1816 shows them in north Louisiana. For Native Americans the trails had three purposes, to lead to the Hot Springs of Arkansas, where their sick could be healed, to find salt, and to follow the buffalo. An important trail ran from the home of Francois Grappe, whom the Native Americans called Touline, at Grappe's Bluff just west of Campté. The trail went north to Touline's cattle pens near the town of Ringgold. This trail branched to the northeast and ran to the Hot Springs. From Touline's home another trail went northeast across Black Lake to the Drake salt licks now in Kisatchee National Forest, near Goldonna. From Touline's home the trail went south to Grand Encore on the Red River near Natchitoches. From Alexandria trails fanned to the east, north and south. One went to Opelousas, two went east, reaching the Mississippi River near Natchez. From Opelousas, trails extended onto the western prairies and south along the west side of Bayou Teche all the way to Berwick Bay. From Natchez a trail came south to St. Francisville, then to Baton Rouge and New Orleans. From Opelousas a trail also went east, splitting just before the Atchafalaya. Each of the two branches crossed Pointe Coupée, one to the south of False River and the other to the north, ending at the ferry to St. Francisville. This was the most southerly east-west trail across Louisiana. Louisiana Highway 190 later followed this route.

While the Native American population of Louisiana plunged in the eighteenth century, the European and African population increased only haltingly. French financier John Law developed the most ambitious program to populate Louisiana, but few of his 3,991 recruits ever actually reached Louisiana By 1731 the population of Louisiana stood at about 3,000 slaves and 2,000 whites. It doubled by the 1750s, and, in 1769, 4,000 blacks and whites farmed along the Mississippi River between New Orleans and Pointe Coupée. The population in the Natchitoches area numbered 740 people in 1769. Of the thousands who actually arrived in Louisiana over the next two centuries, many died from epidemic diseases that came on the same ships as the immigrants.

Because Louis XIV successfully claimed Louisiana, Frenchmen were the first Europeans to settle within Louisiana's boundaries. Those earliest settlements took place along Bayou St. John within the boundaries of present-day New Orleans and along Bayou Amulet in Natchitoches. Soon afterwards the French settled at Pointe Coupée, where the Mississippi cut through a bend and formed the False River. A century later their descendants formed the town of New Roads along the north bank of that False River. In 1718 the formation of New Orleans as the administrative center of Louisiana quickened the pace of growth. By 1730, New Orleans was a real town, while Natchitoches and Pointe Coupée were barely recognizable as villages. By this year New Orleans had a school, convent, goldsmith, locksmith, gunsmith, bakers, carpenters, and the first St. Louis Church. The governor of Louisiana was firmly settled there, as were the members of his superior council. Bienville served three terms as governor, finally departing Louisiana in 1741. He succeeded in making his personal fortune through land grants and trade. Pierre de Rigaud, marquis de Vaudreuil, followed Bienville in the 1740s, and France's Louisiana colony achieved its brightest prospects during his tenure. His departure and replacement in 1753 by Louis Billouart de Kerlérec led to administrative failure that determined the French Crown to donate Louisiana to Spain in 1763.

Connections with Europe helped many achieve prominence in the new Louisiana, yet hard work and ability helped many more. Men like Francois Pascalis de la Barre had useful old-world bourgeois connections, but they also worked hard to fill their offices and obligations. Vincent Ternant, Julien Poydras, and John McDonogh began careers in Louisiana with a pittance. Using their connections and their energy and character, they gradually built large fortunes.

Above: Jean-Baptiste Le Moyne de Bienville was a three-time governor of Louisiana, his terms spanning twenty-eight years. From a Canadian family of eleven children, he set the Creole tone in Louisiana. That tone was acquisitive of land, hard working, family oriented, and status conscious. He knew Native Americans and their languages, but they were only allies or enemies. While the first African Americans came to Louisiana during his tenure, he was no promoter of slavery.

COURTESY OF THE HISTORIC NEW ORLEANS COLLECTION, 1991.34.7.

Left: Coushatta Indians are a growing tribe.

COURTESY OF THE NEW ORLEANS PUBLIC LIBRARY.

Above: This view of the New Orleans waterfront illustrates New Orleans before the coming of the steamboat. Even as late as 1832, flatboats, seen in the foreground, carried the bulk of the exports from New Orleans to world markets. In the distance can be seen the full-rigged sailing ships that carried abroad the cargo of New Orleans. The flatboat brought the foodstuffs of Middle America—ham, wheat, and corn. It was the economic tie that bound the South to the West. The rise of steamboat as a shipping force helped make cotton the dominant product shipped out of the port of New Orleans. This product owed nothing to the western territories, and it epitomized the coming isolation of the South in a dream of self-sufficiency.

COURTESY OF SPECIAL COLLECTIONS, TULANE UNIVERSITY.

Louisiana, like all the English, Dutch, and French colonies in the eighteenth century, commenced with African slavery. In Louisiana, however, the frontier rather than slavery shaped the lifestyle of the people, slave or free. The frontier made the Louisiana slave society fluid and variegated. Within a few years of arriving in Louisiana, a few slaves made the transition to freedom. Africans Simon and Scipion owned land in the vicinity of Marrero as early as the 1720s; Raphael owned land below New Orleans probably near Chalmette. Scipion was hired to bring shipments by barge from New Orleans to Illinois at 250 *livres* per trip.[2]

The French settlers of Louisiana quickly learned that land was cheap. What was decisive was access to slave labor. First the Company of the Indies granted promising French families concessions or grants of land. Then to those who seemed to be the hardest working, the company sold groups of slaves on liberal terms. Those who received the slaves became the successful French planters. Master carpenter Michel Zeringue constructed the first church. He received large land grants at Westwego. Jean Louis Senet, the first captain of the port, also received land on the western bank. Antoine Piquerary was a baker who also was given land to persuade him to remain in the colony. Dr. Louis Vigé was yet another example. They all also received slaves on credit.

The French contribution to Louisiana was above all a looseness in racial relations. As soon as slaves arrived, many were charged with important duties on top of their basic labor. Slaves who supervised other slaves managed most early French plantations. They operated the early sawmills, grew rice and sugar cane, manufactured liquor, and served as messengers and rowers in the shipping business of the eighteenth century. They soon moved into the European crafts, notably ironwork, carpentry, and retail sales.

Between 1719 and 1723, 2,083 slaves arrived in Louisiana, and in 1726, 1,540 slaves remained, a higher survival rate than for the whites. The first Africans brought a Senegambia culture noted for its "powerful, universalist trend." This meant that since Senegambia had long been a crossroads of the world, their culture was already an amalgamation. Senegambians were especially receptive to

Right: Julien de Lalande Poydras stumbled into Louisiana about the time of Alexander O'Reilly. A soldier of fortune-turned-peddler, he spoke the three languages in Louisiana—French, Spanish, and English. The peddler quickly became a merchant and land speculator. Pointe Coupée became the center of his trading empire, but he made large sums in New Orleans selling cotton and sugar. He founded the Female Orphans Asylum in 1817, an institution still in existence. He died a millionaire with a vision of freeing his slaves in twenty-five years. But it took the Civil War, not his last will, for them to acquire their freedom.

COURTESY OF THE HISTORIC NEW ORLEANS COLLECTION, 1991.34.281.

cultural innovation, exceptionally able to incorporate useful aspects of new cultures they encountered. "New Orleans became another crossroads where the river, the bayous, and the sea were open roads, where various nations ruled but the folk continued to reign."[3]

The riverine life of Louisiana must have been very familiar to the Senegambians, whose West African home was watered by the great Senegel and Gambia Rivers. Slaves Jacques and Petit Jean were leased to the sieur de Monbrun, who financed a trip to the Illinois to secure flour. The two were to serve as rowers, much as they might have done at home.[4] Gilbert Dumas, called L'Empileur, leased the Negro Pierrot to Delfau de Pontalba to help him move from Madame Pellerin's and to cook for him. Pontalba liked the slave and took him on a merchandising trip to Pointe Coupée, bringing with them brandy and other goods.[5] Another example of slave life from the earliest records involves Tiocou, a Negro slave freed for his valor at Natchez in 1729. He married slave Marie Aram. She had worked out an agreement with the Ursuline Sisters to work seven years at the new Charity Hospital, from which she received her freedom in 1737.[6]

Where the fortunate Frenchman could accumulate large numbers of slaves, their labor brought them wealth. Within the riverine society, however, individual personalities inevitably led some slaves to flee or simply to go on holiday. These individuals came to be called maroons, those who were temporarily absent from duty. The striking characteristic of maroons is that they did not distance themselves from the plantations; they surrounded the plantations. Maroons never set off on a trek to California, or even to South Carolina, much less to Canada. Most maroons were simply looking for a way of life out from under an individual master or overseer. They worked in their swampy hideouts. Most maroon camps contained fields planted to

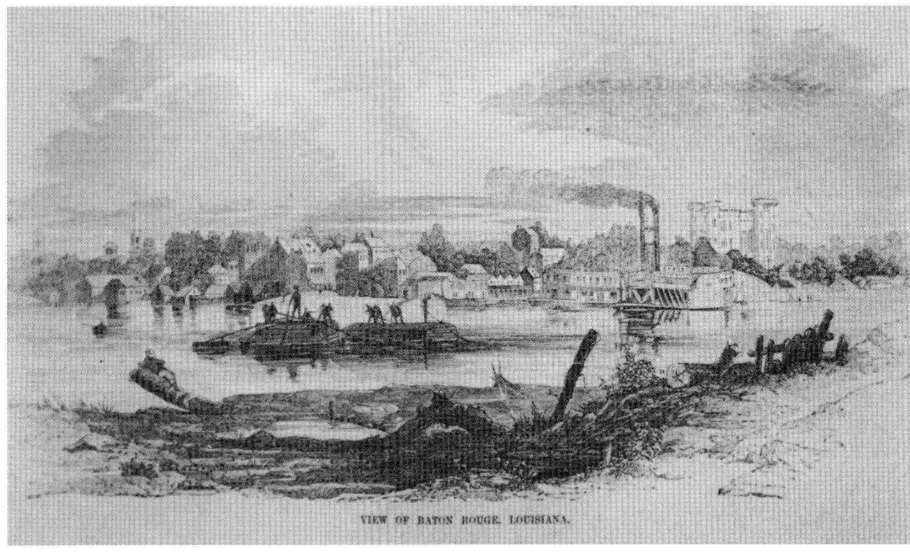

Above: Baton Rouge is the most southern town on the eastern bank of the Mississippi River that can claim high land. In this illustration can be seen the state capitol completed in 1850. The flatboat on the river, reminiscent of Tom Sawyer, *carries goods all the way to New Orleans. The voyagers returned on a steamboat like the sidewheeler seen in the background.*

COURTESY OF NEW ORLEANS PUBLIC LIBRARY.

Left: This drawing by A. R. Waud probably contributed to the American image of Acadians as "cajuns," somewhat shiftless swamp dwellers. Both the vegetation and the home are more Creole than Acadian. The Acadians were diligent farmers who sought out the prairies and banks of the Bayous Lafourche and Teche.

COURTESY OF SPECIAL COLLECTIONS, TULANE UNIVERSITY.

produce foodstuffs. Maroons worked as outside labor for loggers and other individuals charged with producing lumber for the export trade. Maroons cut trees, squared the logs, and hauled them to the sawmills. The sawmills paid cash. "The maroons living in the ciprière maintained a symbiotic relationship with sawmill owners. They cut and squared cypress logs, dragged them to the sawmills, and were paid for each log delivered."[7] The difficulty of maroon life was plain to the slaves who remained on the riverfront. This helps explain why most slaves remained at work on the plantation.

The economic system led to strange behavior in the society of slaves. Usually masters compartmentalized the various aspects of slavery—compulsion, commerce, and humanity. When these aspects conflicted, masters often saw unexpected results. The grandson of Delfau de Pontalba, Joseph Delfau de Pontalba, had a favorite worker in Augustin, who supervised an elaborate drayage business for Pontalba. He arranged to have carts available to haul goods to and from the plantations, as well as to transport the extensive building materials Pontalba purchased to build his houses in New Orleans. Yet, Augustin was also responsible to bring Pontalba a glass of milk early each morning. One week he was consistently late in bringing the milk, so Pontalba's solution was to have him whipped. Augustin promptly fled. Pontalba was disconsolate, more so after he noticed that his carts were not running on time. Fortunately for Pontalba, soon afterwards Augustin's uncle, Simon Charles, paid Pontalba a visit. He said, "that there had never been any runaways in his family, and that he would not have Augustin, his nephew, fall into any such habit; he told me that he was the brother of Marie-Jeanne, mother of Augustin, and he asked me for a note that he might go and fetch him." Pontalba reported to his diary later, "I actually found him at the house when I returned at ten that night; he fetched Augustin before me and asked that the latter be forgiven, pledging himself for his good behavior in the future, this event gave me great pleasure, I can assure you, as no one could replace Augustin in taking care of my drayage, which was

✧

This Cajun girl is cooling off from her exertions in the field.

COURTESY OF SPECIAL COLLECTIONS, TULANE UNIVERSITY.

beginning to fall behind, and you may say that the uncle easily obtained forgiveness for his nephew."[8] The remarkable attitudes conveyed in this incident need to be examined. Simon Charles plainly led a family that did not feel that the end of the world was at hand. He could see that Augustin was in line to be freed; that slavery was only temporary. In short, the society continued to employ slaves, but it was not a slave society. It might very well have been a society where all blacks gradually achieved freedom. It was not yet forced into a mold where blackness meant only slavery.

Across from New Orleans, in the area later to be Harvey, Louisiana, two different families of freed Negroes operated independently on the sawmill canals. In the late eighteenth century, Negro Gabriel Villars lived on a sawmill canal (later Harvey Canal) with his Native-American wife, Tonton, and their daughter, Tonton. Carlotta, a Negresse freed by Claude Joseph Dubreuil, Jr., resided along the Dubreuil Canal. She manufactured an alcoholic beverage, probably the rum-like tafia, and sold it to blacks and whites alike.

The French had come to Louisiana with riches in mind. They were all capitalists or, as they would say, bourgeois. Slavery was a tool to achieve wealth. Three later groups of immigrants were initially anti-slavery in their lifestyle—the Germans, the Acadians, and the Isleños. But they were essentially refugees seeking not wealth but life itself.

One of the strongest foundations of Louisiana was the German settlement. Initiated during the John Law era, the census taken in March 1722 found a total German population of 330 men, women and children settled in some small communities along the river banks of the future St. John the Baptist and St. Charles Parishes. Governor Bienville placed the German coast under the authority of Charles Frederic D'Arensbourg, a young Swedish military officer fluent in German. Since the Germans lacked capital, the Company of the Indies allocated only small parcels to the individual families. Slaves were scarce. The Germans specialized in vegetables, food crops suitable for sale in New Orleans' markets. The Germans grew corn to feed livestock. Rice for the New Orleans market soon became a major product. In this "truck farming" business, German immigrants prospered. By 1776, 1,005 white settlers lived at the German coast on 216 farms with 666 slaves. The population distribution showed that the west bank of the river was still one of small farms, a characteristic it would retain for many decades. Truck farming for the New Orleans' market has remained a viable business up to the present day.

Between 1755 and 1785 a fourth major population entered Louisiana, the Acadians. French residents of Nova Scotia, the British summarily evicted them, sending them fleeing to ports on both sides of the Atlantic. Gradually a majority of them chose to live in Louisiana because of their heritage of private ownership of land and their democratic traditions, which conflicted with the quasi-serf and slave systems of France and the Caribbean islands. After having lived once on the frontier, that is, Canada, where land was essentially free, they again chose the frontier by settling at St. Martinville in May 1765. Where their first frontier choice (Canada) was dictated more by government policy, their second choice (Louisiana) was their own, a choice to preserve a way of life that had already developed.[9] Approximately five thousand Acadians moved to Louisiana by 1785. They settled first on the plains to the west of Bayou Teche, then along Bayou Lafourche. Finally they settled along the Mississippi River upstream from the Germans in the parishes that became St. James and Ascension. Their way of life was frankly agricultural, but agriculture without capital. The consequence was a system of small farms, each workable by a family. For a long time they were at odds with the developing slave society around them, but they eventually partially succumbed. The lure of slaves to increase wealth proved too much for some Acadians as it had for the Creoles.

This village demonstrates the importance of the cottage to early Louisiana. In New Orleans the Creole cottage is one of its most distinctive elements. In Acadiana, it is the Acadian cottage, different in having stairs on the front gallery and not as many square feet.

COURTESY OF THE LOUISIANA OFFICE OF TOURISM.

✧

This early twentieth century photograph by Samuel Locket is entitled Swamp Hunting. *It illustrates cut-over lands during a Spring flood.*

COURTESY OF SPECIAL COLLECTIONS, TULANE UNIVERSITY.

But Acadians remained more oriented to the family farm then the state as a whole.

The Acadian lifestyle has been partially documented. One of the pieces of evidence is the folktale. Storytelling was ubiquitous and popular throughout Acadiana. The Acadian and Black Creole oral traditions developed around the evening visits where stories, called *veillées*, were told. But the surviving evidence tells a surprising story. Acadian life was not one of isolation and rejection, but rather one of inclusion. Like the blacks from Senegambia, the Acadian folktales demonstrate an acceptance of cross-cultural influences totally surprising to purists seeking to link a cultural artifact to one historical root. Examination of the Cajun folktale, one of the preeminent cultural relics of the eighteenth century Acadian settlement, reveals that the French environment subsequently accepted large doses of other cultures, notably African, African American, British American, native American, and Spanish American.[10] The Acadians did not bring a xenophobic culture to Louisiana; they brought a culture that could and did grow. The Cajun repertoire of stories includes the standard categories of animal tales, magic tales, jokes, tall tales, legends, and historical tales. Of the animal tales, it is notable that the malicious spider is missing, a standard feature of African and West Indian stories. France and Africa have influenced modern Cajun and Black Creole culture much less than the experience of being in the multicultural North America. The Black Creole language also borrowed European tales, such as Ben Guiné's remarkably creolized version of "The Ant and the Lazy Cricket." Cultural crossover is evident in animal tales that use both the African Bouki and the French Lapin in conversation. Continuing Acadian creativity is evident in the later invention of a story genre called the Pascal stories. They are told in the town of Mamou in west central Louisiana. True Pascal stories are instant improvisations, centered on a cast of characters named Pascal, Jim Israel, and Olinde.

After the Acadians came the Isleños, Spanish settlers from the Canary Islands. Some two thousand came to Louisiana in the 1780s. They settled in five places in southern Louisiana, but soon they moved in with other groups, moved to New Orleans, or consolidated at Terre Aux Boeufs in St. Bernard Parish. Like the Germans, they specialized in truck farming for the New Orleans market. The neighborhood of the Terre Aux Boeufs was named for the great oxen they used in farming and for transporting their crops to the French Market early each morning. The Isleños were joined by many mainland Spaniards, merchants, and military men, who held a major role in New Orleans.

Louisiana grew on these foundations. Though the French, Acadians, and Isleños gave a decidedly Catholic cast to the territory, the steady influx of Americans and their slaves from the eastern states built up a large Protestant sector across northern Louisiana. Of all the southern states, Louisiana is the only one with some reasonable balance between Protestant and Catholic faiths. The socio-economic structure of the Isleños and the Acadians has also given a decidedly democratic character to the state. Louisiana remains one of the more politically liberal states of the South.

Chapter I Endnotes

1 Fred B. Kniffen, Hiram F. Gregory, and George A. Stokes. *The Historic Indian Tribes of Louisiana*. Baton Rouge: Louisiana State University Press, 1987.

2 *LHQ VI*, 306.

3 Gwendolyn Midlo Hall. *Africans in Colonial Louisiana: The Development of Afro-Creole Culture in the Eighteenth Century*. Baton Rouge: Louisiana State University Press, 1992. p. 200.

4 *LHQ VIII*, 490. 1736

5 *LHQ VIII*, 491. 1736

6 *LHQ XII*, p. 669. See also *LHQ III*, 551.

7 Hall. *Africans in Colonial Louisiana*, 207.

8 Letter from Joseph Xavier Delfau de Pontalba to his wife, May 9, 1796, translated by Henri Delvile de Sinclair, typescript. Collection 590. Manuscripts, Howard-Tilton Library, Tulane University.

9 Glenn R. Conrad, "The Acadians: Myths and Realities" in *Glenn R. Conrad, The Cajuns: Essays on Their History and Culture*. Lafayette, Louisiana: Center for Louisiana Studies, 1978. p. 11-12.

10 The evidence of cultural mixing is very evident in Barry Ancelet's *Cajun and Creole Folktales: The French Oral Tradition of South Louisiana* (Jackson, Mississippi: University Press of Mississippi, 1994). Ancelet has worked for twenty years recording Louisiana French oral narratives. Previous treatments of Louisiana French folktales have dealt exclusively either with black Creoles (e.g. Fortier, 1895) or white Cajuns (Saucier, 1962). Ancelet, however, treats the two groups as a continuum, an approach which he fully justifies by documenting powerful connections between Cajun and Creole tales. Fortier dealt almost exclusively with animal tales, Saucier with magic tales, Bergeron (1980) with personal narratives. Finally, earlier collections such as those by Calvin Claudel (1948) dealt with Old World survivals. In 1993 the folklore archives at LSU had eight hundred hours of recordings and thousands of stories.

Spanish notary and member of the Cabildo, Don Andres Almonaster, provided the funds to construct the new Cabildo in 1796, following the second great fire of 1793. Almonaster also funded the reconstruction of St. Louis Church. That reconstruction endured until a second reconstruction in 1849, leaving the church with its current appearance.

COURTESY OF THE LOUISIANA OFFICE OF TOURISM

LOUISIANA
and part of
ARKANSAS
Scale of Miles
CRAWFORD
POPE
CONWAY
ST FRANCIS
Masserne Mountains
HOT SPRINGS
MILLER
PULASKI
JEFFERSON
MONROE
PHILLIPS
Harrington
Arkansas
CLARK
SEVIER
Washington
HEMSTEAD
UNION
ARKANSAS
Columbus
Ecore Fabre
CHICOT
Villemont or Chicot
LAFAYETTE
Grand L.
CLAIBORNE
CARROLL
Cado L.
Washita
Warrenton
NATCHITOCHES
Saline L.
Natchitoches
L. Cassim
Red River
CATAHOULA
Catahoula
Natches
Concordia
Alexandria
RAPIDES
Marksville
Woodville
MISSISSIPPI
Crocodile L.
Coshatta Indians
ST HELENA
WASHINGTON
Jacksonville
Franklinton
Pearl R.
St. Helena
Springfield
Covington
Madisonville
LIVINGSTON
ST TAMMANY
Opelousas
OPELOUSAS
GT. CALSASIU PRAIRIE
St Martinsville
ST MARTINS
Lake Pontchartrain
Lake Borgne
ORLEANS
ST JAMES
ST JOHN BAPTIST
ST CHARLES
ASCENSION
IBERVILLE
Donaldsonville
LAFOURCHE
Thibadeauxville
Franklin
Sabine L.
Marsh Lake
ATTAKAPAS
Mermenton
PLAQUEMINES
Plaquemines
TERRE BONNE
INTERIOR
Achafalaya Bay
Ship L.
Round B.
Main Pass
South Pass
GULF OF MEXICO
94
93 Lon. W. from London
92
91
90
89

CHAPTER II

THE CREOLE TRANSITION, 1780-1830

In 1803, Louisiana did not spring joyfully into America's arms. In the eighteenth century, she was European and African, not American. But by the 1850s she was a fully Southern state of the Union. The era between the two conditions was the Creole transition. It was a Creole time because native-born people with mixed European and African roots played a significant role in the economy, government, and culture. This variegated state of affairs prevented any one racial, ethnic, or political group from achieving dominance. The happy consequence was a grudging tolerance that facilitated free speech, free love, and free spirits. New Orleans acquired its enduring reputation as a party town.

The Creole transition began in the 1770s under Spanish sovereignty, a comparatively happy, tolerant, and prosperous time. While the American Revolution was underway, between 1779 and 1781 Louisiana military forces won three battles, capturing English forts at Baton Rouge, Mobile, and Pensacola. The Spanish welcomed the Acadians and the Isleños. They provided free land to them and to many Americans moving westward from the English colonies facing the Atlantic Ocean. Spanish governors were among the best Louisiana has ever had, from Bernardo de Gálvez and Estevan Miró to François-Louis Hector, baron de Carondelet. But at the turn of the century the Spanish empire popped like a giant balloon struck by the lightning generated by the French Revolution.

The arrival of refugees from Haiti between the years 1794 and 1810 gave the French influence in Louisiana its greatest boost since the 1720s. In 1809, 3,102 free blacks and 2,731 whites came to New Orleans, accompanied by 3,226 slaves. They all spoke French. Among the many distinguished Haitian refugees were attorney Louis Moreau-Lisle, and professors Jules Davezac and Pierre Lambert of the Collège d'Orléans. The significance of the Haitian influx was the increase it gave to the French-language whites, slaves, and free blacks.

The long-term significance of the Creole transition was the appearance of a group of people of mixed racial background. For almost a century this group, known first as Free People of Color, lived an influential and quasi-free life in Louisiana. It ended in the 1890s as legal segregation clamped down on both freedmen and former Free People of Color.

Free People of Color included those of entirely one race, as well as many descendants of interracial unions. In Natchitoches the first families all produced sons who married Indian women. These included Pierre Bertrand, Louis Joseph Blanpain, Jean Baptiste Brevel, and Barthelemy LaCour. Others created families of mixed French and African heritage, notably the Metoyer family. In Pointe Coupée Parish many Creoles created families with African woman, notably brothers Antoine and Joseph Decuir. In New Orleans in 1760, two French brothers arrived from Provence. Louis and Jean-François Dolliole sailed to America from La Seyne sur Mer near Toulon on France's Mediterranean coast. Jean-François Dolliole began a decades-long liaison with a free woman of color named Catherine, who most likely came from Africa, and became father to four children of color. His brother, Louis, did much the same thing, mating with a woman named Geneviéve "Mamie" Larronde, most likely from the French West Indies, and producing four offspring. The younger Vincent Rillieux produced several sons with his partially African wife Constance Vivant—Edmond, Bartolome, and Norbert Rillieux. Edmond became a New Orleans builder. Norbert invented the vacuum pan process for the manufacture of sugar.

One of the achievements of the Creole transition was the creation of the unique Louisiana system of civil law. Based on Spanish and French precedents, in the nineteenth century it made Louisiana the most progressive state in the Union for family law. In the rest of the country the husband was head of the house and free to sell and dispose of all of the private estate without consulting anyone, especially

A map of Louisiana and Arkansas from 1830. This map highlights the river systems of Louisiana. Notice how in the northeastern portion of the state the Ouchita River flows south from southern Arkansas and creates a parallel valley with the Mississippi. It finally empties in the Red River.

COURTESY OF THE LOUISIANA STATE ARCHIVES COLLECTION.

his wife and children. In Louisiana the ancient clauses of the civil law insisted that at marriage a community of property was formed. All property acquired during the marriage belonged to both husband and wife and the husband could not dispose of it without the wife's free consent. At his death a man could not, as he could anywhere else in the United States, disinherit his children. A forced portion of his estate automatically went to them.

Another portion of the civil law regulated how property was bought and sold. When an item was sold a buyer had an implied warranty, in contrast to the common law that provided no warranty unless explicitly expressed. It placed land sales in the hands of professional notaries, who were charged by law with the preservation of the relevant documents. This simple provision created vast notarial archives where invaluable historical information now safely reposes. For many decades these aspects of the Civil Law were threatened with extinction. In the last decade the legislature has permitted fathers to disinherit their children. But in the last fifty years the fair and democratic nature of Civil Law has spread to the Anglo law. We now find concern for family life and warranties in the larger American society and law.

Above: Joseph Xavier Celestin Delfau de Pontalba left a set of letters describing Creole life in the 1700s. Son of an associate of Bienville, born in Louisiana, he hungered for position. Once a New World bourgeois, Napoleon transformed him into a baron, thus eventually making his daughter-in-law Micaela Antonio Almonester a baroness. That she would refuse to turn her fortune over to him so infuriated Pontalba that he attempted to kill her. His failure to do so resulted in him taking his own life.

COURTESY OF THE HISTORIC NEW ORLEANS COLLECTION, 1991.34.20.

Right: A portrait of Nicholas Augustin Metoyer (1768-1856) painted by J. F. Fuille in 1836. Metoyer donated the land for the St. Augustine Church and Cemetery established in 1803. The present church is the third structure on the site, and has been served by Holy Ghost Fathers since 1913. The original church design can be seen in the background of the painting.

Another of the gifts of the Creole era is Creole architecture, exemplified by the Creole cottage, the Creole countryhouse, and the Creole townhouse. The Creole Cottage dates from the 1790s. A small square house, it is surmounted by a full-hipped roof and sits directly on the street. Four openings face the street and four rooms lie hidden behind the façade. Behind the four rooms are usually two smaller rooms at each of the rear corners called cabinets. Between these two cabinets is an open gallery, open only on one side, the courtyard side. Several arches might define the boundary between gallery and courtyard. Towards the rear of the courtyard is a service building of two stories, with a gallery facing the courtyard. The servants live above the kitchen.

In the countryside the Creole cottage is raised and enlarged. A gallery often surrounds it on all four sides. This gallery shades the house walls and extends the living space outward. Raised eight feet above the ground, the house attracts more breeze and fewer insects, which tend to hug the ground. Draperies often hang on the gallery, closing off some private spaces. The Creole countryhouse sports a square plan, a plan that was emulated by the next generation of homebuilders in Louisiana. Tuscan columns of

of them, and it will be a long time before I have them and you will see to it that they are not in bad shape.

I am sending you also the dictionary of synonyms of Gérard so that you will know that words that have several "rapports" don't mean however the same thing; and to speak well, it is necessary to know the true meaning of each word so as to render your ideas correctly if you want to be well understood by those who hear or listen to you...I am also sending you eight French novels entitled: *La Reine des Fleurs, L'Ange Fidele, Pauvre Ange des Ciecen, La Fleur de Ciel, Aimer Seule, Dieu Soit Toujours Beni, Que les Hivers sont Courts, Vous le Sauvez.*

One of the characteristics of the Creole economy was the relative freedom of the African Americans. Many were literally free, and many slaves acted as if they were free. The typical Creole plantation was run not as a factory, but as a personal enterprise. The way Creoles administered their plantations was fundamentally different from the American system. Benjamin Poydras in Pointe Coupée Parish worked his slaves under the "Creole" plan, where "the masters, instead of feeding their Negroes and requiring them to work all day, gave them tasks which occupied about half the time, and the balance of the time they were allowed to provide for themselves with the necessaries of life." Poydras used the Creole plan on all his plantations because it avoided cash outlays.

One consequence of the Creole plan was the formation of enterprising companies of slaves who organized work gangs for their own benefit. On his main plantation at Pointe Coupée, Poydras had a gang of young Negroes who "had the reputation for picking cotton very well. That gang contracted for a twentieth. There were also women [in the gangs]. Before Poydras departed for France, he sent the gang to the chenal [Alma], also the Isle, and rented them out sometime." The leader of this gang was a woman by the name of Lise. One of their clients was Evariste

Above: The Creole cottage of four rooms and two rear cabinets is one of the architectural jewels of New Orleans. This cottage sits on a corner, so the roof slopes in all four directions.

COURTESY OF THE LOUISIANA OFFICE OF TOURISM.

Below: This rear view of a cottage clearly shows the two rear corner rooms that frame an open gallery. The little rooms are called "cabinets," and the gallery is thus the cabinet gallery. Such galleries are found on raised Creole countryhouses and city cottages. The cabinet gallery is a comfortable space, offering openness with a modicum of privacy.

COURTESY OF THE LOUISIANA STATE MUSEUM.

✧

Above: The Parlange Creole Countryhouse.

COURTESY OF THE LOUISIANA OFFICE OF TOURISM.

Above: The Houmas House, erected in 1830 by Wade Hampton, represents the new Louisiana housing design style called "Tuscan." Shaped roughly square, it has monumnetal columns of the Tuscan order. It combines the simplicity of design inherited from the Creole raised cottage with the new American pride expressed in monumentality.

COURTESY OF THE LOUISIANA OFFICE OF TOURISM.

Boudreau, who lived next door to Alma Plantation. In 1836 he made a very good harvest, with seventeen workers he made 209 bales of cotton. He did not, however, pick all the harvest with his own Negroes. He hired Negroes from the Poydras plantation after their tasks finished at noon. The Negroes came to his place at noon, and he employed them the rest of the day. They picked about 80 to 100 bales of cotton at his place. When he didn't hire them, they went to the neighbors." This Creole plan of labor illustrates how the slave system in Creole society gave room for slaves to live their own life. It permitted them to prepare and to hope for freedom. It also foreshadowed the labor systems to come after the Civil War.

Sugar as well as cotton could be worked on the Creole plan. The Jesuits brought sugar cane to Louisiana in the 1750s and planted it on their plantation, now the location of New Orleans' central business district. Since the 1680s sugar had grown profitably in the West Indies. Its success in Louisiana could have brought additional investment to the colony. Numerous planters took up the cane brought by the Jesuits. In 1766, English surveyor

Philip Pittman noted the presence of many sugarhouses up the Mississippi from New Orleans. In 1766, Alexandrine de La Chaise, Charles Pradel's widow, sought to re-establish the sugarhouse after she purchased part of the Jesuit plantation.

In 1769, in St. Charles Parish, a Dutch sugar maker named Jean Jonas lived between the plantations of Francois Lemelle and Charles Brasseaux where the Boggs Bridge now crosses the Mississippi. In the 1760s, Jean Baptiste Destrehan operated a large, twenty-arpent plantation below New Orleans with 170 slaves. He grew sugar and operated a sugarhouse and distillery. The latter was to produce rum or the easier substitute called "tafia."

When Alexander O'Reilly imposed Spanish control over Louisiana, he stopped sugar shipments to French ports. In compensation, he granted Louisiana the authority to make sugar boxes for the Cuban sugar industry. This business utilized the enormous Louisiana timber stand, but it led to the temporary withering of sugar planting. In the 1790s the Spanish loosened up their control, and markets for sugar began to appear in the new American nation. Simultaneously numerous planters began replanting sugar, spurred by the perception that the revolution in Haiti would eliminate a major supplier in the world market. Sugar was replanted in Pointe Coupée as well as near New Orleans. Evidence indicates that sugar boilers were in use along the south bank of False River by the mid-1790s, when Margaret Farrar employed Abraham Ellis as a sugar maker.

Yet the man most often credited as the father of the Louisiana sugar industry is Creole Etienne Boré. Born December 27, 1741, at Kaskaskia, Illinois, Boré entered the French army, where he became a cavalry officer, eventually reaching the position of captain. But agriculture was his calling. By 1771, Boré was thirty years old, well respected in both military and planting circles. He married a Creole, a Destrehan daughter, and devoted himself to his lands and family.

In the 1780s, Boré purchased the twenty-arpent plantation in uptown New Orleans extending from Joseph Street to near the lower boundary of Audubon Park. He erected a large home with a garden about a block square surrounded by a brick revetment and a moat of water filled with frogs, fish, and eels. There in 1794 he began planting sugar cane, determined to develop a new cash crop in the face of the failure of the hitherto profitable indigo crop. He employed sugar makers from Haiti who had already succeeded in granulating sugar. His new mill successfully ground and granulated the crop, and he sold it for an estimated $12,000. Immediately planters up and down the river began erecting new sugarhouses and planting cane.

Boré's brother-in-law was St. Charles Parish planter Jean Noel Destrehan. Destrehan's

✧

Left: Jean Etrienne Boré (1741-1820) successfully cultivated and granulated sugar cane on his plantation in uptown New Orleans during the 1790s. His son-in-law, historian Charles Gayarre, memorialized this feat. Boré's wife was the daughter of Jean Baptiste Destrehan, the colonial treasurer. Boré eventually took charge of his wife's family affairs. Boré was a military man and farmer, not a cultured Creole.

COURTESY OF SPECIAL COLLECTIONS, TULANE UNIVERSITY.

Right: Jean Noel Destrehan, a Creole planter in St. Charles Parish, was an early convert to sugar growing. His brother-in-law was Etienne Boré, who produced the first commercially successful sugar crop. Destrehan was widely admired for his probity. During the territorial period (1804-1812), he was the spokesman for the Creoles. He employed the Creole system of planting, a system that offered slaves considerable personal freedom. This painting is attributed to Matthew Harris Jouett, c. 1818.

COURTESY OF THE LOUISIANA STATE MUSEUM.

✧

Right: The Second Municipality of New Orleans (now the American business district) decided to construct a city hall for its own use. Designed by James Gallier and completed in 1849, the city hall asserts the values of a Greek temple. It is rectangular, with the narrow side facing the street. The columns on the front of the building evoke the majesty of the forest.

COURTESY OF THE LOUISIANA OFFICE OF TOURISM.

Below: This negro wood sawyer cut firewood and trees in New Orleans.

COURTESY OF THE LOUISIANA STATE MUSEUM.

plantation operated on the Creole plan. In 1803, Pierre Clément de Laussat found Madame Destrehan, with her four daughters, supervising the salting and preserving of beef. Destrehan himself took time out from grinding to give Laussat a tour of his plantation. They began in the quarters, where the slaves worked on the "Creole" plan. Laussat observed that each slave had his own garden plot, which he was encouraged to cultivate. He also noticed that Destrehan did not give clothing to his slaves; he sold it to them at wholesale prices. Under the Creole plan, slaves worked either in their own gardens on their own time and sold the produce for cash, or worked for others for cash. Since it was grinding season, most slaves were working in the sugar mill. But they did not work around the clock, as at many plantations. Laussat noticed that Destrehan employed the workers on "three-quarter watches," consisting of tours of duty of six hours each. Normally, slaves on the Creole plan had to provide their own food, but during grinding Destrehan provided the food. He was told that slaves took the opportunity to fatten up. He also learned that under Destrehan's plan slaves were better clothed and did not run away.

At Oakland Plantation near Natchitoches slaves owned their own cattle. In one list of cattle in 1839, six slaves owned four heifers and seven bulls. The slaves raised corn for their own account. In the winter months they often worked for the masters cutting wood in the swamps. An entire gang would depart under their own supervision and return in a month with shingles and lumber.

The Creole plan could have paved the way for gradual emancipation, a road out of the dead end of slavery. But in the following decades American rule gradually snuffed out the idea that slaves could organize and work on their own. New England landscape architect Frederick Law Olmstead toured the South in the 1850s. In New Orleans, he found it awful that unskilled Irishmen labored for skilled black masons. In that same decade white and black cotton screwmen became the aristocrats of the New Orleans riverfront. These were the men who loaded the ships with cotton bales and then operated screw presses in the ships' holds to maximize the cargo. They first organized in 1851. They struck successfully in 1854 and 1858. In 1866 they got their pay above $5 a day. A visitor reported seeing the strikers as they "marched up the levee in a long procession, white and black together."

The pluralistic Creole system was significant because it was utterly unacceptable to the American racial system in place across the South and struggling for dominance in Louisiana. Nineteenth and twentieth century racial segregation suppressed Louisiana's racially variegated society. But it did not destroy it.

Left: Lafcadio Hearn, an Irishman and a reporter, spent ten years in New Orleans. An early marriage to a Creole of color ended quickly in divorce, but his sensibility for Louisiana was acute. He published Chita: A Memory of Last Island *in 1889. After his death his Creole sketches were issued. He was a member of the early Louisiana literary blossoming which consisted of writers such as George Cable, Adrien Rouguette, Grace King, Rudolph Matas, and Elizabeth Bisland.*

COURTESY OF SPECIAL COLLECTIONS, TULANE UNIVERSITY.

Below: A miniature of Madame Marigny Livaudais, c. 1812.

COURTESY OF THE LOUISIANA STATE MUSEUM.

Chapter III

LOUISIANA AND THE UNITED STATES

Though the past two centuries have witnessed a world-wide homogenizing of peoples, Louisiana has retained a sense of its individual origin and identity. Louisiana's relationship to the American government has been distinctive. As part of the South, Louisiana experienced what the rest of the United States did not, the loss of a war. On the other hand, in 1815 it was the site of the Battle of New Orleans that ratified America's independence. While it often sought to be aloof, it truly needed the resources and power of the Federal Government to develop its economy. The Civil War created a powerful new federal government that wielded tariffs to protect the steel and sugar industries, that leveed the Mississippi River, and that fought yellow fever, a particular scourge of Louisiana.

In 1803 the United States purchased an unwilling Louisiana. She was the first people to be forced into the Union. But the only evidence of discontent came from the African Americans. At a time of Napoleons and kings, people were more resigned to their fate then they are today. For the next ten years Louisiana remained a territory, virtually a colony, of the young republic.

Ironically, Americans were the last group of settlers to arrive in Louisiana. Some were refugees from the American Revolution, Tories whose loyalty to their Mother Country made life in the new United States impossible. Point Coupée received a wealthy South Carolina planter and surveyor named Benjamin Farrar. His son and two daughters became prominent members of the Anglo planting class along the Mississippi River. At the other end of the political spectrum was one David Bradford of western Pennsylvania. He was a lawyer and a leader of the Whiskey Rebellion of 1795. He judged it prudent to escape the clutches of the new United States, and settled near Bayou Sarah in West Feliciana Parish, where he prospered. Judge John Perkins, a Maryland native, was a representative Louisiana cotton planter throughout the antebellum years. He came to Louisiana in 1802 In 1813, Governor W. C. C. Claiborne appointed Perkins parish judge for Concordia Parish, where he began acquiring plantations south of Bayou Vidal. All were contiguous, and eventually his "Somerset Estate," as he called it, totaled 17,500 acres. On April 7, 1857, the judge donated his estate, valued at more than $600,000, to his son John Perkins, Jr., in return for an annuity. John, Jr., served as secretary of the Louisiana Historical Society and even journeyed to France to collect documents pertaining to Louisiana history. He played an important role in the Civil War government of Jefferson Davis and fled to Mexico upon its conclusion.

A wave of American officeholders also invaded the territory, setting off a scramble for position between the French, the Creoles, and the new Americans. President Thomas Jefferson appointed William Charles Cole Claiborne governor of the new territory. The ambitious young man had begun his career as a clerk in the brand-new United States House of Representatives. He then commenced a legal practice in territorial Tennessee aided by political appointments facilitated by his national contacts. As a member of the House of Representatives from Tennessee, he voted for Thomas Jefferson in 1801 after the electoral college deadlocked. As soon as Jefferson took office, he appointed Claiborne to be territorial governor of Mississippi, followed in 1803 by his appointment to Louisiana. Former New York City Mayor Edward Livingston came to town to rebuild his fortune. Brothers John and Thomas Slidell moved to Louisiana in the 1820s. The sons of a New York City merchant, they were extremely able lawyers who reached the pinnacle of political power in Louisiana, John Slidell as United States Senator and tutor of President James Buchanan, and Thomas Slidell as chief justice of the Louisiana Supreme Court.

While these Americans embraced Creole society, others despised it. Wade Hampton made a fortune growing cotton in South Carolina. Then, the U.S. government sent him to Louisiana as a general in the U.S. Army, where he quickly purchased one of the largest land holdings along the

✧

The Riverlake Sugar House *by Adrien Persac, c. 1858. This painting shows the process of harvesting sugarcane in the nineteenth century. Workers cut the cane, loaded it onto carts, and then drove them to the sugarhouse. On the left is the sugar shed where the cane was dumped. In the center is the conveyor that carried the cane under the rollers. Steam engines supplied the motive power. Slaves cut wood to fuel the engines. This plantation belonged to Arthur Denis, a prominent New Orleans lawyer whose wife, Antoinette Decuir, inherited the plantation from her father, Antoine Decuir. The sugarhouse in the painting burned in 1870. Antoine and Joseph Decuir were prominent, wealthy planters on the lower False River in Pointe Coupée Parish. Both men established families with free women of color, families that led to many free people of color in Louisiana.*

COURTESY OF CHARLES DENIS FOURIER.

✧

Right: The Miles Branch settlement in Washington Parish contributed several structures to the Washington Parish Fair held annually in the fall in Franklintown. The log cabin was once the ordinary dwelling for the Americans who came into Louisiana after the Louisiana Purchase. The cabin was built out of "pens" or rooms. To a one-pen structure, a second pen was added. Sometimes an open hall separated the two pens, creating a dogtrot.

COURTESY OF THE LOUISIANA OFFICE OF TOURISM.

Bottom, left: William Charles Cole Claiborne (1775-1817) was the first American governor of Louisiana, both the territory and the state. Unlike many Louisiana governors before him, Claiborne spent comparatively little time enriching himself in office. Creole life and women quickly captured his loyalty, to the degree that he suffered through a duel. He worried most about the grasping successful Americans around him, men such as Edward Livingston and Daniel Clark. Such giants made him feel small. Nevertheless, he successfully navigated the political perils to get himself elected the state's first governor.

COURTESY OF THE HISTORIC NEW ORLEANS COLLECTION.

Bottom, right: A daguerrotype of John Perkins, c. 1843. Representative of the Anglo cotton planters of antebellum Louisiana, the John Perkins family played a leading role in Concordia and Tensas Parishes and the state. John Perkins, Sr., was an early judge of the parish, and then a planter of thousands of acres of cotton (Somerset Plantation). His son, John Perkins, Jr., became the secretary-treasurer of the Louisiana Historical Society and visited Europe repeatedly to collect documents pertaining to early Louisiana history. He was, however, a vehement Confederate. The loss of the war sent him to Mexico, where he started a coffee plantation. By 1870 he moved to Europe, where he remained until 1878.

COURTESY OF JEREMY PRESCOTT.

Mississippi River, the Houmas claim just downriver from the new town of Donaldsonville. William Donaldson, like most successful men in the colony, spoke the three languages of Louisiana. A successful merchant from England, Donaldson was selected by Governor Claiborne to be one of the first members of the legislative council for the new American Territory of Louisiana. The Louisiana Bank elected him to its board of directors. A few years after purchasing half of the Houmas tract, he founded the town of Donaldsonville at the junction of the Mississippi River and Bayou Lafourche. This town grew to be the county seat of Ascension Parish, the site of the U.S. Land Office for Louisiana, and even for two years the state capital. Ever the developer, he married the daughter of the first registrar of public lands, B. F. Van Predelles, thus guaranteeing himself an inside look at what lands were unclaimed. In cooperation with John Scott, Donaldson also built the first

Top, left: Jacque Philippe Villére was the first Creole governor of Louisiana and served from 1816 to 1820. Son of the insurrectionists of 1768, the court of Louis XVI took him in as a page. Returning to Louisiana, he eventually settled below New Orleans on land the British had occupied in their failed attempt to invade New Orleans. He became the ranking general of the militia. This lithograph was made by J. B. Pointel du Portail and dates from the late 1830s.

COURTESY OF THE LOUISIANA STATE MUSEUM.

Top, right: Attorney Edward Livingston came to New Orleans in 1804 from an abbreviated and damaging term as mayor of New York City. He rebuilt his fortune speculating in batture lands and practicing law in Louisiana. He helped draft the Civil Code for Louisiana, and represented the state in the House of Representatives and the U.S. Senate. President Andrew Jackson made him secretary of state.

COURTESY OF THE HISTORIC NEW ORLEANS COLLECTION.

Bottom, left: John Slidell and his brother Thomas came to New Orleans in the 1820s. Both became political powers, one as chief justice of the Louisiana Supreme Court, and the other as a Democratic senator from Louisiana. They embodied the American takeover of Creole Louisiana.

COURTESY OF THE LOUISIANA STATE ARCHIVES COLLECTION.

Bottom, right: Edward Douglass White served as chief justice of the United States from 1910 until his death in 1921. Son of Louisiana Governor Edward Douglas White, he was born in Bayou Lafourche and grew up as a New Orleans lawyer. His grandfather, James White, came to Louisiana around 1807 after an exciting career as congressional Indian agent, territorial representative, and land speculator in five states. While in his first term as a U.S. senator, President Grover Cleveland selected White for the U.S. Supreme Court. Later, President William Howard Taft made him the first sitting justice to be appointed chief justice.

COURTESY OF THE LOUISIANA STATE ARCHIVES COLLECTION.

steam-powered sawmill in the territory. Significantly, he installed it at the mouth of Bayou Manchac, the upper end of the Houmas claim.

One of the most remarkable Americans to come to Louisiana was Dr. James White, who also spoke English, French, and Spanish. Son of a successful Irish merchant in Philadelphia and well-educated in Europe, White moved first to North Carolina, where he was promptly elected to the Continental Congress. There he became the superintendent for Indian affairs for the South, a position that required more travel, especially to the territory of Tennessee. He secured several land grants and moved to Nashville. When Tennessee organized as a territory, it selected White its territorial representative to the United States Congress, the first such representative in American history. White made the contacts that brought Tennessee into the Union in 1796. As soon as Tennessee became a state, he moved on to the

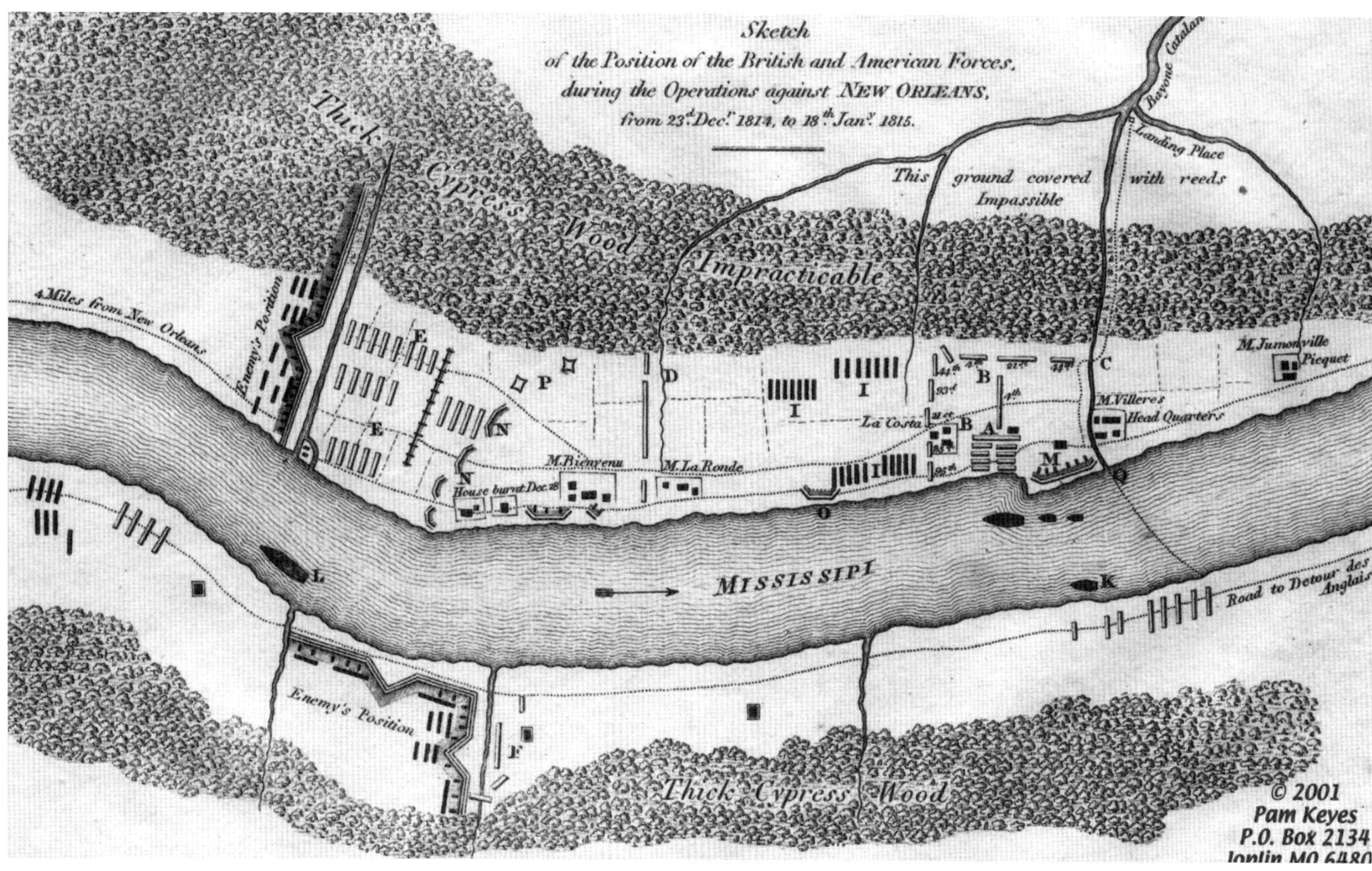

Historian and genealogist Pat Keyes discovered this map and an account of the Battle of New Orleans. This map represents the first published view of the battle and predates Latour's Historical Memoir of the War in West Florida and Louisiana by several months. The map appeared in the summer of 1815 in the Naval Chronicle of London. The map's author is anonymous. References on the map include: A) The bivouac of the troops on December 23; B) The position on the night ditto; C) Ditto on December 24; D) Ditto, after the advance on December 28; E) The attack on January 8; F) Thorton's attack; G) unknown; H) unknown; I) The enemy's attack on December 23; J) unknown; K) An American schooner blown up on December 27; L) An American twenty-four-gun warship; M) Batteries against the schooner; N) Batteries thrown up by the English; O) Ditto to protect the flank; P) Redoubts; and Q) Canal cut to pass boats.

COURTESY OF PAM KEYES.

Mississippi Territory. After settling in Natchez, then along the Pearl River, he journeyed to Pascagoula, where he lived for several years under the Spanish regime. After the Louisiana Purchase his affiliation with Thomas Jefferson brought him the appointment as judge for the Attakapas District, where he died in 1809. But he left a son, Edward Douglas White, who likewise spoke French and English, practiced law, and entered politics. He served five terms in Congress, interrupted in 1835 by a term as governor of Louisiana. E. D. White left five children, but none of them left any children. His namesake, Edward Douglass White, pursued a legal career, went to Washington in 1890 as a United States senator and died chief justice of the United States. All three generations of the Whites were charming storytellers, naturally political, and the very essence of personality. They combined in themselves Louisiana's Catholicism and Francophonism with an indisputable Philadelphia heritage.

Since the dominant Jeffersonian political party wanted new western states, Congress admitted Louisiana to the Union in 1812. This did not please all Creoles. The legislature elected Jean Noel Destrehan as the first United States senator from Louisiana, but he promptly resigned to show his disdain for the new American power. Governor Claiborne could not succeed himself in 1816. The resulting election went to Jacques Philippe Villeré, the first Creole (native-born) governor since the founding of Louisiana in 1699. The popular vote provided Villeré with 2,314 votes to Judge Joshua Lewis' 2,145 votes. Lewis carried East Baton Rouge and everything west and north except the old French settlements at Natchitoches, Pointe Coupée, and West Baton Rouge. The four years of Villeré's administration were prosperous, but continued American immigration ended Creole control. In 1820, Thomas Bolling Robertson won the governorship.

The last time Louisiana played a role in international affairs was the Battle of New Orleans on January 8, 1815. This was the final thrust of England's three-pronged offensive against the United States that concluded the War of 1812. Though the

battle occurred after the signing of the preliminary articles of peace, the decisive American victory sent a message around the world that the new United States was able to defend itself. Its domestic impact was equally important. It increased American self-confidence. The Battle of New Orleans was a victory for Louisiana, but just as important it was a victory for Tennessee and everyone along the western border. General Andrew Jackson, who commanded the American forces at the Chalmette battle site, became the first famous westerner and the first western president. The battle's impact on internal Louisiana affairs was also important. For the first time the French in Louisiana had a common cause with the Americans, for both hated the British. Many of the Tennessee troops who marched south with Jackson had Irish roots. The French had fought the British for centuries for dominance in Europe. The Louisiana French and their Creole descendants thoroughly relished the opportunity to humble England, a cause that all Frenchmen, be they Napoleonic or royalist, could support. Could it be a surprise that Villeré became governor in 1816, the fruit of the common good feelings between the Americans and the Creoles?

Besides Jackson, the most famous "participant" in the Battle of New Orleans was the pirate Jean Laffite. Born in Haiti, he and his brother Pierre entered the privateering business in the 1790s. By 1806 or so they established a port south of New Orleans to which they could bring their captured ships and goods for sale. The most profitable items were the slave ships taken from the cruise to Cuba or the French or English islands. After the United States Constitution in 1808 abolished the legal right to import slaves, Laffite's pirating became exceptionally profitable. Eventually Governor Claiborne's government tried to halt this evasion of the ban on slave imports. Several skirmishes with the pirates took place at their auction site called the Little Temple, a shell mound at the lower end of Barataria Island. Laffite established his warehouse on Grand Terre, one of four swellings in the marsh, beginning on the east with Cheniere Ronquillo, Grande Terre, Grande Isle, and concluding on the west with Cheniere Caminada. In 1814, when the British decided to attack New Orleans, they sent an emissary to Laffite to secure his cooperation. Laffite's undying fame is due to his stout refusal. He sent the original messages to Governor Claiborne to prove his willingness to resist the English. When General Andrew Jackson arrived in Louisiana he immediately asked for the pirates' support. Laffite is credited with providing flints and artillerymen used in the battle. Following the victory at the Battle of New Orleans, Laffite and other privateers organized a new venture directed at taking Texas from Spain. In 1817 they moved onto Galveston Island, where

Left: Andrew Jackson, like George Washington, possessed the charisma of leadership. He could not avoid it. Neither permitted education or family to handicap them. Generals James Wilkinson and Wade Hampton preceded Jackson to New Orleans, but it was Jackson to whom the great opportunity for victory was given. He organized the defense of New Orleans in December 1814 that led to the defeat of the British at the Battle of New Orleans on January 8, 1815. Elected president of the United States in 1828, Jackson shaped a new popular electoral system and founded the Democratic Party.

COURTESY OF THE LOUISIANA STATE MUSEUM.

Below: Felix Achille de Saint-Aulaire came to New Orleans as a young painter in 1820. This view is probably a pilot boat off the mouth of the Mississippi River prior to the age of steam. A few years later, bar pilots operated from steam launches.

COURTESY OF SPECIAL COLLECTIONS, TULANE UNIVERSITY.

they stayed for two years before being evicted by American naval forces. The Laffite brothers public career ended at this point, lost in the confusion of Latin American revolutions.

International trade with its attendant private bankers ensured that Louisiana's products traveled the routes of the world. American control of Louisiana brought banks, signalling the beginning of the integration of Louisiana into the greater American economy. Under the French and Spanish colonial regimes, banks had been unthinkable in Louisiana. But the new American economy encouraged the consolidation of capital. The first bank was the Bank of Louisiana, a private bank. A branch of the Bank of the United States (BUS) soon appeared in New Orleans. For a brief period the BUS did wonders for American economic growth, serving as a central bank. During its reign Louisiana agriculture and trade expanded steadily. In 1829 the Planters Bank opened its doors, followed by the Citizens and the Union Banks. In 1832 President Andrew Jackson effectively circumscribed the power of the Bank of the United States. By the mid-1830s, excessive speculation had spread through the economy. The economic crash of 1837 was so severe that after a few years even the exceptionally solid New Orleans banks closed their doors.

New Orleans banks recovered in the 1840s, helped along by silver from Mexico and investments in the new Texas Republic. As the Civil War loomed, New Orleans banks had the highest ratio of specie to loans of any American banks. They limped through the Civil War, but the slow economic recovery of the late nineteenth century doomed the remnants to extinction. The Canal Bank and Trust Company, founded in 1833 to finance the digging of the New Basin Canal, continued through the nineteenth century and up to the

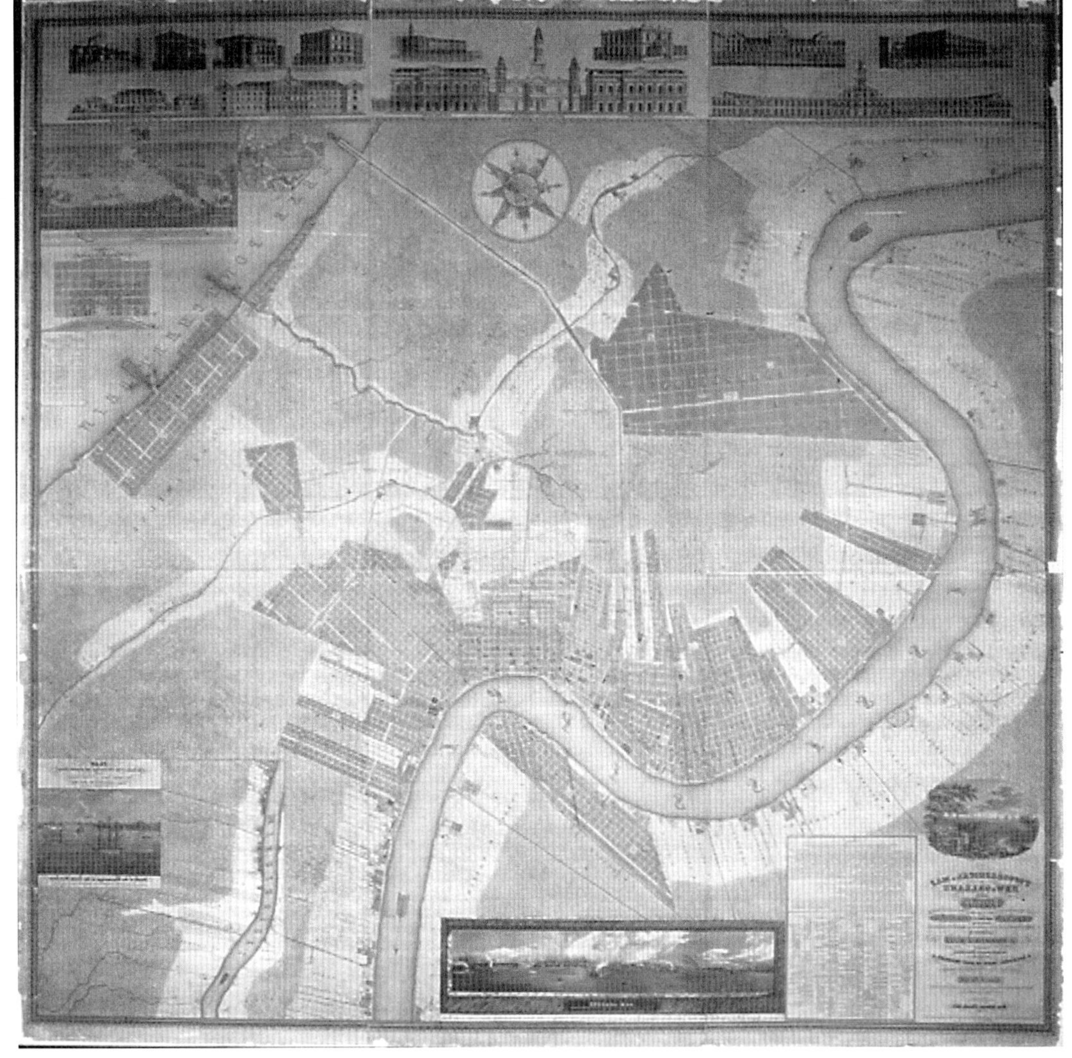

Charles Frederick Zimpel seems to have been a Prussian surveyor and cartographer in Louisiana in the 1800s. He spent the 1830s in New Orleans where he compiled the city's most famous map, the Zimpel map of 1833. An uptown street recalls his work on the New Orleans & Carrollton Railroad. As an architect he designed Banks Arcade and the Bank of New Orleans.

COURTESY OF THE HISTORIC NEW ORLEANS COLLECTION, 1945.13.

Great Depression before it finally succumbed. The oldest bank operating today is the Hibernia, which dates back to the 1870s. The Whitney Bank opened its doors in the 1880s.

A weak to non-existent federal monetary policy hurt Louisiana, while two other federal economic interventions helped its economic growth. Federal Indian removal policy paved the way for the founding of Shreveport. Federal navigation policy provided the funding to Henry Shreve that made the clearance of the Red River raft a reality. With two snag boats of Shreve's design, he began work in 1833, effectively completing a channel to the site of Shreveport by 1839.

An activist Federal Indian policy led to the eviction of Indians from Louisiana as land-holding tribes. The Caddo of northwestern Louisiana were the last group of Indians with a territorial claim in Louisiana. On July 1, 1835, the United States government signed a treaty with the compliant Caddo whereby they gave up their claim to most of Caddo Parish for a payment of $50,000. The Indians, however, reserved 640 acres, which they gave to their white friend and interpreter Larkin Edwards. Edwards had come to the region decades earlier.

After his first wife died, Edwards married a Caddo Indian woman. In 1837 he sold his 640 acres to Henry Shreve, Angus McNeill, Bushrod Jenkins, and five others. These eight purchasers paid Edwards $5,000 for his land and laid out the town of Shreveport. Larkin Edwards' daughter, Mary, married Jacob Irwin, long-time gunsmith for the Caddo Indians. His brother, James Irwin, married Ann Brown Clay, the daughter of U. S. Senator Henry Clay. James Irwin and his family later moved to the vicinity. Their daughter married a son of Dr. John Sibley, who had come to Natchitoches in 1803 and was a friend and informer to President Thomas Jefferson.

Shreveport was the only site along the upper Red River where western bluffs reach to the water's edge, thus eliminating the need to cross the wide morass of boggy marsh adjacent to most of the Red River's course. The Texas Trail crossed the river at this spot, and many Americans were crossing into Texas here. An important stage coach line later followed this route, running from Monroe, on the Ouachita River, via Mount Lebanon and Minden to Shreveport and on to Marshall, Texas.

The Shreve Town Company laid out Shreveport with eight streets running each way, Commerce Street along the river. Even before the survey of the town Bushrod Jenkins had contracted with John Craig of Woodford County, Kentucky, for the construction of a cotton gin. Similarly, Shreve contracted with E. J. Smedley, a millwright of Louisville, Kentucky, to erect a sawmill. Settlers flocked in, and on March 20, 1839 the Legislature chartered the new town. A year earlier the Legislature had created Caddo Parish. Shreve sold his interest in the town for $7,900. John O. Sewall became the first mayor of Shreveport, but he died soon afterwards in a duel.[1] In the 1840s, Shreveport got its first bank, and, by 1850, had one thousand settlers. She went through the Civil War unscathed, and, by 1873, had a population of twelve thousand, making it the same size as Houston and Dallas. That year yellow fever struck Shreveport, causing one of the worst epidemics in the late nineteenth century. Thousands died and the city emptied. Not until the oil boom thirty years later did Shreveport recover.

Alexandria became the principal town of the lower Red River. Located at falls that defined the upper limit of navigation for most of the year, it grew with its parish, Rapides. Alexander Fulton laid out the town of Alexandria between 1805 and 1810, thirteen arpents front by the

✧

Above: Henry M. Shreve (1775-1851) was a self-taught engineer. He built steamboats, an occupation that made him quickly realize the need to clear the Mississippi River of the infamous snags, or large trees, that punctured and sank steamboats. He designed a snag-removal boat and worked for years clearing the Red River. He founded the town of Shreveport in 1837.

COURTESY OF THE HISTORIC NEW ORLEANS COLLECTION, 1974.25.27.400

Below: Shreveport, with its easy access to the cattle markets of East Texas, had an Armour meat-packing plant.

COURTESY OF THE LOUISIANA STATE MUSEUM.

✧

Barksdale Field was dedicated in 1933. It occupies twenty-two thousand acres near Shreveport and Bossier City. Barksdale was host in the 1930s to the Twentieth Pursuit Group. In 1940, Barksdale hosted major army maneuvers in preparation for World War II. Subsequently, Barksdale has been a bomber base, with the first B-52 arriving in 1958. Barksdale is the home of the Eighth Air Force and its museum.

COURTESY OF THE LOUISIANA STATE MUSEUM.

same depth. His business partner was William Miller, the first judge for the parish. Miller was a Pennsylvania merchant who had moved to Louisiana during the Spanish occupation. The principal politician of Rapides quickly became Josiah Stoddard Johnston, who went on to become a Whig United States senator. One of Johnston's brothers remained a prominent planter, and another of his brothers, Albert Sidney Johnston, went on to become a Confederate general. Alexandria became the hub of the district that grew both cotton and sugar in the antebellum period. The first railroad west of the Mississippi went into construction in 1837, extending from the Alexandria courthouse to Bayou Hauffpaur below Cheneyville. It did not survive the Civil War.

By the Civil War, Alexandria was an important center for Confederate supplies. The Confederacy operated a major packing plant that pickled meat to be shipped to their eastern armies. A large foundry and machine shop were the only ones left in Confederate hands in Louisiana save Shreveport. A shipyard turned steamboats into gunboats. With the return of the Union Army in 1864, the town was entirely burned, including the courthouse.

Shreve's snag removal boats worked the Mississippi River for decades. Snag removal was an essential component in the spectacular rise of steamboating, a mode of transportation that for decades rivaled railroads. For Louisiana, steamboating ensured that the principal artery of transportation went north to south, rather than west to east. Louisiana was the beneficiary. Louisiana's first railroads were links between towns and water routes.

In 1830 the New Orleans-Pontchartrain Railroad, one of the first in the nation, tied the city proper to the steamboat routes on Lake Pontchartrain which extended east to Mobile. It took forty more years for the railroad to cross the Rigolets and extend to Mobile. The Opelousas and Great Western Railroad commenced at Algiers across from New Orleans, but extended no farther than Morgan City. Prior to the Civil War it simply shortened the water route to Texas on the west. The Nashville and Great Northern Railroad was the one railroad that never included a water link. Intended to strengthen the north-south trade axis, before the Civil War it could only reach Jackson, Mississippi. As an aftermath of the Civil War, Henry Simpson McComb scooped up the pieces of the railroad and assembled the southern portion into an acceptable line that soon ended up as the southern link of the Chicago-owned Illinois Central. He founded the town that became McComb, Mississippi, to be the railroad repair yards for the line.

Following the Civil War, the success of Louisiana agriculture soon came to depend on another federal policy—flood control. In the eighteenth century and up to the Civil War, the responsibility for the levees belonged to the riparian owner. Nevertheless, some parishes contributed to the cost of levees, notably Concordia, which spent $600,000 on levees before 1861. Just out of law school, young Edward Douglass White, the future chief justice of the United States, won his first case by arguing that the State of Louisiana, with federal funds, had acquired the responsibility to maintain the levees, not the individual riparian owners. The immediate consequence was the creation of the Louisiana Levee Company, a carpetbagger scheme that milked the state. Louisiana began contracting with parish governments to build levees, but by the 1890s reformers began insisting that a new governmental body was needed—the levee board. With federal assistance in the form of donated marshlands, the new levee boards took over the powers and responsibilities of levee construction. The results were dramatic, if the means were environmentally destructive. The levee boards along the Bayou Lafourche used their public powers to manipulate the Federal Government into permitting the closure of Bayou Lafourche. The temporary dam placed at Donaldsonville in 1900 became permanent, and landowners seized and built on the former water bed of the Bayou Lafourche. Many of the old levees were removed. The former water route to the plantations was replaced by a railroad line in 1899, a branch of the Texas Pacific Railroad.

That the United States Army Corps of Engineers should become the dominant agency in channeling the Mississippi River was a vagary of Civil War politics. The basic work was in the former occupied lands of the South, so instead of creating a staff for the civilian Mississippi River Commission, it co-opted the military Corps of Engineers. It was at this point that a second great river engineer helped to change the course of Louisiana history, James Eads. He introduced the idea of jetties at the mouth of the Mississippi that employed the force of the river to scour the channel. Silt that had formerly filled the channel now surged out to deeper water. The jetty system worked marvelously for a century, but apparently has reached the limits of its effectiveness. The immense draft of modern ships again require continuous dredging to maintain the required depth of almost one hundred feet.

From the creation of the Mississippi River Commission in 1879 until 1928, the dominant policy had called for flood control through a levees-only policy. But it was not until 1917 that Congress passed a bill explicitly to fund additional levees to control floods. Most of the smaller earlier appropriations had been disguised as navigational improvements employing earlier rationales that extended back to the Whig days. The impetus for the 1917 act was the failure of the levee system in 1912, 1913 and to a lesser extent in 1916 that led to massive flooding all along the Mississippi River Valley. By the mid-1920s, however, the main line levees had been created and flood control was achieved. The devastating flood of 1927 erased that conclusion and forced a multi pronged flood control effort legislated in the 1928 act known as the Yadwin plan. This plan created extensive flood plains along the Mississippi River in Missouri and down the Atchafalaya River in Louisiana. As extended in the 1930s, the plan envisaged the creation of dams on the rivers that fed into the Mississippi, dams that would impound water in flood times and permit gradual release in low water periods. As amplified by the works of the Tennessee Valley Authority, it led to an extensive set of recreational lakes and lakes that held drinking water for the growing cities of the southeast. All of this was an offshoot of the need to stop flooding on the Mississippi.

Alexandria was a transhipment point at the headwaters for the transportation on the Red River for many years. Cotton was grown on all sides of the city. The Kisatchee National Forest surrounds Alexandria and has provided many jobs.

COURTESY OF THE LOUISIANA STATE MUSEUM.

For the first time the Corps employed nature to help restrain the Mississippi. In the next century it seems clear the river will have to be untied from its levees so that marshlands can be reflooded to prevent south Louisiana from sinking beneath the Gulf of Mexico.

For south Louisiana the most important monument to the 1927 flood is the Old River Control Structure. This dam with spillway is designed to ensure that no more than thirty percent of the Mississippi River water ever flows down the Atchafalaya River. To put it another way, it is designed to take thirty percent of the Mississippi's water so that water height on the main line levees can be reduced in flood years. It has worked for the last sixty years, but many question how much longer. The underlying issue is the fate of the port of New Orleans. If the Mississippi changes its mouth, will the port remain viable?

Another federal program that had a dramatic effect on Louisiana was the campaign to eradicate yellow fever. As a port, New Orleans had attracted both immigrants and their diseases. Throughout the nineteenth century yellow fever had regularly devastated Louisiana. Since the 1790s this plague of the tropics had visited New Orleans aboard ships coming from Martinique or Cuba. It came in the bloodstream of sick sailors or passengers. One mosquito bite sent the virus spiraling across the marshes of Louisiana on the wings of the *Aedes aegypti*. Epidemics in 1796, the 1820s, especially 1853 and 1854, 1878, and 1897 set back the growth of Louisiana by killing thousands of people.

Finally experiments in Cuba following the Spanish-American War showed that it was the mosquito that transmitted the disease. At experimental stations just outside Havana, Walter Reed and his assistants James Carroll, Aristides Agramonte, and Jesse Lazear proved that the *Aedes aegypti* mosquito was the carrier for the yellow fever virus. Their work destroyed the popular notion that yellow fever spread by direct contact with infected people or "contaminated" objects and focused the people's efforts on the eradication of the *Aedes* mosquito. The last yellow fever epidemic hit New Orleans in 1905. The announcement of the way to prevent the disease sparked a general cleanup of the city by the eradication of open pools of water, the destruction of old cisterns, and the introduction of the screen porch.

✧

In 1845, Captain Thomas B. Leathers (1816-1896) launched the line of Mississippi River steamboats named the Natchez. *He lived in prominent homes in New Orleans. His boats established the speed record from New Orleans to St. Louis of 3 days, 21 hours, and 50 minutes. He was the most famous for the steamboat races between the* Natchez VI *and the* Robert E. Lee. *He died after being hit by a St. Charles Avenue streetcar.*

COURTESY OF SPECIAL COLLECTIONS, TULANE UNIVERSITY.

Even before the Federal Government had begun the campaign against yellow fever, Louisiana public health doctors began a campaign to control Hansen's Disease. In the eighteenth century, Andres Almonaster had funded the creation of a retreat house behind the city where leprosy victims could live. A century later reporter John Smith Kendall of the *New Orleans Picayune* wrote a series of articles pointing out a rise in the number of leprosy cases. The members of the Orleans Parish Medical Society, led by the great dermatologist Dr. Isadore Dyer, turned their attention to the disease. Their fundamental public health tool was isolation, but they determined to try it outside of the urban pest house and in a healthful farm setting. But they knew that isolation was not a cure. They were determined that the asylum should be a place of treatment and research for a cure—not simply a place of detention. They were humanitarians who believed the asylum should be a place a refuge, not of reproach.

In 1894 the state purchased a site for a new facility that came to be known as Carville. An order of Catholic nuns, the Daughters of Charity, agreed to provide the staffing for

Carville, a task few lay people could bring themselves to undertake. The Daughters served at Carville from its founding until its closing in the 1990s.

Between 1905 and 1916, the state of Louisiana embarked on two major building programs for Carville. In 1905 it began constructing numerous bungalow-style cottages for use as patient, medical, and chaplain facilities, and added a clinic and dining facilities, a laboratory and operating room, and a central steam plant for heating. By 1916 it had added $30,000 worth of cottages, a waterworks, fire protection and sanitary sewer systems, an electrical plant, a cold storage plant, and a new clinic.

One of the great architectural features of the early campus was the introduction in 1905 of the first covered walkways, prototypes of the elegant two-story, enclosed walkways that distinguish the campus today. These early raised boardwalks connected the bungalows from building to building at porch level, "making it possible for a patient to walk or be conveyed under cover from any building to another, without ever having to negotiate steps or try to roll a wheel chair across wet grass.

When Senator Joseph Ransdell of Louisiana became acquainted with Carville, he realized that the cure of leprosy was a national concern. He introduced legislation to provide for the funding of a national hospital Founding and developing the state leprosarium may well be the single most progressive act of the state's history, and it le eventually to the Congressional act, passed in 1917, that permitted the U.S. Public Health Service to purchase the Louisiana Leper Home. World War I delayed implementation, but the sale culminated in 1921. From 1921 until 1941 hundreds of experiments were undertaken at Carville to find cures for Hansen's Disease. In the 1930s the New Deal poured funding into Carville to create a new facility of double quadrangles with covered walkways and complete laboratories.

In 1940, Dr. Guy Faget arrived at Carville as chief medical officer in charge. As the name suggests, Dr. Faget was no stranger to Louisiana. A tuberculin specialist, he had a background in treating acid-fast diseases, such as leprosy. Before the close of his first year, Dr. Faget had begun to correspond with researchers at Parke-Davis Company, and, in March 1921, his first volunteers were injected with the Sulfone drug Promine. After the first volunteers received treatment with Promine, improvements were slow but dramatic. Early cases recovered in six months, and advanced cases got better in two to three years. Soon other drugs were added. Abbott Laboratories unveiled Diason in 1943, and Promizole came on the market in 1945. Through careful testing, Carville doctors, with important contributions from the Daughters of Charity nursing staff, learned to regulate dosages to limit side effects. For the first time in history, Hansen's Disease patients began to get well and be discharged in large numbers from Carville.

Louisiana's relations with the United States perfectly exemplify the complexity of human relations. Twice an unwilling partner, Louisiana has reveled in her Americanisms. She has profited from the wealth of America She has given her port, her sugar, her timber, and her oil to the greater partner. Only two things she has held back—her sense of self and her sense of place.

James Buchanan Eads (1820-1887) was a civil engineer, though untrained, who constructed the first bridge across the Mississippi River. Built of brick and steel, its central span stretched five hundred feet. Salvage operations on the Mississippi gave him an acute knowledge of hydrology. He conceived the idea of jetties to funnel and scour the channel at the mouth of the Mississippi. The splendid success in 1879 made him a household name in Louisiana. His achievement earned him recognition worldwide.

COURTESY OF THE HISTORIC NEW ORLEANS COLLECTION, 1974.25.27.122.

Chapter III Endnotes

[1] 1 J. Fair Hardin, "An Outline of Shreveport and Caddo Parish History" *The Louisiana Historical Quarterly,* Volume 18 no. 4 (October, 1935), 759-871.

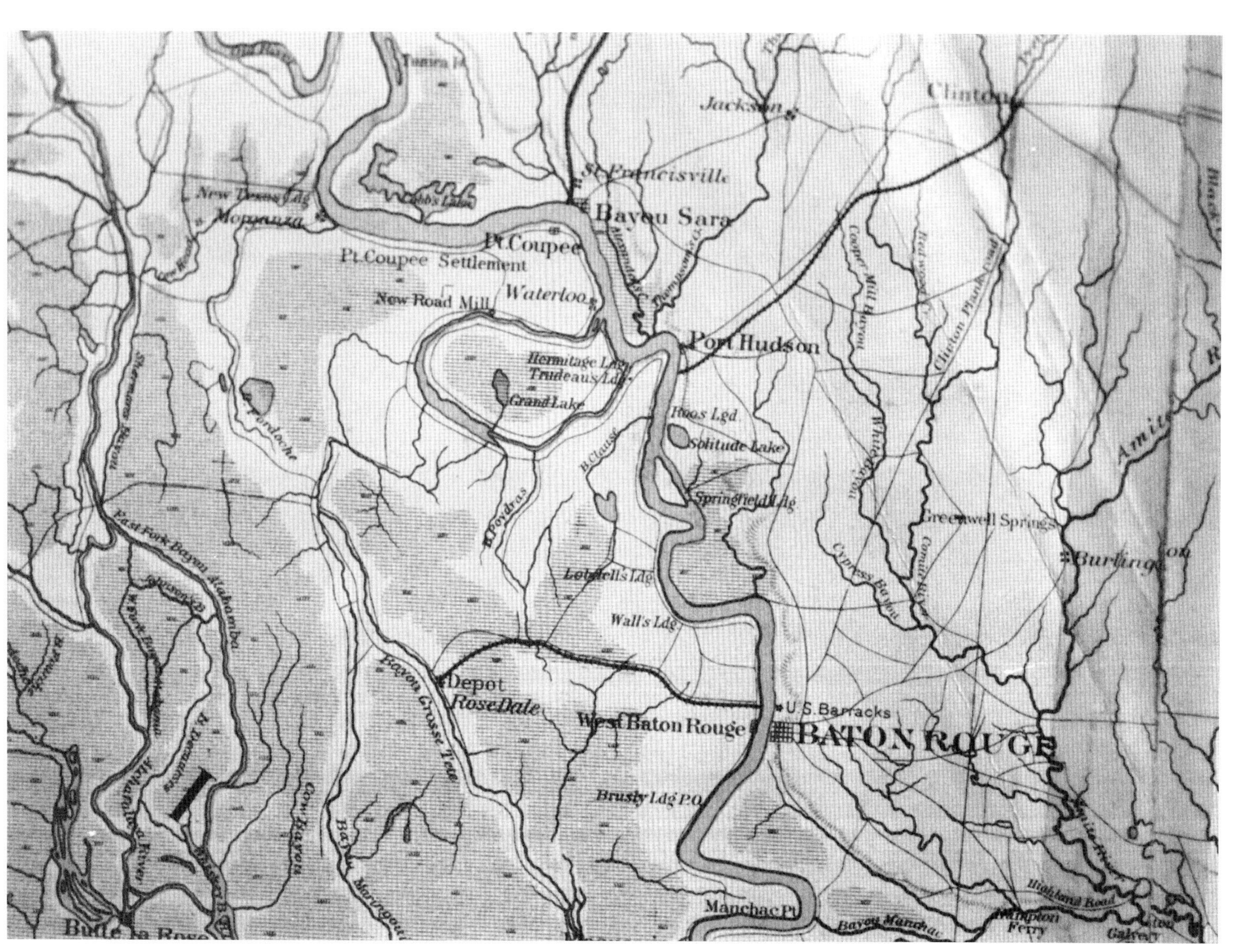

Jackson
Clinton
St. Francisville
Bayou Sara
Pt. Coupee
Pt. Coupee Settlement
New Road Mill
Waterloo
Port Hudson
Hermitage Ldg
Grand Lake
Roos Lgd.
Solitude Lake
Springfield Ldg
Greenwell Springs
Lobdell's Ldg
Wall's Ldg
Cypress Bayou
Depot
Rose Dale
West Baton Rouge
U.S. Barracks
BATON ROUGE
Brusly Ldg P.O.
Manchac Pt
Bayou Manchac
Highland Road
Ferry
East Fork Bayou Alabama
Bayou Grosse Tete
Cow Bayou

CHAPTER IV

MAKING A LIVING: AGRICULTURE

Louisiana's economy in the eighteenth and nineteenth centuries depended almost exclusively on the renewable resource called agriculture. Her great export crops of cotton, sugar and rice made parts of Louisiana prosperous. This prosperity drew people to the state, slaves by coercion and whites seeking wealth. By 1860, Louisiana had the largest percentage of the United States population in its history—2.25 percent. In contrast, by 2000 Louisiana's percentage of the United States population was 1.56 percent, a drop in influence of thirty percent. Of Louisiana's population in 1860, the overwhelming majority worked in agriculture. Of her 700,000 souls, only 8,800 worked in manufacturing. The value of all the farms was $204 million, compared to only $7 million invested in manufacturing. More than 300,000 slaves worked in agriculture along with 50,000 whites. Living and working the land was the life and business for most Louisianians.

Even today, though the number of farm laborers is under forty thousand, Louisiana's renewable resources—her agriculture, seafood, commerce, and tourism—are a significant part of her economy. Of Louisiana's renewable resources, timber is the most productive, sugarcane is second in value at $306 million a year, rice third at $275 million, and cotton fourth at $241 million. The seafood industry was worth $231 million in 1995. Louisiana supplies twenty-five percent of the nation's seafood harvest. Soybeans are the fifth ranked crop at $123 million. Just as soybeans and cotton alternate in north Louisiana, in south Louisiana rice and sugar have alternated. Though timber and rice have long been important crops in Louisiana, their national significance only dates to the late nineteenth century, when northern capital transformed the crop from merely local to national production.

This map of Baton Rouge from around 1861 shows three railroads bringing cotton to the Mississippi River. The St. Francisville-Woodville Railroad extends north from Bayou Sarah. The Port Hudson-Clinton Railroad extends to East Feliciana. The Baton Rouge-Grosse Tete Railroad also brought sugar to market from the fields along Bayou Grosse Tete and Bayou Maringuin.

SUGAR

Sugar has been the crop grown longest in Louisiana and for many years was its largest employer. Though sugar planting had its roots in the Creole transition, American planters such as John Randolph and Wade Hampton dominated it by the 1830s. Not surprisingly, they did not copy the Creole plan but operated their plantations as systems of total control. One of the great sugar plantations of Louisiana was at the Houmas, just downriver from the new town of Donaldsonville. The Houmas Indians occupied the site from 1704 until 1776, when their chiefs put the land on the market. Consisting of a square league, it had ninety arpents front on the Mississippi and a depth of three miles. In 1811, South Carolina cotton planter Wade Hampton purchased part of Houmas to grow sugar. Recognizing its immense potential, Hampton immediately ordered his son to bring over eighty slaves from his South Carolina estates. At the conclusion of the War of 1812, Hampton ordered new sugar equipment to be shipped to Houmas from New York. The equipment included eight new copper kettles valued at $2,910, each weighing from 300 to 800 pounds.

To sell his sugar, Hampton developed efficient modes of transportation and finance. He arranged with his northern correspondents to have sea-going ships come up the Mississippi River to receive the sugar directly from his docks at White Hall, Point Houmas, and Houmas. When the German trader J. G. Flugel passed the Houmas in 1817, he recorded in his journal that he had seen a three-masted ship loading at Hampton's place. "Passed General Hampton's plantation (sugar), where a three-master lies which sight is pleasing to me." In the late fall of 1828 the brig *Artic* picked up 41 hogsheads from White Hall and the Brig Dodge Healy loaded 273 hogsheads at Point Houmas. Hampton maintained agents in many cities—Liverpool (Wm Forde & Co.), Baltimore (Harrison & Sterett), and New York (Goodhue & Co.). The agent accepted the hogsheads of sugar, divided them into reasonable size lots, and auctioned them off. In one sale, for example, five of his hogsheads from

✧

Right: Wade Hampton, Jr. (1791-1858), exemplifies a recurring figure in Louisiana history: the man who comes to Louisiana to operate a business and then departs. For many planters, timber and oil men, Louisiana was only a place to make money, not to live. Son of General Wade Hampton, he operated Houmas Plantation, as well as the only cotton lands in South Carolina and Mississippi. His political influence in South Carolina was extreme. His son, also named Wade Hampton, succeeded his father's influence. In the Civil War, Wade III rose to the rank of major general of the Confederacy and later became the governor of South Carolina.

COURTESY OF THE HISTORIC NEW ORLEANS COLLECTION, 1987.43.21.

Below: The lavish interior of the steamboat Great Republic.

COURTESY OF THE LOUISIANA STATE MUSEUM.

the ship *Sarah Thornton* sold for eight-and-a-half cents a pound. The hogsheads were weighed at a gross weight of 5,824 pounds, less a tare weight of 699 pounds, leaving 5,125 net salable pounds (1,024 pounds per hogshead) worth $435.62. By this method of shipment Hampton avoided all the New Orleans middlemen charges, not to mention the risks and delay attendant on transshipment there. The same method is used today as ocean going ships pass New Orleans headed for the great chemical refineries that have replaced the sugar plantations. Houmas became more and more profitable. On December 27, 1834, Jesse Strong reported to Hampton that he had made the largest crop ever at the Houmas, twelve hundred hogsheads. A few weeks later the eighty-one year-old Hampton read his overseer's report and penciled in his profit for that year, "$119,000."

In 1848, Hampton's sons-in-law, John Manning and John Preston, partitioned Houmas Plantation. The buildings and machinery on the Mannings part of Houmas were extensive and first-rate. The principal building was the brick overseer's house of eight rooms and an office. Each of the thirty-three slave cabins had a front gallery, two sitting rooms, and four sleeping rooms. Half were of brick, half of cypress. The plantation had 2 two-story stables, each 106 feet long by 50 feet wide. There was a blacksmith shop made of brick, as well as a carpenters, wheelwright, and coopers shop. The sugarhouse was 320 feet by 52 feet, with a height of seventeen feet to the eaves and a roof of slate. It used an open kettle system and made fair brown sugar.

Hampton's second son-in-law, John Preston, brought William Seale down from South Carolina in the early 1850s to oversee his nine thousand acres. Seale's diary provides a valuable look at what the workers did day-by-day on a large sugar plantation in the 1850s. He began it on January 1, 1853, and kept it faithfully for nine months, after which he made occasional entries for several years.

Sugar requires dry land. The first job of workers on sugar plantations was ditching. In January on Houmas dozens of men and women worked clearing the ditches. Ditching was hard dangerous work, and on many plantations the work was contracted out to gangs of Irish laborers. English journalist William Howard Russell observed that "the labor of ditching, trenching, cleaning the waste lands, and hewing down the forests, is generally done by Irish laborers, who travel about the country under contractors." On Houmas the ditches ran back to the rear levee that cost $100,000 to build. A great drainage machine pumped 175,000 gallons of rainwater a minute over the levee. The drainage machine was a cast-iron thirty-foot wheel that lifted water over the rear levees. A $30,000 steam engine of 140 horsepower operated the wheel and also drove a sawmill.

The second job on the sugar plantation was chopping wood to feed the steam engines at next season's grinding. Workers chopped wood more or less continuously from January to August, accumulating about three thousand cords of wood. But the slave workers also had to cut shingles and make barrel staves. In February on Houmas five men worked to cut shingles, and another five brought out six thousand staves for barrels. A highly respected slave named Peter Nott supervised a gang that made thirty thousand staves and a new cistern for the quarters.

The preparation of the fields for a new cane crop also continued after the end of January. The preceding fall workers had plowed two hundred and twenty acres of cane land, and actually planted one hundred acres. In January, while some men were ditching and others were cutting wood, most were planting. Planting meant that the cane seedlings were laid across the furrow, four inches apart, alternating and overlapping eight inches on each side of the furrow. The heads all faced the same direction. The canes were then covered with soil. The slaves planted fourteen acres on January 3, another twelve on January 4. Three ox carts hauled the cane seedlings. Six three-horse plows prepared another hundred acres and then turned to plowing for the corn crop, the essential food source for the plantation.

Once the planting was done at Houmas, sixty men began scraping cane, all the while continuing to plant additional acreage in corn. Scraping was the process of reducing the amount of soil covering the plant cane to no more than two inches, so that the heat of the sun would induce sprouting. Yet another March activity was the planting of twelve acres of pumpkins, considered an experiment. In May the workers were running thirty plows in the cane to control weeds.

The slaves were simultaneously hauling sugar and molasses from the sugar house to ships tied up in the river. The process of shipping sugar directly from the plantation to refineries in the east that Hampton had inaugurated continued up to the Civil War. On January 27, 1853, the bark *Parson Warren* loaded sixty-five hogsheads of sugar from the Conway sugarhouse. The next day they hauled 127 hogsheads out of the Clark sugarhouse. On the twenty-ninth the gang turned to filling barrels with molasses and completed two hundred and ten barrels by 3 p.m.

Left: Young sugarcane with the sugar mill in the background.

COURTESY OF THE LOUISIANA STATE MUSEUM.

Right: A pair of oxen pulling a cart to town. These animals were the principal power source until the introduction of mules in the nineteenth century.

COURTESY OF THE LOUISIANA STATE MUSEUM.

✧

For a century and a half, the waterboy was a staple of the Louisiana sugar and cotton plantations.

COURTESY OF THE LOUISIANA STATE MUSEUM.

Two days later they hauled one hundred and thirty barrels of molasses down to the ship.

Besides spring planting, cutting wood, ditching, scraping, and hauling molasses, the workers also built new sugarhouses. On February 28, 1853, workers commenced pulling down the machinery in the old sugar-house, and four carts were set to hauling brick for the new cooling room and purgery. Peter Nott, the slave who had built the cistern, was assigned to frame the windows and doors. By March 11 they had commenced pulling down the walls of the old mill, and by the eighteenth all hands were cleaning the mill and engine off the old foundation. Four days later they started building the new foundation. A month later, on April 25, the new machinery arrived at the plantation aboard the *Mideastern*. By the middle of May twenty-three hands were working installing the bed-plates and cylinders, as well as the boilers. By the first of June the crew had finished the chimney for the boiler.

In the sugarhouse, immense rollers flattened and squeezed the cane, extracting sugar-laden juice that ran into kettles. For many decades the smaller plantations used horse or oxen power to operate the rollers. At first the Louisiana planter employed the open kettle system. Under that system, the sugar-maker boiled the juice in four open kettles of successive sizes, consuming a great deal of fuel wood in the process. In the early years, the juice was also clarified, or skimmed of impurities, as it boiled. The sugar-maker added lime during the boiling to cause dirt, bits of stalk, and other impurities to float to the surface, and then skimmed them off. But he unavoidably remixed any remaining impurities into the juice as he ladled it progressively into the smaller kettles. The juice came to its thickest concentration in the smallest kettle, the "battery," where it had to be boiled just enough but not too much. Undercooking would increase the amount of syrup that failed to crystallize, and too much boiling would scorch the sugar. When the sugar maker decided that he had allowed the right amount of boiling, he made a "strike" and ladled the sugar into cooling troughs, at which point it began to crystallize.

Even after boiling, skimming, and cooling, some of the juice would fail to crystallize, and the sticky residue that remained in the crystals had to be separated out from the pure sugar and marketed as molasses. The molasses was collected in a building called the "purgery," a long structure much like a wine-aging room, where the molasses dripped slowly out of perforated hogsheads of sugar into larger molasses barrels. Visualizing this, one can easily imagine the source of the expression "slow as molasses."

The vacuum pan boiling system addressed the problems of fuel consumption, scorching, and crystallization by replacing the smallest open iron kettle (the "battery") with a closed copper pan with a dome-shaped cover. In it, the reduced juice could be boiled in a vacuum at a lower temperature, precluding scorching and allowing reboiling of the juice to make more sugar crystals and less molasses.

In 1830, free man of color Norbert Rillieux invented the multiple effect evaporating process. His parents sent him to Paris to study, where he became a civil engineer.

Edmond Forstall hired Rillieux to install the system on his plantation, but a longstanding feud between the Rillieux family and Forstall ended the engagement. Rillieux first demonstrated the effectiveness of the steam train on the plantation of Theodore Packwood in 1843. The Rillieux system used a copper tubing system to pipe exhaust steam from the grinding mill to a jacket under the first kettle. It was called a train because the four kettles were hooked together by copper steam pipes. The heat released by the boiling liquid in the first kettle then traveled in the copper tube to the second kettle, and so on. This system consumed much less energy than the open pan system, for the same steam was used three times to heat the kettles, while the vacuum pan used a lower temperature for the final boiling. The Rillieux system cut the energy consumption of sugar making in half while simultaneously increasing the efficiency of the process. His machinery remains the foundation of sugar making today.

In 1860, slaves made up forty-six percent of Louisiana's population. Nearly all worked on sugar or cotton plantations. On Houmas Plantation available information shows that, compared to inner cities today, these rural workers lived within a strong family structure that carried over from generation to generation. Families grew large, sent out young shoots, and other families started, formed of marriages between the large old-line families. From about one hundred slaves in 1815, Houmas steadily increased in numbers. By 1844, Houmas had 526 slaves serving in more than two dozen occupations. Though most did field work, a substantial minority practiced a variety of professions. They erected the largest structures and the smallest. Black carpenters and masons such as Peter Nott built the various sugar houses, as well as the fences and barrels.

Besides its size, the Houmas had another remarkable characteristic. The slaves lived in families headed by both a mother and father. In 1848 there were 584 individuals on Houmas, of which 518 (eighty-nine percent) lived in family groups and only 66 were unrelated individuals. Most remarkable of all is that 105 of the 127 family groups contained both the man and woman or father and mother as the case may be. Of everyone on the Houmas, 444 or seventy-six percent lived in families headed by both a man and a woman. Only twenty-two of the family groups were single-parent families. There was thus a remarkably strong family structure amongst the slave workers of Houmas plantation.

The families continued right up to the Civil War. Eighteen of the families had six or more members. Marcellas and Kitty Haines had nine

Left: Norbert Rillieux was the natural son of Vincent Rillieux, a merchant and inventor, and of free woman of color Constance Vivant. His scientific mind led him to address the most useful and useless questions of the day, from how to refine sugar to how to decode the Rosetta Stone. Trained, like many Creoles, in Paris schools as an engineer, he developed a multiple effect evaporator that replaced the antique system of open kettles with ladles used in the manufacture of sugar. By 1850, fourteen major plantations employed the Rillieux process and his ideas remain the basis for sugar making today.

COURTESY OF THE LOUISIANA STATE MUSEUM.

Below: An aerial view of the modern town of Monroe facing the Ouchita River.

January 10, 1844. Daily Report of...employment on the Houmas.

Field work	293	Ostlers	9
Wood cutters	9	Blacksmith	4
Brass founders	-	Wheelwright	5
Cooper	3	Carpenters	5
Bricklayers	2	Saw mill	5
Cook	3	Laundresses	3
Seamstresses	1	Barn house	9
Grist mill	10 on Sat.	Gap minders	1
Stock minders	5	Harness makers	1
Collar makers	2	Foremen	1
Nursing children	19	Hospital nurses	4
Midwife	2	Pregnant	5
Child under 7	130		
Light workers	5(convalescent)		
Total	**526**		

Above: A slave inventory for Houmas Plantation in the mid-1800s.

Bottom, left: The sugar district was just below Canal Street.

COURTESY OF THE LOUISIANA STATE MUSEUM.

Bottom, right: Plantation workers harvesting sugarcane.

COURTESY OF THE LOUISIANA STATE MUSEUM.

children by 1858, ranging from Caroline, age twenty, down to Joseph, just born. Their boys were named Isaac, Gabriel, Luke, John, Mark, and Joseph. Notice the old Gospel nature of the names they gave their boys. Part of the family, perhaps a large part, stayed in Ascension Parish after the Civil War. Their second youngest son, Mark, presided over a large family in 1890, with his wife, Charlotte, and eight children. Tom and Rose Milan had eight children, ranging from seventeen-year-old Lott to newly born Patuner. Included was a set of twins, age ten. Archy and Dido Davis also had eight children, ranging in age from twelve-year-old John to one-year-old Milford. Archy Junior was two. There were many sons with the same name as their father and the appellation "Junior." These included George Whitesides, Jr., Toby Ward, Jr., and Dandridge Claiborne, Jr.

Billy Easy had been born in Africa. He and his wife Sally had brought fourteen children into the world. When journalist William Russell met him in 1862, he was living by the river's edge, engaged in the work of a "porter." Typically the porter lived in a finely ornamented "porter's lodge," such as is still found at Manresa in Convent, Louisiana. At Houmas, he was called "Boatswain." He lived with his old wife, Sally Bartley, in a wooden hut close by the margin of the Mississippi. They were both born in 1788. His business was to go to Donaldsonville for letters, meat, or ice for the house. "Boatswain" told Russell that though he was born in Africa, he had no desire to return. "I'm getting very old, massa. Massa Burnside very good to Boatswain.... Golla Mighty gave me fourteen children, but he took them all away again from Sally and me."

In the 1840s the United States consumed about 550 million pounds of sugar annually, with 300 million pounds coming from Louisiana and Texas. Cuba supplied the difference. American expansionism in the 1840s occasionally looked Cuba's way. Small armies of adventurers occasionally organized in New Orleans to invade Cuba, a phenomena that continued into the 1960s. But many of Louisiana sugar planters opposed any effort to annex Cuba for the good reason that it would lead to the wholesale importation of Cuban sugar without benefit of tariff. Why, they reasoned, should Louisiana sugar planters be put out of business to help Cuban planters?

The Louisiana sugar industry today is essentially the same size as the industry in the 1850s. In 1850 there were 865 steam operated sugar mills and 681 horsepower sugar mills producing 270 million pounds of sugar in Louisiana. In the 1850s sugar output doubled to 528 million pounds. By 1990, Louisiana sugar production had only increased to 860 million pounds, a nominal increase over 140 years. The number of steam operated mills increased to 1,027, but consolidation and efficiency reduced the number of horsepower mills to 264. By 1990 the number of Louisiana sugar mills had dropped to nineteen.

Sugar mills produce the raw sugar from the cane, but sugar refineries make it white, thus more marketable. The seasonal nature of Louisiana's sugar industry worked against establishing many refineries in the state, but there were always a few. From the 1840s there was a sugar refinery at the Chalmette Battlefield known by the name of Battle-Ground Refinery. It can be considered the antecedent to the great refinery erected by the American Sugar Trust in 1909 in the same general location. The Louisiana Steam Refinery operated in New Orleans, as did the Lafayette refinery. Valcour Aime operated his St. James refinery on his plantation near Oak Alley. Besides granulating Louisiana sugar, the refineries all imported Cuban sugar. The latter was available year round because of the long growing season in Cuba. Bringing in the sugar was an idea that helped support Louisiana refineries and has been used continuously until the present day. Louisiana raw sugar was also shipped north up the Mississippi. In the late 1840s, twenty-five thousand hogsheads of sugar a year were shipped upstream to St. Louis and Cincinnati.

COTTON

Cotton and sugar have traditionally divided Louisiana. Sugar dominates the south and cotton the north of the state. Though cotton is considered an upland crop, in Louisiana its growth is synonymous with the river bottomlands along the Mississippi and Red Rivers. Cotton was and is grown on the richest lands, not the poorest.

Unlike sugar, the commercial expansion of cotton growing in the nineteenth century was

Left: These quarters are excellent examples of Creole cottages.

COURTESY OF THE LOUISIANA STATE MUSEUM.

Bottom, left: An intriguing image of longshoremen resting atop hogsheads of sugar.

COURTESY OF THE LOUISIANA STATE MUSEUM.

Bottom, right: The sugar exchange followed the cotton exchange by a few years. The sugar landing was just below Canal Street at Iberville. The sugar refinery, sugar analysis laboratories, and related warehouses were clustered in this area.

COURTESY OF THE LOUISIANA STATE MUSEUM.

✧

Right: *The American Sugar Refinery resulted from the sugar monopoly of the 1890s. This refinery opened in 1909 near a site that had a sugar refinery since the early nineteenth century. American refined the Louisiana cane, but also imported Cuban sugar.*

COURTESY OF THE NEW ORLEANS PUBLIC LIBRARY.

Below: A picnic at Southdown Plantation near Houma commemorates the importance Southdown played in the survival of Louisiana's sugar industry. In the early nineteenth century, the mosaic virus ravaged the industry. Sugar production had reached an all-time high of nearly 400,000 tons in 1904, but by 1926 was less than 50,000 tons. In 1922, Southdown had begun planting the new P.O.J. varieties of sugarcane imported by the U.S. Department of Agriculture. In 1925, Southdown, the USDA, and the American Sugar Cane League began distributing the disease-resistant varieties throughout the state. This image came from an exhibit at the LSU libraries in 1996, entitled " Sugar at LSU: Archiving the Past, Researching the Future."

COURTESY OF THE LOUISIANA OFFICE OF TOURISM.

the consequence of one simple invention. Eli Whitney graduated from Yale in 1792, and two years later patented the cotton gin on March 14, 1794. The cotton gin is a machine that separates seeds, hulls and other unwanted materials from cotton after it has been picked. The machine was so valuable and so easy to duplicate that Whitney's patent gave him no protection and no income. Three years later he abandoned efforts to protect his patent. It was almost 150 years before another mechanical invention revolutionized cotton production. The mechanical cotton harvesters are of two types, strippers and pickers. Stripper harvesters strip the entire plant of both open and unopened bolls along with many leaves and stems. Picker machines, often called spindle-type harvesters, remove the cotton from open bolls and leave the bur on the plant.

The antebellum South witnessed an immense expansion in the cotton crop. In 1800 the United States exported forty-five thousand bales of cotton. Between 1815 and 1840, cotton output in the South jumped from 200,000 to 1.35 million bales weighing 400

Top, left: *Whites also worked in the fields picking cotton. These men could also be part owners of the tract, the small farmers of Northern Louisiana.*

COURTESY OF THE LOUISIANA STATE MUSEUM.

Top, right: *The second Cotton Exchange Building. Prior to the Civil War, planters received news about cotton prices from their factor or newspapers. In 1871, cotton merchants and bankers organized the New Orleans Cotton Exchange to improve the flow of information, mainly pricing. Grading standards and their administration was also an important duty of the new association. The first Cotton Exchange was in a building on the corner of Carondelet and Gravier Streets in New Orleans. On the same corner in 1883, the second Exchange opened in a new structure, ornamented with large allegorical figures. It lasted only forty years before the third exchange building replaced it. Such regional exchanges have largely disappeared.*

COURTESY OF THE LOUISIANA STATE MUSEUM.

pounds each. By 1849 output had reached 2.85 million bales and continued until 1860, when 4.8 million bales of cotton were produced. Reflecting the westward drift of population, Mississippi by 1860 had become the nation's leading cotton state with a production of 1.2 million bales (or about a quarter of all cotton produced in the United States). The largest cotton plantations housed thousands of slaves and produced hundreds of bales of cotton a year. Stephen Duncan, for example, was a planter who lived near Natchez, Mississippi. In 1850, he had more than one thousand slaves and an income from cotton, after deducting expenses, of $169,354. Frederick Stanton, also from Natchez, had a slave force of 444 on his three plantations. His operation produced 3,054 bales valued at $122,000 in 1858.

By the 1820s, New Orleans had become the chief cotton exporter in the world. In the antebellum years the great merchants in New Orleans administered the cotton trade. Vincent Nolte issued the first market letter in New Orleans in 1818, and it induced cotton brokers to consider speculating in cotton. In 1825 and 1839 great cotton "corners" appeared as combinations of merchants sought to buy all the cotton coming to market and hold it until prices rose. In 1825 these merchant speculators thought the Liverpool and Manchester cotton mills would continue to buy cotton as prices soared upward from under 10 cents a pound to 40 cents a pound. However, Brazil cotton planters, who normally shipped only 175,000 bales to market, dumped 350,000 bales at Liverpool. The merchants could not hold on and prices plummeted. The consequence was the failure of the House of Baring, the largest merchant house in England, the very same one that had financed the Louisiana Purchase. In New Orleans, Vincent Nolte's French merchants had been purchasing everything that came on the market. The collapse crushed his firm. The second great cotton speculation, the one in 1839, failed because of an unusual coincidence—the failure of the American wheat crop. As wheat prices soared worldwide, Manchester cotton mills stopped spinning. The failure of the mills to buy cotton ended the merchants'

Below: *Cotton was compressed and stored in the cotton warehouses. But as it moved towards the ships, it often remained for days on the levee.*

COURTESY OF THE LOUISIANA STATE MUSEUM.

ability to hold cotton off the market and the "corner" collapsed.

Cotton growing hardly changed for a century and a half. The worker began his preparations for planting in February. Land was laid off into rows from three to four feet apart, then ridged up by throwing two furrows of a turning-plow together. A small shovel-plow made a trench in the ridge to receive the seed. A man and a mule followed with a "board" which lightly covered the seed with earth. When the cotton was up and growing well, cultivation began by throwing earth to it with a "cotton sweep," and the space between the rows was plowed up and thoroughly pulverized and the "sweeping" repeated. As soon as the plants strengthened sufficiently, they were cut out "to a stand" by a small hoe, spaced from eight to eighteen inches. The hoe performed a double duty, for it cut out also the fine grass that sprang up about the young plants. Plowing and hoeing now continued as rapidly as possible—taking into consideration that ten days, at least, must elapse between each operation—until the cotton shaded the land sufficiently to protect itself against the growth of grass, and until the plow injured the plant by breaking branches. The cotton was now said to be "laid by."

✧

The Eads jetties at the mouth of the Mississippi River narrow the water's flow to assist in scouring the channel. For many years the jetties were sufficient, but the greatly increased draft of contemporary ships requires the U.S. Army Corps of Engineers to dredge constantly to maintain a channel depth in excess of ninety-five feet.

COURTESY OF THE HISTORIC NEW ORLEANS COLLECTION, 1958.59.5

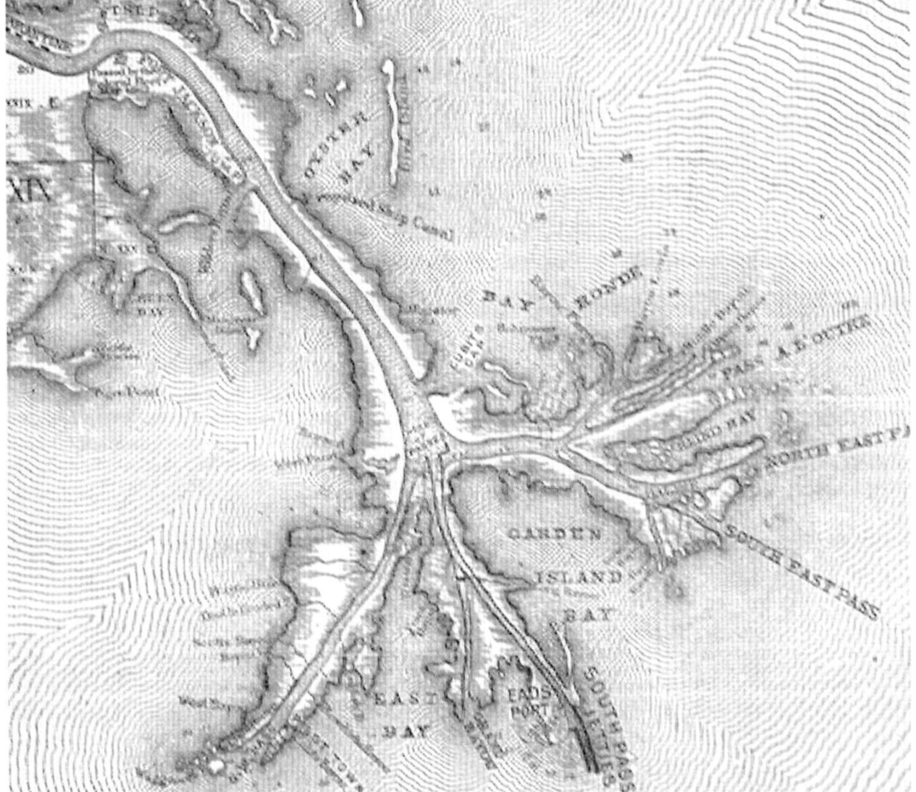

After about two months, flower buds called "squares" appeared on the cotton plants. In another three weeks, the blossoms opened. Their petals changed from creamy white, to yellow, to pink and finally dark red. After three days, they withered and fell, leaving green pods called cotton bolls. Inside the boll, which is shaped like a mini football, moist fibers formed and pushed the newly formed seeds outward. As the boll ripened, it stayed green. The fibers continued to expand under the warm sun. Finally, they split the boll apart, and the fluffy cotton came forth. It looked like cotton candy, only white. Cotton pickers then went down the rows transferring the cotton to their bags. After weighing, the cotton was spread out to be dried and sunned, then "ginned," that is, the soft white lint was separated from the seeds. The "cleaned," or "ginned," cotton was now pressed into bales ready for the market. The planter marked the bales with his initials and separated it into eight grades—"stained," "tinged," "ordinary," "good ordinary," "low middling," "middling," "good middling," and "fancy." "Stained" and "tinged" indicated cotton injured by frost. The remaining grades ranged from those soiled by dust, leaves, and trash to the "fancy," which is the finest of all and perfectly clean. The seed went to the cotton-seed-oil factories to be pressed for oil, or converted into cake for feeding stock or into a material for making paper.

It was 150 years after the cotton gin before there was another comparable improvement in efficiency in the cotton business. In the 1940s mechanized planting and harvesting began to reduce the number of man hours required to produce one hundred pounds of cotton. In 1945, forty-two labor hours were required. By 1965 that number had been reduced to five, a reduction of eighty-eight percent. Since then hours required to produce one hundred pounds of cotton have declined further.

Louisiana is sixth among the states in average cotton production. Texas is first with 4.56 million bales, followed by California, Mississippi, Arkansas, and Georgia. Worldwide production has recently averaged eighty-seven million bales per year.

RICE

Rice was first successfully grown in South Carolina in 1699, and the Carolinas soon became the center of rice production in North America. They remained dominant until the Civil War. In 1860 they produced virtually all of the 117 million pounds of marketed rice. Early rice growing in Louisiana was centered in Plaquemines Parish. In 1860 the parish produced two-thirds of the six million pounds grown in Louisiana. The end of slavery witnessed a remarkable expansion of free labor farming in Louisiana, carried on by former slaves but also by immigrants from the middle west who knew how to farm and knew the value of Louisiana's lands. By and large, they also had some capital.

Rice farming was the outstanding success story that transformed southwestern Louisiana during the late nineteenth century. As early as 1870, Louisiana marketed 13 million pounds of rice, compared to 40 million pounds for the Carolinas and Georgia. By 1881, Louisiana marketed 51 million pounds to 59 million pounds for the other three states. By 1889, Louisiana was marketing 81 million pounds to 44 million for the Carolinas and Georgia. In 1896, Louisiana marketed 127 million pounds of rice, compared to 40 million for the former dominant producers. In 1890 84,377 acres were planted in rice, a number that increased to 201,685 acres by 1900. By 1890 the largest rice producing parishes were Acadia, Plaquemines, and St. James. Much of the rice was produced on former sugar plantations or on the rear of still-producing sugar plantations. Today the rice crop of Louisiana is more valuable than the cotton crop.

Rice, like sugar before it, was consciously introduced into Louisiana because the geography and climate seemed to favor it. The striking quality of the western prairies was their flatness and a clay strata just below the surface that was impermeable. Bayous and wells were quickly tapped to flood the new rice fields. The Southern Pacific Railroad pushed its line through western Louisiana in the 1870s and received many thousands of bonus acres from the Federal Government. The railroad hired Iowan S. L. Cary to serve as stationmaster at Jennings and to advertise inexpensive lands to his Iowa friends. Hundreds came south. He induced Maurice Bryne of Iowa to settle in Louisiana, and in 1884, Bryne brought the first twine binder from the wheat lands to the rice lands. Six years later one thousand twine binders were in use in Louisiana.

Salmon "Sol" Lusk Wright was a Yankee wheat farmer "transplant" who came to Louisiana in 1890. After working with seed rice imported from Japan for several years, Wright embarked on the experimental quest of developing a purebred American rice seed. The result is the Blue Rose variety, which became commercially available in 1912. He was known around the world for his efforts and was referred to affectionately as, "the Wizard of Rice", the "Burbank of Rice" and "the gentle genius." Frances Parkerson Keyes based her novel *Blue Camelia* on Wright's work. Today, the Blue Rose Museum stands as a testimony to Wright and his work. Wright Laboratories are still in operation today.

Above: The quarters at Bel Air Plantation in the late nineteenth century. One of the remarkable characteristics of the 1870 and 1880 census is the degree to which the former slaves formed families of the traditional nuclear type. In this image we see fathers and children, the mothers are hidden in the houses.

COURTESY OF THE LOUISIANA STATE MUSEUM.

Below: A country store in the late nineteenth century.

COURTESY OF THE LOUISIANA STATE MUSEUM.

✧

Above: Seine netting for river shrimp was popular in the nineteenth century, long before the great mechanized shrimping fleets of today went to sea for shrimp.

COURTESY OF THE LOUISIANA STATE MUSEUM.

Below: Tonging for oysters. The cultivation of oysters is and was hard labor. Immigrants from the Dalmatian coast specialized in the business, taking the oyster leases on both sides of the Mississippi River. Oyster cultivation requires that all oysters be moved by hand from one bed to another.

COURTESY OF THE LOUISIANA STATE MUSEUM.

Opposite, top: This 1872 image of an oyster cannery was drawn just after the commencement of the canning process. Men like George Dunbar made fortunes from exporting canned Louisiana seafood. The exporting of oysters was also made possible by the arrival of the national railroad network to Louisiana following the Civil War. This image shows how the new industry created work for women.

COURTESY OF SPECIAL COLLECTIONS, TULANE UNIVERSITY.

Opposite, bottom: The shrimping industry has been a way of life in Louisiana for over a century. Trawling from motorized boats began in the 1890s and has provided a good life for thousands in the fertile Louisiana marshes.

COURTESY OF THE LOUISIANA OFFICE OF TOURISM.

Wright settled in the town of Crowley in the heart of Acadia Parish. The establishment of Crowley began with the sale of 174 acres of land for $80 in 1886 to the Southwest Louisiana Land Company. Lots were sold the next year, and in 1888 the village of Crowley was incorporated. It was named after Pat Crowley, an Irish roadmaster employed by the Louisiana Western Railroad (his name was first given to the "Crowley Switch" or railroad spur where all construction materials for the new town were unloaded). People came, and the town grew from 240 in 1890 to 6,000 by 1917. The merchants erected a mill street corridor along the railroad, most of which remains standing. Within a few years after its founding, Crowley was the recognized center of rice production in Louisiana. The large turn-of-the-century homes also remain in beautiful condition. The thirty-two block historic residential section of Crowley has a large collection of Queen Anne Revival and Eastlake architecture. Their complex rooflines, elaborate ornamentation, and size give a weight and attractiveness to the town. There is also a fine mixture of two- or more storied homes among many raised, one-story, and bungalow style homes.

SEAFOOD

Louisiana is the nation's largest producer of shrimp, crayfish, oysters, and crabs. Louisiana's seafood industry originated in the eighteenth century, when various peoples began bringing

oysters into New Orleans. Records at the Dubreuil Canal, the predecessor of the Harvey Canal, show oyster shipments to New Orleans. The Yugoslavs, who began arriving in New Orleans in the 1840s, made oyster growing an industry. They introduced the oyster tong and began the cultivation of the large oyster eaten on the half shell. Natural oysters had long grown on the reefs on the east side of the Mississippi River estuary. The Yugoslavs noticed they could transplant oysters from the east to the west side of the Mississippi onto artificial reefs where the oysters would grow to a large size. The transplanting became the hardest part of the business, but it was also the part that brought the most profit. An early settlement on the west bank was at Bayou Cook above Bastian Bay. By 1893 some four hundred people lived around that bayou. The hurricane of that year destroyed the settlement and cost many lives. That same hurricane obliterated Cheniere Caminada and drove that French population up Bayou Lafourche and eventually to Westwego.

Two factors in the late nineteenth century revolutionized the seafood industry—the invention of artificial ice and the invention of the gasoline-powered lugger. The Dunbars pioneered the canning of shrimp in 1868. The great schools of white and brown shrimp in the Louisiana marshes soon became the target of fleets of sailing luggers. Small shrimp were dried first on large drying platforms developed in the 1870s. Gradually icehouses moved southward, bringing more fish into market. The gasoline-

powered luggers soon acquired the ability to stay at sea for many days at a time because ice was used to preserve the catch. A series of seafood ports opened in the first half of the twentieth century, notably at Harvey, Westwego, and Dulac in central Louisiana. Fleets of luggers used these ports to bring their catch to market. Seafood wholesalers also gathered, and canners operated their plants in the area.

Crayfish were long harvested from the natural swamps where they grew. Towards the end of the twentieth century, crayfish farming became more profitable than simple gathering. The seafood industry also witnessed the introduction of catfish farming, a phenomenon extending across the South.

By the end of the twentieth century Louisiana's economy had grown much larger than it was at the beginning of the century. But manufacturing products, including the extractive industries, greatly surpassed agricultural production. In 1998 the total farm value of Louisiana's crops equaled $2.7 billion and timber made up $1.3 billion of that total. This compares with a 1996 value of natural gas output from Louisiana of $3.44 billion and oil at $2.41 billion. The value of all manufactured products shipped in 1995 totaled $64 billion, two-thirds of which were supplied by the chemical and petroleum industries. Though comparatively little of the profit from this business remains in Louisiana, the state reaps its reward from the industry's payroll of $3.4 billion, more than the value of her agricultural business.

Renewable and non-renewable resources are important ways to evaluate the historical success of Louisiana's economy. Perhaps her greatest renewable resource has been the Mississippi River. This geographical feature has brought commerce and the port, the marshlands, and the chemical industry. Its management is the single greatest determinant of the future of Louisiana. Louisiana's historic crops continue to feed and clothe a significant portion of Louisiana's population. The timber industry falls somewhere between renewable and non-renewable. While new forests are growing to replace the clear-cut forests of the late nineteenth and early twentieth century, the new forests are not duplicates. The variety and types of trees are fundamentally different. In a word, they are inferior. For the timber industry to become truly a renewable resource, government will have to insist on true replacement. The renewable seafood industry is dependent on the health of the Louisiana marshes and vigorous government prevention of overcropping. Whether Louisiana and America have the will to save Louisiana's marshes is still an unanswered question. Since the marshes depend on the Mississippi River and its control, the battle over levees will continue to shape the future of major Louisiana industries.

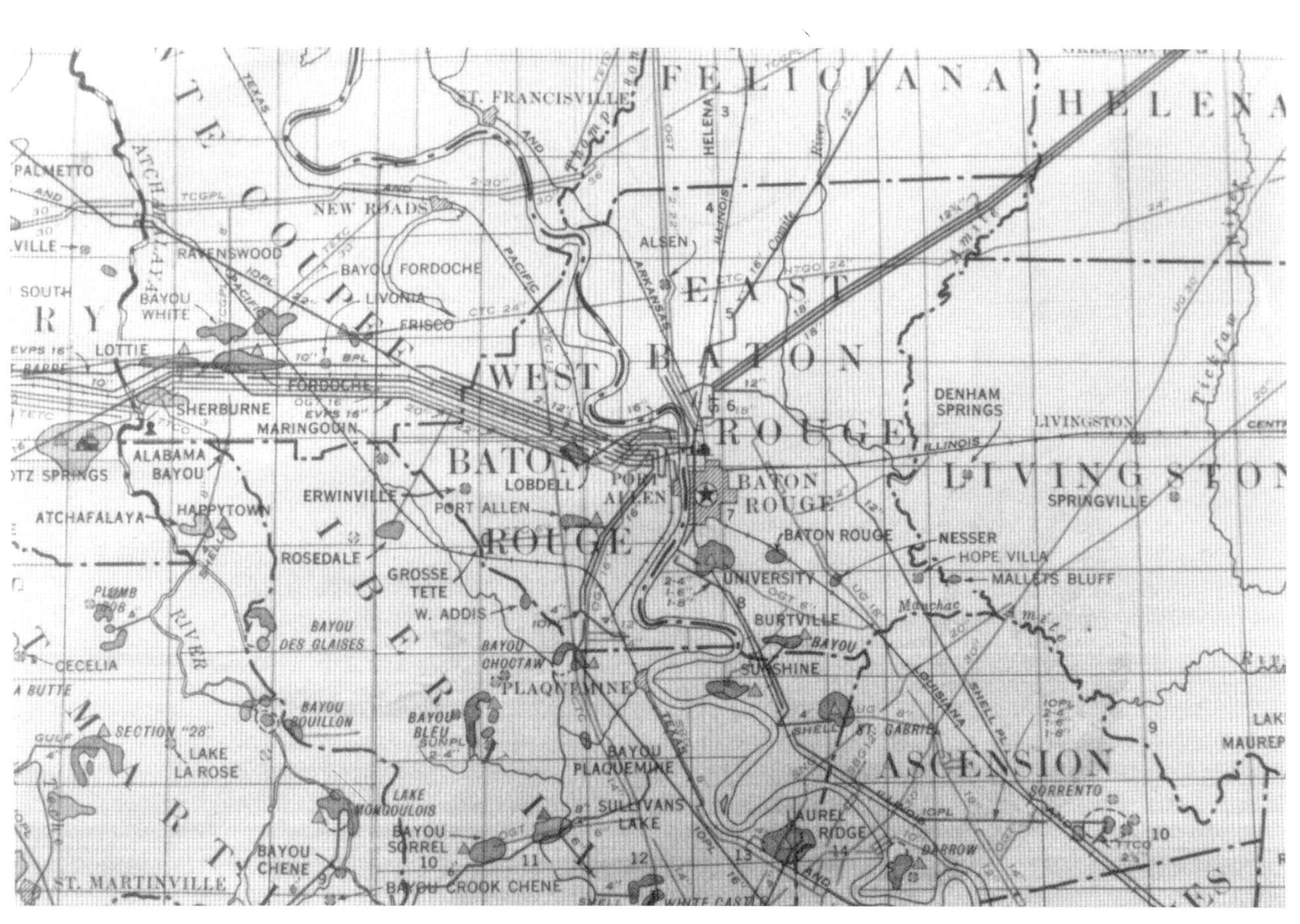
FELICIANA
HELENA
ST. FRANCISVILLE
NEW ROADS
PALMETTO
RAVENSWOOD
BAYOU FORDOCHE
LIVONIA
FRISCO
BAYOU WHITE
LOTTIE
FORDOCHE
SHERBURNE
MARINGOUIN
ALABAMA BAYOU
ATCHAFALAYA
HAPPYTOWN
ERWINVILLE
ROSEDALE
GROSSE TETE
W. ADDIS
BAYOU DES GLAISES
PLUMB BOB
CECELIA
SECTION "28"
LAKE LA ROSE
BAYOU BOUILLON
BAYOU CHOCTAW
PLAQUEMINE
BAYOU BLEU
BAYOU PLAQUEMINE
LAKE MONGOULOIS
SULLIVANS LAKE
BAYOU SORREL
BAYOU CHENE
ST. MARTINVILLE
BAYOU CROOK CHENE
WEST
BATON
ROUGE
EAST
ALSEN
LOBDELL
PORT ALLEN
BATON ROUGE
UNIVERSITY
BURTVILLE
SUNSHINE
ST. GABRIEL
LAUREL RIDGE
DARROW
ASCENSION
SORRENTO
DENHAM SPRINGS
LIVINGSTON
SPRINGVILLE
NESSER
HOPE VILLA
MALLETS BLUFF
MAUREPAS

CHAPTER V

MAKING A LIVING: INDUSTRY

Large-scale industry spurred Louisiana's growth in wealth and population in the twentieth century. The great industries have been timber, oil and gas, chemicals, sulphur, and shipbuilding. The capital and the ownership of these industries have generally come from outside the state of Louisiana. The large Louisiana chemical industry replaced the nineteenth century sugar industry as the primary Mississippi River landowner. Oil, gas, sulphur, and abundant fresh water has made Louisiana a major force in the United States chemical industry. An increasing percentage of Louisiana workers are employed by national firms, and an increasing percentage work in service industries.

Timber was the first major export industry of Louisiana. Despite its ups and down over the past three centuries, today timber alone accounts for half of the value of Louisiana's agricultural products. Frenchmen and Acadians began lumbering from the earliest days. Cypress was recognized at an early date as a unique wood for shipbuilding, because it was extremely light and totally resistant to worms. The French, Spanish, and later, the United States reserved the largest trees to serve as masts and spars on their military sailing ships. Louisiana barrel staves and boxes became of prime importance to the Caribbean sugar islands that were devoid of wood for the casking of molasses and sugar. Logging grew in the 1780s as two new groups entered the market. The partnership of Louis Judice, the Acadian coast commandant; Joseph Landry, a Lafourche militia officer; and Laurent Sigur purchased trees for sale to the Spanish Royal Navy at Havana. Pierre Belly of Iberville Parish led another partnership from the 1780s and assembled a group of investors "to supply ...masts and spars to the King...."

Within Louisiana, New Orleans was the largest market for timber. In 1773, builder Alexander Latil, a resident of Bayou Road, purchased supplies for wooden flooring in New Orleans houses. The following year he entered into a partnership with Maurice Conway to purchase the Houmas Indian site for its lumbering possibilities.

The introduction of steam-powered sawmills at the beginning of the nineteenth century spurred the timber industry, but even by 1880 hardly a tenth of Louisiana's first growth timber had been harvested. One reason was that most of Louisiana's land belonged to the Federal Government as a result of the Louisiana Purchase. But in 1849, Congress enacted the Swampland Act. By this act the United States gave ten million Louisiana acres (one third of the entire state) to the State government. This "swampland" was to be sold and the proceeds used to build levees. Civil War and Reconstruction intervened, but finally the State government began transferring its swamplands to local levee boards. Valuable cypress forests often covered the swamplands. The swamplands often covered salt domes and oil and gas deposits.

With the final clearing of the large forests in the upper midwest in the 1880s, northern lumbermen turned to Louisiana. They found pliable levee boards anxious to make a deal in return for cash to build levees. Until the 1880s, men known as "swampers" felled the cypress trees in the winter and early spring in anticipation of the rise in the Mississippi River that flooded the swamps. The logs would then be floated out to the waiting sawmills. Northern investors turned the Louisiana industry from a handcraft to an industrial enterprise. In 1888, Joseph Rathborne founded the Louisiana Cypress Lumber Company. He came to the United States soon after the Civil War and settled in Chicago, where he started in the lumber business with Kelley, Wood & Co. handling white pine. Rathborne later bought out Wood and the firm became Kelley, Rathborne & Co., operating two lumberyards. After twenty years Rathborne formed his own firm to handle white pine and the newly discovered Louisiana cypress. Two years later he moved down to New Orleans and leased the land where the Harvey Canal joined the Mississippi River. He introduced

✧

The Exxon refinery (once Standard Oil) in Baton Rouge is a large pipeline hub, bringing oil and gas from the Louisiana fields in the marsh to the west.

✧

Above: A skidder in loading logs. Powerful engines "snake" the logs with cables from the forests, sometimes from as far as a mile away. These machines straddle a railroad track. As soon as one car is loaded, another is shoved into place to be filled. The loader could load a car in eight minutes.

COURTESY OF THE LOUISIANA STATE ARCHIVES COLLECTION.

Below: The Frank B. Williams sawmill near Patterson, Louisiana. With the sawmill, Williams created on of the largest fortunes in Louisiana history.

COURTESY OF THE NEW ORLEANS PUBLIC LIBRARY.

the first pullboat that employed steam engines attached to giant drums from which one inch cables were attached to logs as much as a mile and half into the forest from the boat.

The Louisiana Red Cypress Company of Patterson, Louisiana, and the Ruddock Cypress Company competed with Rathborne. William Baptist of New Orleans invented the pull boat. Woodward, Wight, and Company of Louisiana later built engines designed by Baptist. Quickly the engines were mounted on railroads for skidding on dry ground. Another tool was the Cableway Skidder, known as the overhead-suspended swamp skidder. Rathborne also introduced the first bandsaw into Louisiana. One of the principal products of the first mills was shingles used to roof the houses of the state. In 1897, *The Southern Lumberman* ranked the Rathborne mill as the largest cypress mill in the world, followed closely by Lutcher and Moore Cypress Lumber Company of Lutcher, Louisiana. H. J. Lutcher was a Pennsylvania native who sold much of the firm's lumber back north to the Pennsylvania oil fields. In 1874, John N. Pharr and Francis Bennett Williams organized the company that became the major enterprise in the Atchafalaya at Patterson. Early in life Williams worked on the railroads, including engineering work for the Louisville and Nashville Railroad. He then went to work for Morgan's Louisiana and Texas Railroad. When the railroad went bankrupt in 1870, he found himself at the end of the line in Patterson, where he decided to enter the lumber business. Despite reverses, in 1896 he bought out Pharr and had surpassed the Rathborne company by 1908. Then the F. B. Williams Cypress Company owned more sixty thousand acres of timberland with one and a half billion feet of timber. Like Pharr he was a Republican in politics. In 1896, Pharr made a strong bid for the governorship, a campaign that, had it been successful, might have stopped the escalation towards segregation in Louisiana.

From 1907 to 1925, Louisiana was either first, second, or third in the nation in the production of lumber. It ranked first in just one year 1914, producing almost four billion board feet. Most of this total was yellow pine. By 1925, two-thirds of Louisiana's production was yellow pine. The cypress industry cut 1.62 million acres of cypress forest in the fifty years of its existence. By 1934 only 22,000 acres of cypresslands remained. It was the impending prospect of the exhaustion of timberlands that led to the creation of Louisiana's first severance tax in 1912. Largely ineffective at first, it played an important role in state finances for the balance of the twentieth century. Occasionally mill workers attempted to organize to increase their pay. A strike at the lumber mills in 1903 lasted several days as the workers sought to reduce their hours from eleven to ten per day. It failed.

Yellow pine was the choice wood of Calcasieu Parish in southwestern Louisiana.

Jacob Ryan introduced the first sawmill, and many others followed. In 1840 the two thousand residents of Calcasieu carved their own parish from the giant St. Landry Parish. It was not until the arrival of Michigan lumber men that the business took off. The decisive step was the completion of the Southern Pacific line from New Orleans to Houston in 1880. One of the first large companies was the Bradley-Ramsay Lumber Company, whose mills operated in Goosport, a suburb of Lake Charles. The latter town was named for Charles Sallier, a merchant and planter in the early part of the century. By 1911, eleven large mills produced over four million board feet a day in Calcasieu. An English company originally formed to develop timber, the North American Land and Timber Company, transferred its interest to agricultural land, acquiring some nine hundred thousand acres. It built irrigation canals, drained land, and then sold it in small parcels to farmers. One of its successor companies was the Sweet Lake Land & Oil Co., which farmed ten thousand acres of rice irrigated by two massive fresh water irrigating canals.

By the 1920s virtually all of the cypress and most of the yellow pine had been cut from Louisiana. In the mid-1930s only 1.2 million acres of merchantable timber remained. Ten million acres had been replanted. In the following decades the lumber industry began to replant privately owned forests. In addition, the Federal Government began purchasing large tracts of land that it formed in 1936 into a patchwork of national forests across seven parishes of Louisiana under the name Kisatchee National Forest. The total acreage is 600,000, and just one of the sections of the national forest, the Vernon Ranger District, contains 88,000 acres or 132 square miles. Longleaf pines dominate this part of the Kisatchee. They shelter many rare birds and plants, including the endangered Red-cockaded woodpecker and the rare, fly-eating pitcher plant. The biggest threat to the Kisatchee is the military's need for training lands.

The presence of the virgin forest naturally gave rise to Louisiana's shipbuilding industry. It commenced along the riverfront of New Orleans in the eighteenth century. Carpenters laid a keel right out on the batture at

Above: The Kisatchee National Forest falls into three or more parts extending across central Louisiana. It serves as a timber resource, recreational resource, and also as a military training facility. Exercises held around Alexandria prior to America's entrance into World War II demonstrated the skills and talents of some of America's future generals.

COURTESY OF THE LOUISIANA OFFICE OF TOURISM.

Below: The New Basin Canal, constructed in 1833, brought building material into uptown New Orleans. In this photo a tug is pulling a log raft up to one of the many lumberyards that line the canal.

COURTESY OF THE LOUISIANA STATE MUSEUM.

Above: *Bernardo de Gálvez (1746-1786) was a military leader akin to Pierre Le Moyne d'Iberville. His lasting importance to Louisiana was a result of his three successful military campaigns during the Revolutionary War in which Gálvez's Spanish forces drove British troops from forts at Baton Rouge, Louisiana; Mobile, Alabama; and Pensacola, Florida. These Spanish territories would later fall into the waiting lap of America instead of remaining British outposts whose importance would have greatly magnified the danger to New Orleans in 1815. Gálvez married a Creole widow who named the Feliciana parishes.*

COURTESY OF THE HISTORIC NEW ORLEANS COLLECTION, 1991.34.15.

Right: In 1820, New Orleans banned shipbuilding from the east bank. Shipbuilding was then moved to Algiers. In the 1930s, a new shipbuilder opened on the west bank at Avondale Plantation. By the 1980s, Avondale was one of the largest industries in the state. Drydocks can still be found at Algiers.

COURTESY OF THE LOUISIANA STATE MUSEUM.

water's edge. Soon after 1770, Bordeaux shipbuilder Arnold Magnon opened a yard on the riverbank adjacent to the Ursuline Convent. In 1780 when Bernardo de Gálvez planned his attack on Pensacola, he needed a flotilla of thirty-two vessels. Magnon worked on many of them. He successfully kept his shipyard operating in front of the city until 1819, employing as many as twenty-six slaves. Another early shipbuilder just down river from Magnon was Andre Seguin. With the onset of the embargo of 1808, the U.S. Navy presence in New Orleans dramatically increased. The local commander, David Porter, received three hundred feet along the river front between Dumaine and St. Philip Streets to use as a navy dockyard.

In 1819 the city council evicted shipbuilding from the New Orleans side, so shipbuilders moved across the river to Algiers. That very year the owner of Algiers point, Bernard Duverjé, began subdividing his tract of land. The first shipbuilder to move was Seguin. By 1842 half the population of Algiers was in the shipbuilding business. The greatest antebellum shipbuilder was Peter Marcey. Dry docks were a staple of the ship repair business, and the earliest dry docks appeared at Algiers by 1840. Eleven different dry docks lined the Algiers river front before 1860. The largest was the Pelican Dry Dock, which could lift a vessel four hundred feet in length. There were eight shipbuilding firms in Algiers by 1850. The Confederate abandonment of New Orleans led to the destruction of some shipbuilding property, but the presence of the Union fleet insured much work for the duration of the war.

After the Civil War shipbuilding transformed itself from a branch of carpentry to a branch of metallurgy. In 1903 the Algiers Iron Works and Dry Docks appeared just upstream from the Canal Street ferry. A dry dock remains at this site to this day. At the turn of the century, Lewis Johnson moved his ironworks across the river. The firm was one of the largest in the city, and it went into ship repair. In the 1950s it became the

Left: The great iron foundry and machine works stood at the corner of Tulane and Jefferson Davis in New Orleans. The New Basin Canal ran right behind the factory and provided some transportation. The foundry provided machinery for the sugar industry and employed hundreds of Louisianans.

COURTESY OF THE LOUISIANA STATE MUSEUM.

Below: The Southern Pacific Railroad yard at Algiers became a major industrial center for New Orleans. Until the erection of the Huey P. Long Bridge in the 1930s, railroad cars and passengers crossed the Mississippi from the foot of Elysian Fields to begin the journey westward. The Southern Pacific maintained a major locomotive repair facility that employed many hundreds with comparatively good wages.

COURTESY OF THE NEW ORLEANS PUBLIC LIBRARY.

Todd Shipyards. Shipbuilding in Algiers was greatly facilitated by the presence of the large Southern Pacific Railroad yards just downstream from Algiers Point. Constructed in the 1880s, this repair facility employed many men who could work equally on the railroad and in shipbuilding. The Southern Pacific Railroad maintained a fleet of ships to bring freight from the east coast to its Algiers dock at New Orleans. Six or seven ships with names like *El Paso* and *El Monte* operated constantly on the line. The ships were unloaded in Algiers, and their freight was transferred to the cars of the Southern Pacific, which then dashed across the country. Their longshoremen were both black and white. Four hundred men worked thirty-six hours to unload and reload each forty-seven-hundred-ton ship.

The opening of the Industrial Canal in 1923 gave new sites for shipbuilders. By World War II numerous shipbuilders were located along it, including Alexander Shipyards. But the greatest shipbuilder appeared upstream at Avondale. The Texas Pacific had chosen this spot to bring railroad cars across the river for connection with the other lines owned by Collis P. Huntington, the New Orleans & Mississippi Valley. This railroad ferry featured a

thousand-foot track that descended into the river. With the completion of the Huey P. Long Railroad Bridge in 1935, the ferry became obsolete. In 1937, James G. Viavant, Harry Koch, and Perry N. Ellis identified the site as an excellent barge repair facility. The predecessor company had been operating using a borrowed dry dock at Algiers. The men leased the site and formed Avondale Marine Ways, Inc. By the time World War II erupted, it was employing two hundred men. In 1959 it was sold to the Ogden Corporation. By the 1960s it was the largest industrial employer in New Orleans, with five thousand employees. In 1999, Avondale Marine Ways, Inc. was merged with Litton Industries.

The chemical and petroleum industries of Louisiana were born and raised together. Salt from Avery Island entered the markets in the late nineteenth century. About the same time large deposits of sulphur were discovered in Calcasieu Parish further west. At first quicksand and other dangers made it impossible to remove the sulphur with conventional mining techniques. In the 1890s, Standard Oil Company sent Herman Frasch to investigate the oil possibilities of the parish, and, in the course of his investigation, he came up with the idea of using boiling water to dissolve the sulphur and pump it to the surface. Once on the surface, the boiling sulphur-laden water was dumped into giant flat pits where, once the water drained, the sulphur formed huge solid cakes. It was absolutely pure. By 1909, ninety-nine percent of the United States sulphur production came from Calcasieu Parish.

The Freeport Sulphur Company was born in Texas in 1912. In 1933, Freeport adapted the Frasch method to opening the giant sulphur mine at the Grande Ecaille district in Plaquemines Parish. The company constructed the town of Port Sulphur to serve as quarters for its workers. The mine produced for forty years. Today, Freeport-McMoRan is producing sulphur from an offshore mine at Main Pass almost as large as the Grande Ecaille. The chemical, papermaking, pigment, pharmaceutical, mining, oil-refining, fertilizer, and fiber manufacturing industries all depend on sulphur.

The first Louisiana oil company was formed in 1866 to drill for oil near the oil bubbles reported in Calcasieu Parish. The Louisiana Petroleum and Coal Oil Company had no success. Thirty years later Anthony Lucas drilled at Belle Isle unsuccessfully before he hit the gusher at Spindletop near Beaumont, Texas. Just a few months later, W. Scott Heywood and his brothers brought in another gusher at Jennings, Louisiana. Jennings, like the town of Crowley, originated in the 1880s as a rice-growing center inspired by the promotional work of S. L. Cary. The first oil refinery in Louisiana, the Royal Petroleum Company, opened in Jennings in 1903. In 1910 the Vinton Dome became a big producer. Its champion was John Geddings Gray, who pushed the drilling and was rewarded with enormously valuable royalties. Like so many in the oil business, initially he was in timber and rice. His parents had been prominent in South Carolina and Mississippi. He attended Soulé's Business College in New Orleans, but then went into the timber business. He began buying land in the vicinity of Vinton, where he both timbered and operated a rice farm. To irrigate his land, he dug a canal to bring in water from the Sabine River.

In 1905 the brothers J. S. and W. A. Savage brought in the first well in the Shreveport oil field. Uncontrollable natural gas jetted from the ground, causing numerous explosions for years in the area. One giant gas well burned for five years. The waste at Shreveport led to Louisiana's first conservation law in 1906, prohibiting oil companies from simply letting gas wells burn. By 1910, Shreveport produced three-quarters of the Louisiana oil. Caddo Lake was a part of the Shreveport field, so it was not long before oil exploration went "offshore." It was on Caddo Lake that Gulf Oil Company set up the first oil drilling rigs on barges, a technique later brought south to the Gulf of Mexico. Shreveport had the first African-American-owned oil company, an independent named Universal Oil, Gas, and Mining Company, owned by Odessa Strickland. He invented the "electronometer," a sensitive instrument that helped locate drilling sites. Shreveport became a major stop on the principal Standard Oil pipeline commenced in 1909 and running from the Oklahoma fields, through the Shreveport fields, and down the Red River to Baton Rouge.

The Louisiana oil industry really began when Standard Oil Company erected its giant refinery at Baton Rouge in 1909. Pipelines were laid across Louisiana, bringing oil to the deep water at Baton Rouge. The Standard Oil Company originated in the 1870s, and, by 1879, John D. Rockefeller's Standard Oil Company controlled ninety percent of the refining capacity in the United States. In 1911 the United States broke Standard Oil into Standard Oil of California (Chevron), Standard Oil of Texas (Texaco), Standard Oil of New Jersey (Exxon), and Standard Oil of Indiana (later Amoco).

British Petroleum evolved with capital from the Hudson's Bay Company, from the Burmah Oil Company, and the Anglo-Iranian (or Persian) Oil Company. The Samuelson Trading Company in the Dutch East Indies (now Indonesia) began trading in oil at the end of the nineteenth century, under its family logo—a pecten seashell. At the beginning of the twentieth century, this company merged with the Royal Dutch Trading Company to form the Royal Dutch Shell Oil Company. The company embarked on an aggressive expansion into Venezuela and Mexico.

The impetus provided by the Standard Oil Refinery brought several refineries to the Mississippi River. In 1914 the Mexican Petroleum Company purchased Destrehan Plantation, and in 1916 the New Orleans Refinery Company made its acquisition at the town of Sellers. During WWI, the site served

Opposite, top: Oil field work paid well and provided jobs for both white and black workers.

Opposite, bottom: An oil field near Jennings, Louisiana.

COURTESY OF THE NEW ORLEANS PUBLIC LIBRARY.

Above: Sulphur mining began in western Louisiana, then moved to Port Sulphur. Now sulphur production has moved offshore.

COURTESY OF THE NEW ORLEANS PUBLIC LIBRARY.

✧

Above: Leeville near the lower end of Bayou Lafourche was an early oil field during the 1930s. At Leeville, drillers learned to work half on land and half in the water.

COURTESY OF THE LOUISIANA STATE MUSEUM.

Below: Prosperity came to Monroe, Louisiana, with the discovery of their great gas fields. One product of this prosperity was the G. B. Cooley house, originally constructed in 1910 in the Prairie Style reminiscent of Frank Lloyd Wright. The actual architect of the house was Walter Burley Griffin. Beautiful interior details tie furnishings to the exterior of the building.

as storage for petroleum products used for the war. The first refinery installations were built in 1920, producing asphalt. In 1925 the town renamed itself after the refinery (Norco). In 1928, Shell purchased the 460 acres belonging to New Orleans Refinery Company and established its major refinery at Norco. When Shell took over the plant, the town of Norco was a maze of tents and shacks.

In the 1930s, oil discoveries in the Louisiana marshes suggested that the next frontier would be offshore. In 1937 the first offshore well was drilled in the "Creole" field off of Cameron Parish. World War II stopped that trend, but as soon as the war was over, drillers began exploring offshore once more. Drilling was done from barges or ships, anything that would float. Each drill site required the erection of a new rig and assembly of the support workers. A young naval engineer from Marksville named Alden J. "Doc" LaBorde invented the idea of a permanent drilling barge, with a rig permanently assembled on one barge. The barge would then be brought to a site where the rig would be sunk, and, when resting on the bottom, would become a stable drilling platform. The key was reuse. He realized that the barge could be refloated and taken to another location. Murphy Oil Company eventually put up the money and a new company was formed named Ocean Drilling & Exploration Company or ODECO. This company went on to become one of the premier deepwater exploration companies in the world. Its first successful drilling rig, "Mr. Charlie," went to work in 1954. Laborde then turned his attention to offshore support vessels and founded Tidewater Marine, the world's largest offshore vessel operator. Next Laborde developed semi-submersible oil rigs. With the major oil companies competing to drill in the Gulf, the Louisiana oil patch boomed in the second half of the twentieth century.

At the beginning of the century the town of Lafayette boasted a population of over three thousand and proudly announced that commercial establishments existed in sufficient number and variety to serve the needs of the townspeople. For the next fifty years, the major factors influencing growth were the railroad, the state university created in 1900, and establishment of the community

as the retail hub of a eight-parish (county) trade area. Farming was still the principal economic generator. But by the 1950s the steady progress of the oil industry led to the scattering of company offices along the Intracoastal Canal between Lafayette and Lake Charles. Lafayette entrepreneur Maurice Heymann recognized the need for an oil center, and an office park for the oil industry, and the Heymann Oil Center was born. The oil companies quickly began to open offices there, and the immigration of oil people accelerated immensely.

The oil industry created a new set of support jobs in Louisiana, impacting communities from Lake Charles to Harvey. The latter, across the Mississippi River from New Orleans, is the site of the crucial link of the Intracoastal Waterway that carries barge traffic from Florida and the East Coast to Texas. The U.S. Army Corps of Engineers began digging the waterway in 1912. Much of it came by way of purchase as the Corps bought both the Harvey Canal that extended from the Mississippi to Bayou Barataria and large sections of the Barataria and Lafourche Canal, extending westward from Bayou Lafourche. The Harvey Canal owners began selling lots next to the canal in the 1940s, and oil-related industries crowded in. Ship repair and platform support were the most common businesses. In the 1950s the Harvey Canal became so crowded that the Corps dug a new barge canal down river extending from the Mississippi just above English Turn directly to the intersection of the Harvey Canal and Bayou Barataria. At its peak in 1984, the oil and gas industry provided 94,700 jobs in Louisiana and the chemical another 33,000.

The completion of the Intracoastal Canal to Lake Charles brought such additional business that in 1923 the citizens of Lake Charles voted to tax themselves to build a deepwater port. The port formally opened on the east bank of the Calcasieu River on November 30, 1926, with two transit sheds. Initially the route used seventy-nine miles of natural waterways. In 1938, the Corps constructed a direct channel, shortening the length to the Gulf to thirty-eight miles. In 1938 the port operated two terminals, with 3,200 feet of modern docks located one and a quarter miles below the city of Lake Charles. The port also built a public belt railroad similar in purpose to the one in New Orleans. In the late 1930s, private docks were already quite extensive. Oil companies operated five crude oil transfer stations between deep draft vessels and storage tanks. Today the port has ten transit sheds. In 1980 the port shipped 4,139,360 tons of cargo. The Lake Charles Harbor and Terminal District is a political subdivision of the State of Louisiana that embraces an area of 203 square miles in Calcasieu Parish. It grew from an original area of ninety-three square miles.

While much of the western Louisiana oil industry sprang from the rice and lumber industries, the oil industry of southeastern Louisiana largely originated on Wisner land. Like the lumbermen and rice farmers of the west, Edward Wisner believed Louisiana swamplands would make excellent farmland. But he took the concept of converting Louisiana swamplands into productive farmland further than the rest. The railroads regularly issued promotional pamphlets to entice settlers from the north to the various reclamation projects. Wisner came to

✧

The hazards of the early oil industry were great.

COURTESY OF THE LOUISIANA STATE MUSEUM.

✧

Houma in the early 1950s still had the look of a small town. Today it is a prosperous medical and oil center.

COURTESY OF THE NEW ORLEANS PUBLIC LIBRARY.

Louisiana from Michigan about 1900. He soon began purchasing land at levee board sales and elsewhere. He paid prices ranging from twelve and a half cents an acre to $8 an acre for the 4,900 acres he purchased in the Labranche wetlands. Both the railroads and a new federal agency, the Office of Experiment Stations in the United States Department of Agriculture, helped him develop the techniques for land reclamation. In 1909, Professor W. Gregory of Tulane University persuaded the office to endorse research on the ways swamps could be drained. The experiment station hired its first drainage engineer in the person of A. M. Shaw.

From 1900 to 1915, Wisner acquired a million acres of wetlands, and developed 250,000 acres using the techniques of reclamation. He began at a project near Raceland, and developed forty-five more sites. In 1906 he began assembling the land in Labranche, and, during the following years, dug canals, cleared land, and built a steam pumping station. Wisner concentrated his efforts on Section 39 at the mouth of Bayou Labranche and apparently did little elsewhere on the Labranche wetlands. He surveyed the east bank of the bayou and laid out subdivisions along the two thousand feet of Illinois Central railroad track extending eastward from the bayou. Along the lakeshore he created farm sites of twenty acres and through the center of the tract he drew an "Avenue." The eastern boundary was another canal with a levee, running perpendicular to the railroad and extending to the lake. This canal emptied into a canal paralleling the railroad, which the pumping station emptied. Another canal paralleled the lakeshore and the bayou just inside the levee, providing the earth for the levee. The entire tract drained by the pumping station amounted to about 140 acres. The pumping station was a corrugated tin shed with engine and pumping apparatus. It was oriented to drain the east-west canal paralleling the railroad tracks and dump into Bayou Labranche. The pump seems to have been a type known as the low-lift Menge pump. It contained an impeller wheel attached to a vertical shaft, set in a large wooden body. A belt attached to an engine drove the shaft. When the water reached the height of the discharge mouth, it spilled over into the outlet, in this case, Bayou Labranche. A residence, perhaps a keeper's house, appears to have been attached to the pumping structure on the north end.

By 1911, Wisner's Suburban Land Company was ready to begin selling parcels to individuals. The first purchaser was Louis M. Rountree, a gardener in New Orleans. In June 1911 he was a resident of St. Charles Parish, probably already living at Labranche. On June 16, Rountree purchased the point of land at the juncture of the lake and the bayou, identified in the act of sale as part of Lot 1 or the "ten acres of the northwest lot." This point was also referred to as the junction of the main drainage canal and Bayou Labranche. Although Lot 1 contained twenty acres, Rountree purchased only ten acres at first. The following March he purchased the other ten acres, and then six months later purchased the adjoining lots, Lots Seven and Eight. Rountree presumably cultivated corn and vegetables there, typical truck farming crops of the suburbs, perhaps with some early success. In 1915, his wife used her separate funds to purchase ten acres of Lot 2 adjoining their tract. The plan attached to the act of sale clearly shows their house sitting at the northwest corner of Lot 1 on Bayou Labranche at the Lake. The authorizing resolution referred

to Rountree as residing at "Labranche, La." The price of this lot was at twice the rate of the earlier sales, but the act of sale referred to the existence of buildings that the purchaser was to keep insured.

Six months after the fourth sale to Rountree, the land company sold the remaining lots to Louis Mouledous for $2,208. These lots totaled 27.08 acres. No evidence has been found to show that Mouledous lived there. Louis Mouledous purchased his lot on September 13, just fifteen days before the giant hurricane of 1915. The storm approached New Orleans from the south and pounded Grande Isle with 140 mile an hour winds. The eye passed over Tulane University, where the barometer was measured at 28.11 inches of mercury. Damage was widespread through the area. The windows in the Hibernia Bank and the St. Charles Hotel were blown out, and ninety percent of the structures in New Orleans suffered damage. After passing over New Orleans, the eye continued over Lakes Pontchartrain and Maurepas with a course that pushed an enormous storm surge onto the south shores of these lakes. At the Rigolets, fifty people drowned in a thirteen-foot tide that swept the Rigolets railroad bridge away. In Lake Borgne and the Louisiana marshes, seventy Biloxi schooners were sunk.

The water that poured into Lake Pontchartrain is probably what ended the Labranche Reclamation project. The *Times-Picayune* reported that thirty-five people died at Labranche, and twenty-three at Frenier. The double tracks of the Illinois Central from Labranche westward to Pass Manchac were torn up bodily and twisted around trees in the swamp. The pumping station and levees were destroyed, not to mention the houses. Between 1916 and 1925 the Labranche swamplands were abandoned. In 1925, Suburban Realty sold its eight thousand acres of lakefront to Lake Front Land Company. The survey attached to the sale noted that the individual parcels owned by Rountree and Mouledous were no longer surveyable. The following year Mouledous sold his twenty-seven acres to Alfred D. Danzinger, another land speculator.

Even without the hurricane, the fate of virtually all of the Wisner developments would have been the same. Cultivation, after a few years, made the peat-like soil extremely acidic, making crops increasingly difficult to grow. Cultivation also had the effect of compacting the soil so that the land level dropped three to four feet. Not long after abandonment, a break in the levee would flood the leveed land, creating a regular shaped pond. The farms of Rountree and Mouledous were visible ponds for many years. In the 1990s the U.S. Army Corps of Engineers began a program of marsh reclamation projects. Among the first were their farms, and today the marsh adjacent to Bayou Labranche resembles its nineteenth century appearance.

After Wisner's death in 1915, his widow transferred the land to Wisner Estates, Inc. H. H. Timken, a large creditor of Wisner, sued the company successfully and forced a sheriff's sale of much Wisner land in 1923. Timken had founded a successful carriage business in St. Louis soon after the Civil War. An inventor, when he established the Timken Roller Bearing Company in 1899, he was already quite wealthy. Timken's sons purchased most of the Wisner property in 1923, and three

✧

Cultural tourists love Louisiana's antique shops, whether the shops are in West Monroe or on Royal and Magazine Streets in New Orleans.

COURTESY OF THE LOUISIANA OFFICE OF TOURISM.

years later, they transferred it to Border Research Corporation. This corporation changed its name to Louisiana Land & Exploration Company on May 19, 1927. Timken heirs in Ohio became shareholders of Louisiana Land & Exploration and served on the board of directors. The Timkens continued to hold marshland in Louisiana until 1996, when they donated Couba Island to the New Orleans City Park. This four-thousand acre tract may become a frontier for City Park in the course of the twenty-first century.

By the 1990s, Louisiana Land & Exploration Company, headquartered in New Orleans, ranked 983 on the 1995 Fortune 1000 list. At the time, LL&E's proved oil and gas reserves were equivalent to 260 million barrels of oil. Approximately sixty-eight percent of LL&E's reserves were domestic. LL&E was the largest owner of environmentally sensitive wetlands in the continental U.S., with 600,000 acres or about one-seventh of the wetlands in coastal Louisiana in its portfolio. Louisiana, in turn, comprises forty percent of the wetlands in the lower forty-eight states. In 1996, LL&E merged into Burlington Resources.

Right: Cultural tourism becomes more important with each passing year. Writer Anne Rice not only creates an intellectual aura around her native city of New Orleans, but renovates and preserves threatened structures.

COURTESY OF THE LOUISIANA OFFICE OF TOURISM.

Below: The St. Charles Hotel in New Orleans.

Another northerner with excess capital to invest in Louisiana land was Chester Congdon of Duluth, Minnesota. He had made a small fortune early in the twentieth century from the development of iron mines in Minnesota and copper mines in Arizona. He had heard of the availability of large tracts from Louisiana levee boards at rock bottom prices. Beginning in 1900, Congdon and four associates from the mining industry—Guilford Hartley, David Adams, A. L. Ordean, and A. S. Chase—acquired twenty-five thousand acres of lands on the Gulf Coast of Louisiana for $11,000. They incorporated the St. Mary's Parish Land Company in 1908. By 1935 they had spent $68,000 for not much.

But in the 1930s exploration companies along the Louisiana coast drilled deeper and deeper. Since the St. Mary lands abutted the Belle Isle Salt Dome, hope had persisted that something would hit. In 1933, Texaco's predecessor, using its lease from the State of Louisiana, drilled a producing well on State of Louisiana water bottoms near St. Mary's lands. On May 6, 1938, the St. Mary No. 1 was completed at a depth of 9,910 feet for 335 barrels of oil per day, establishing the Horseshoe Bayou Field, which would become one of the

"giants" of the United States. In 1941, St. Mary leased four thousand acres to Atlantic Richfield, the forerunner of Vastar, and the Bayou Sale Field was discovered on the eve of Pearl Harbor. Oil development and production in both these fields were accelerated to serve the needs of World War II. Vastar still explores in these fields.

Until World War II natural gas had been seen as just a worthless nuisance. After the war pipelines were converted to transport gas. In 1941, Sun Oil Company, the predecessor of Oryx, discovered gas at Belle Isle adjacent to St. Mary's lands. In 1950, Sun leased their land, completing its first St. Mary well in 1955 at the then extraordinary depth of 15,500 feet. Sun declared the Belle Isle Field in 1961 to be "one of the major hydrocarbon reserves in the Gulf Coast." Like LL&E, St. Mary remained a simple holding company for many decades. But it too converted into an exploration and drilling company with the realization that their Louisiana fields might expire. St. Mary Parish Land Company is now a $200-million, Denver-based company with comparatively little interest in Louisiana.

LL&E and St. Mary exemplify the pattern of the extractive industries. The investment and companies come only so long as the resource lasts. Both have now departed from the state. The first Louisiana Purchase transferred seventy percent Louisiana's land to the ownership of the Federal Government. The second Louisiana Purchase transferred seventy percent of the natural wealth to investors from out of state.

Oil & gas and sulphur are mining industries, and the declining production of oil and gas signals that the twenty-first century will be as different from the twentieth century as the twentieth century was from the nineteenth. In the twenty-first century, service and tourism industries will contribute more and more to Louisiana's prosperity. Wholesale destruction of historic houses has virtually stopped as communities and investors have stepped forward to rehabilitate places like Whitney and Destrehan Plantations. New Orleans has become the epicenter for Louisiana tourism, and most downtown office buildings have been converted to hotels. Cultural tourism has teamed up with sports events as economic generators. The Louisiana Superdome, completed in 1975, spurred the conversion of New Orleans downtown from an office to a service complex. The Superdome has hosted more Superbowls than any other facility. When the Rolling Stones drew 87,500 fans in 1981, the Superdome set a record for the largest indoor concert. Tourism is now the leading employment generator in the New Orleans region.

There is hardly a better opportunity for the cultural tourist than a visit to the National D-Day Museum in New Orleans.

COURTESY OF THE NEW ORLEANS OFFICE OF TOURISM.

Chapter VI

LOUISIANA: A STATE OF CONTRADICTION

Louisiana's history for the last century has played out contradictions. North Louisiana has differed with South Louisiana; Catholic Louisiana with Protestant Louisiana; French Louisiana from Anglo Louisiana. Yet another pair of contradicting forces has been even more influential in shaping Louisiana history. Unlike the relatively simple geographical or cultural factions, the political divide in the state is a "wild card," to use an image from the state's most popular business—gambling. Political leaders fall into two competing factions, dividing in ways that depend surprisingly not on economic or cultural forces, but innate personality. "Reformers" have sought an honest, decisive and limited government. They tend to favor the cultural status quo, the already established order. They have an aroma of elitism. "Populists" have sought a government responsive to the individuals that elected it. Exemplified by Governor Huey Long and New Orleans Mayor Martin Behrman, they doled out benefits to individuals in return for political support. All too often the price for the benefits has included pay-offs that went into the pockets of the populist leaders. The populist has often been the corruptionist.

The Civil War began a populist cycle in Louisiana, one that sought to bring African Americans into the political texture of the state. The cycle quickly mutated into Reconstruction and its aftermath, Redemption, eras dominated by those who shared a common attitude that government was to be exploited for the private benefit of the dominant faction. Railroads marched through Louisiana with the overwhelming support of the legislature. Northern timber barons bought up Louisiana's vast timber resources. The state treasurer ran off to Mexico with a million dollars of state funds. In 1881 the criminal sheriff of New Orleans likewise departed with a substantial sum from the city treasury. In New Orleans every city jobholder was a political appointee committed to the status quo. The all-time highest tax rate in New Orleans occurred in 1883, when it reached 317.5 mills on assessed valuation. This almost equals one-third of the value of property to be paid in taxes each year. A man next in line to be mayor was convicted of organizing the murder of a political opponent. In December 1885 the grand jury reported "hoodlumism rampant throughout the city by day and burglars plying their avocation throughout the night, the city is in a deplorable condition, and every citizen's house is liable to be entered at any hour of the day or night, his family insulted, and his house robbed, unless there is a male protector on the premises ready and armed for resistance."

A characteristic Huey Long pose, before the new state capitol.

COURTESY OF SPECIAL COLLECTIONS, TULANE UNIVERSITY.

In the 1880s a reform cycle began in Louisiana. The reformers were a young, new breed of middle-class men anxious to make the state a better place to live. "Anything which benefits the masses should prevail over every other selfish consideration." They sought to accomplish what slavery and sectional conflict had made impossible. They were not averse to employing the power of the Federal Government to accomplish their agenda. At their instigation the Federal Government began the process of deepening the port of New Orleans to make it accessible to the new ocean-going steamship. It put the Louisiana Lottery out of business. And it put the seal of federal authority on segregation.

The first signs of reform appeared in 1885 with the formation of a committee of one hundred. Young men like Edward Douglass White and Felix Dreyfous were determined to improve Louisiana. They were not held back by fears of northern political power or enmity to the capitalistic forces shaping the American economy. They wanted Louisiana to be part of what Henry Grady, the Atlanta journalist, had labeled three years earlier the "New South." The genius of the reformers was their ability to focus on the basics underlying the capitalistic economy. They saw that what Louisiana needed were not "quick fixes" like a lottery, but the construction of an infrastructure that would enable population and business to grow and prosper.

✧

Modern Louisiana political history began in reaction to O. J. Dunn (right) and P. B. S. Pinchback (left), leaders of the new Republican Party in Louisiana during Reconstruction. Dunn resided in New Orleans prior to the Civil War and became a prominent Prince Hall Mason. Pinchback came to New Orleans during the Civil War and later became lieutenant governor and governor. Dunn died mysteriously in 1871. Pinchback lived until 1921.

COURTESY OF THE LOUISIANA STATE ARCHIVES COLLECTION.

The issue that galvanized Louisiana reform was the lottery. The legislature chartered the lottery in 1868 at the instance of a number of individuals from Texas, Alabama, and Louisiana. A piece of Reconstruction corruption, not surprisingly the Redeemers sought to cancel the charter. Skillful use of money and promises, especially the promise the lottery would close in 1895, led to the insertion of a clause in the Louisiana Constitution of 1880 legalizing the Louisiana Lottery until 1895.

The Louisiana Lottery was a private corporation that drew its income from two sources. The main source was the monthly drawings that yielded each month more than three thousand winners. Early on the Lottery Company established a reputation for honest drawings by using Confederate generals and an elaborate mechanical system to ensure fairness. In its almost forty years, the largest winner was a New Orleans barber who collected $300,000 in one draw (the equivalent to about $30 million today). Unlike today's lottery, the state lottery of the 1800s paid winnings quickly. The second source of income, and the one that drew the most reform ire, was the policy drawings.

Policy drawings were three numbers pulled twice daily. Guessing the right numbers yielded a return on a small bet. The lottery company opened more than a hundred policy shops across the city in the 1880s. They were thronged by the masses, and it was the sight of large numbers of the poor gambling that fueled the fire of the reform impulse. As one historian noted, there were "policy booths in front of laundries, bar-rooms, groceries, and markets." New Orleans was policy mad.

With its enormous profits, the Lottery became a patron of politicians and charities. Astutely they supported relief efforts after floods, and subscribed to every fundraiser in the city and state. But the 1880s witnessed the first anti-monopolistic movement in American history, and in 1890 the Sherman Anti-Trust Act passed Congress. Reform public opinion quickly jelled in opposition to the power of large private combines, irrespective of their moral worth. The anti-lottery effort, however, drew additional strength from the Protestant Churches, whose pastors regularly preached against gambling.

With the charter of the lottery company set to expire in 1895, the company chose the year 1890 to amend the state constitution so as to permit the continuation of the lottery. As an inducement, it offered to pay the state $1 million a year, more than twenty times what it had been paying.

Immediately, Edward Douglass White, Felix Dreyfous, and others met at the offices of Charles Parlange to organize the Anti-Lottery League. Since the lottery's advertising budget kept the established press in line, the new

League felt it essential to have its own organ. It formed a new newspaper, the *New Delta*.

The reformers plunged into the grassroots work of campaigning. In spite of the efforts of the anti-lottery faction, a substantial majority of the legislature approved a constitutional amendment in 1890 to recharter the lottery. Reform Governor Francis T. Nicholls vetoed the amendment. On July 16, 1890, the anti-lottery forces celebrated at the Grunewald Hall. It was the largest meeting site in New Orleans, and it was jammed. Hundreds were turned away. Large banners on each side of the stage honored Governor Francis T. Nicholls, Lieutenant Governor James Jeffries, Attorney General Walter H. Rogers, Senators Joseph H. Duggan, Euclid Borland, Felix J. Dreyfous, Joseph C. Gilmore, and Frank Marquez. Letters were read and addresses received. Charles Parlange delivered the first major speech, followed by Samuel Gilmore.

The jubilation of July soon turned to dismay as the lottery forces persuaded the majority in the legislature to declare that such an amendment did not require the Governor's signature. The secretary of state merely needed to promulgate the act. When the secretary of state refused, J. A. Morris, on behalf of the lottery company, moved to obtain a writ of mandamus against the secretary of state. The district judge ruled against the lottery company, but a narrow Supreme Court majority, made up of Edward Bermudez, Samuel D. McEnery, and Lynn Boyd Watkins, reversed the district judge. This put the amendment on the ballot for April 1892. This election coincided with the statewide governors race. Thus the struggle switched to a fight for control of the state Democratic party. Eerily, a century later this struggle was repeated when lottery forces again won a narrow Supreme Court decision declaring that the explicit provision of the Louisiana Constitution against gambling did not include a prohibition against gaming.

The reformers portrayed the fight as one between patriotism and money. True love of country and family required that the lottery be tamed. They portrayed the lottery wing of the Democratic Party as one dominated by "rich" Albert Baldwin, "yankee" John A. Morris, and "carpet-bagger" P. B. S. Pinchback. The reformers hated all the newspapers (except the *New Delta*) because they unabashedly received large sums from the lottery in advertising. In the fall of 1891, anti-lottery meetings were held in all of the wards of New Orleans to lay the groundwork for beating the lottery at the polls.

For governor the regular Democrats recruited Samuel D. McEnery, the Louisiana

Aside from political parties, the first institution to promote itself in Louisiana history was the Louisiana Lottery. All the tools of public relations, so well known in the twenty-first century, were put into play in the nineteenth century promoting the lottery. This advertisement that ran in all pro-lottery newspapers illustrates the "care" to which the lottery company ensured the fairness of its drawings. Generals P. G. T. Beauregard and Jubal Early are seated on the left and right, respectively.

Above: Felix J. Dreyfous (1857-1946) was one of the great Jewish reformers of New Orleans. He practiced the notarial profession in its most thorough and complete form for more than half a century. One of the early reformers, he supported the creation of levee boards, the New Orleans Dock Board, school reform, and drainage reform.

COURTESY OF THE NEW ORLEANS CITY PARK.

Opposite: One of the greatest achievements of reform was the construction of the New Orleans sewerage and drainage system. Mostly below sea level, it pumps every drop of rain out to Lake Ponchartrain. It was not until the late 1970s that it began to break down. In the twenty-first century, due to major federal funding, rebuilding the great underground canals has begun. This map shows that Broad Street is the major axis because it is the lowest portion of the city. From Broad Street water is pumped out to secondary stations as the Seventeenth Street Canal, Orleans Avenue, and the Main Outfall Channel. The map is taken from the Twenty-Eighth Semi-Annual Report of the Sewerage and Water Board of New Orleans.

State Supreme Court judge who had just voted for the lottery company in its appeal for a writ of mandamus. They mustered control of the Democratic Convention that met on December 15, 1891. The anti-lottery faction bolted, called their own convention, and reached an agreement with the Farmers' Alliance. They selected Murphy Foster for governor and Charles Parlange for lieutenant governor, both staunch opponents of the lottery. The election in April 1892, led to a reform victory and the lottery amendment lost overwhelmingly. The future of the lottery had already been sealed by actions of the Federal Government. On September 19, 1890, Congress passed a measure prohibiting lottery solicitations or tickets from the mails. Prosecutions of those violating the law followed. In 1895 the Louisiana Lottery moved to Honduras and became the Honduras National Lottery.

After using the state's power to suppress the lottery, reformers turned to the state to solve a variety of New Orleans' ills. In 1900 the state's largest city, almost ten times larger than the second largest city, operated much as it had in 1800. Its population of 287,000 accounted for more than a quarter of the state's population. The reform agenda was a campaign for public works. These public works comprised drainage, flood protection, municipally supplied pure water, the removal of sewerage, and public ownership of the docks.

Early in April 1888, reformer and notary Felix Dreyfous ran an advertisement in a newspaper seeking anyone with a plan for protection of the city from floods. Some parishes had already tried levee boards. A New Orleans Levee Board became the goal for the reformers. The legislature approved it in 1890. It was a state agency with its board appointed by the governor. The new board had the power to tax and to expropriate land necessary for levees, either in New Orleans or the surrounding parishes. Action was needed immediately, because 1890 brought flooding right up to the city. Many areas upriver from New Orleans, especially around Convent, Louisiana, suffered from deep floods. The river broke through the levee along the western bank of Jefferson Parish, making the Ames crevasse on Missouri and Pacific Railroad property next to Westwego. The New Orleans Levee Board's initial work went into Algiers because the Ames Crevasse channeled water around to the rear of Algiers. Under the direction of Major Benjamin Harrod, the board constructed the rear levee during the winter of 1890-91. It cost $14,000 and was paid for in one year by the one mill tax. The levee board sent Commissioner Ed Eisenhauer to Holland to gather data on their dikes and levees.

By Spring 1892 the board had built twenty-one miles of new levees. All the levees along both riverfronts, as well as the Old and New Basin Canals, were expected to be completed in 1892. The new levees used the most up to date engineering data, calling for a 3-on-1 slope with an 8-foot crown. They were designed to extend as far as three feet above the flood stage of 1890. Almost a million board feet of cypress was employed in revetting or facing the levees. The reformers did not hesitate to oppose powerful industrial forces in order to secure the city from floods. As chairman of the levee board, Felix Dreyfous sued the New Orleans and Northeastern Railroad Company to compel it to build a levee along Florida Walk. The Board received a favorable decision in the local court, and the Supreme Court turned down the railroad's appeal.

By 1896 the reformers were champing to take control of city government from the ring. With the assistance of Governor Murphy Foster, who was running for reelection, Walter Flower and a reform council swept into power. The first step of the Flower administration was to draft a new city charter, one approved immediately by the legislature in 1896. The new charter was thoroughly "reform" and provided for the first real civil service system.[1] At the next election the city council was to be cut from twenty seven to seventeen members. The new council members also received $20 a month, an innovation. The new charter followed the recommendations of the Municipal Reform League and enhanced the power of the mayor. He now appointed most department heads.

The reformers went right to work and, with the help of the state legislature, created a

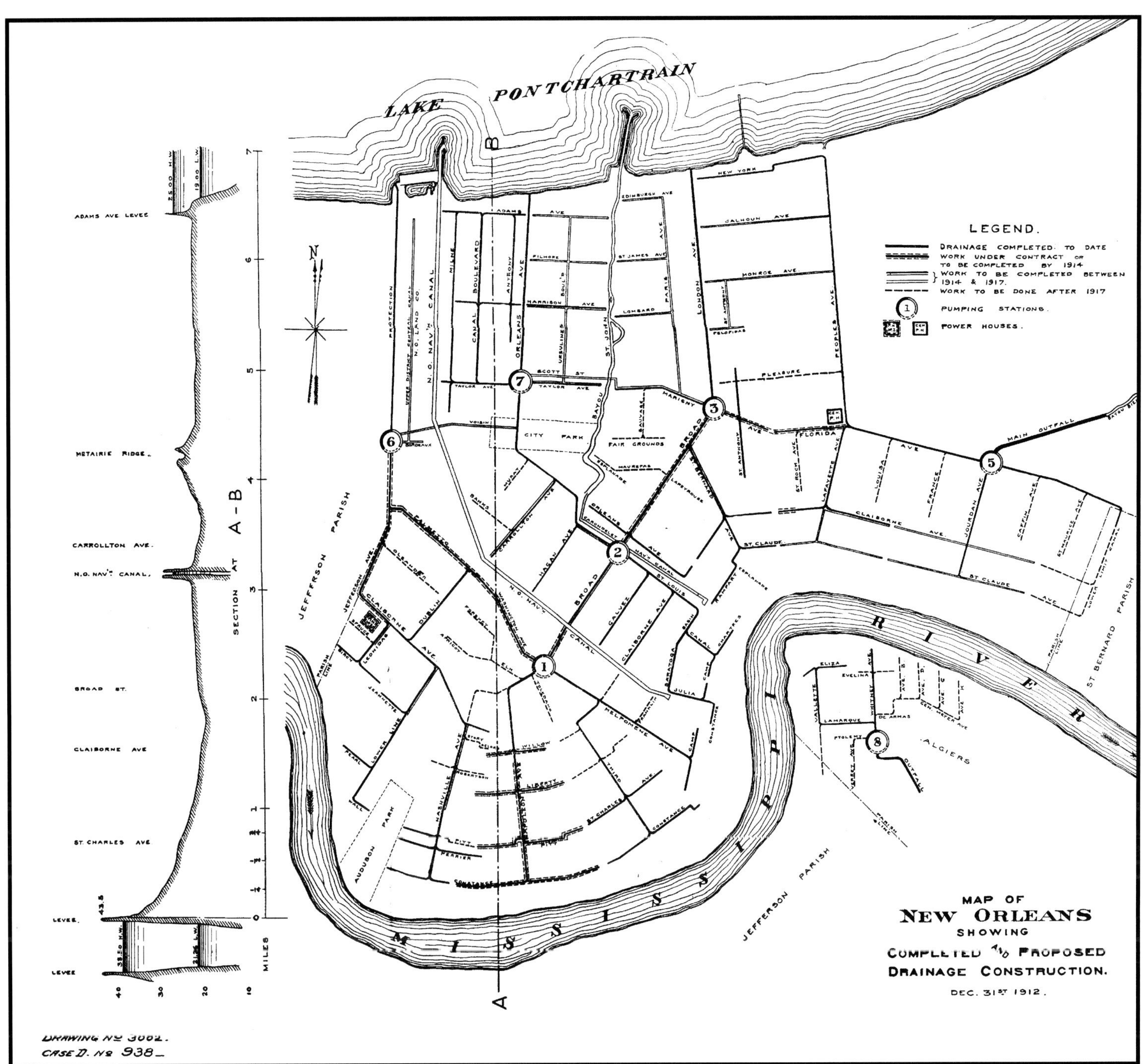

drainage commission for the city. But everyone quickly realized the problem was much broader. Throughout the nineteenth century New Orleans had been conspicuous for its shortage of potable water and lack of sewerage systems. For two decades two companies had been working at a water and sewerage system. But both the New Orleans Waterworks Company and the New Orleans Sewerage Company were demonstrable failures by the arrival of the twentieth century. There were only 5,000 subscribers to the water system out of a population of 290,000.

The turning point in the sewerage and water struggle came in 1898. The *Daily States* reported that talk of ways to improve the city had become so feverish it had almost become utopian. The government had no money, and the scope of a sewerage system was simply too great for private companies. The president of the city council finally came up with the idea that if the government did not have the money, the effort would have to go to the people. He proposed a 2 1/2 mill tax, estimated to yield $250,000, to fund a bond issue sufficient to pay for the entire system at once.

✧

John Milliken Parker (1863-1939) was the leading early twentieth century reformer in Louisiana government. He supported Theodore Roosevelt's Progressive Party and won the governorship of Louisiana in 1920. He fought the lottery, Martin Behrman's political faction in New Orleans, and, later, Huey Long. Parker supported federal funding for flood control, increased regulation of the oil industry, and an oil severance tax. Long took his positions and ran them to the Left, leaving Parker out of power. Like many progressives, he was blind to the evils of segregation. His reform successors were Sam Jones, Robert Kennon, and M. J. "Mike" Foster.

COURTESY OF THE LOUISIANA STATE MUSEUM.

The council estimated that the sewerage system could be laid for $2 million, and the present water work purchased for $2 million. The whole project might not cost more than $5.5 million.[2]

The implementation of the plan required five levels of votes. First was the Council resolution calling for the election in the City of New Orleans to approve the necessary taxes. Second came the election itself. Third was another council resolution laying out the details of the operation of the system and petitioning the legislature for permission. The legislature then had to approve a constitutional amendment. That amendment finally had to be voted on by the people of the entire state. In this election, women would vote for the first time in Louisiana as property holders. The city council then created a special committee on water, sewerage, and drainage.

In 1899 the struggle over sewerage and water reached a crescendo. The reformers stressed the seriousness of the death rate that again was the highest in the nation at 28 per 1,000 for the white population. It was characteristic of reformers not to count the black death rate. Cutting the death rate would bring immigration, then capital, then real estate development. The only opposition came from the "ill-informed" small property owner.

Calling the tax election required more than just a city council vote. A giant petition had to be secured, an effort that the reformers undertook themselves. Some business supporters offered a medal to the city official who raised the most signatures. The contestants for the medal were E. H. Farrar, assisted by Mayor Flower, City Attorney Samuel L. Gilmore, City Treasurer George B. Penrose, Tommy Nolan, and Felix J. Dreyfous. The campaign was successful, and the New Orleans voters approved the sewerage and drainage tax of two mills on June 6, 1899. This led the city council to draft an extensive ordinance providing for the implementation of the water, sewerage, and drainage system.[3] The tax ordinance levied the tax for the year 1899 and subsequently for forty-three years. Bonds were to be issued with a duration of fifty years, subject to the ratification of the legislature and then another popular vote on a constitutional amendment. The bonds and the tax were to be in the hands of the Board of Liquidation, City Debt. Terms of members of the Sewerage and Water Board extended from two to fourteen years, so that the mayor could only replace a member every two years. Among the many clauses of this long act is one now familiar—contractors on work for the Sewerage & Water Board shall only employ residents of the City of New Orleans. All permanent employees of the board shall pass the Civil Service Exam and be residents of New Orleans.

Yet another major innovation of the last years of the nineteenth century was the reform of the administration of the wharves. Until the Civil War the City of New Orleans had built and operated the wharves. Following the war, shortage of money forced the City to lease the wharves to a private company that would charge what it could and be responsible for the construction and maintenance of the wharves. But the private companies did not maintain the wharves and levees adequately. Finally the legislature accepted responsibility for the wharves by creating another state agency, the New Orleans Dock Board. Its powers extended throughout the port of New Orleans, including the river frontage in Jefferson and St. Bernard Parishes. In many ways it was a model super agency akin to port authorities created elsewhere in the course of the twentieth century.

As the reform city council of the 1890s left office at the dawn of the new century, defeated again by the old regulars, future Governor John M. Parker drew a contrast. "I could not help thinking of the wonderful contrast between the last council and the present. For four long years that council dragged the fair name of this city in the mud, and it was openly said abroad that by money one could come here and get anything. I think we can let the mantle of charity fall upon that black record. The record of this council has blotted it out of existence…not a single newspaper in this city has ever made a single insinuation against its honesty. Before, it had gotten so that all one could hear was 'job, job," until it got so that a man was ashamed to say that he came from New Orleans."[4]

The decade of the 1890s witnessed the flowering of reform. Unfortunately reform was rooted in racism. Its dark underside was segregation. In 1890 the murder of D. C. Hennessy, New Orleans chief of police, revealed a serious flaw in the reformers mentality. For ten years Hennessy had waged an effective war against an Italian "mafia" organization. His murder the night of October 15, 1890, was quickly traced to the Mafia and a dozen suspects were arrested and tried. The trial led to a hung jury, however, and the following day the "better" element of the community organized and armed themselves to enforce justice. A crowd of armed men seized parish prison and summarily executed eleven Italians. The leader of this movement was none other than W. S. Parkerson, the president of the Young Men's Democratic League.

The same year the Louisiana legislature required railroads to provide separate railroad cars for blacks and whites. Segregation had existed before and during the Civil War. It was the attack on this act by the Creole blacks of New Orleans that led to the *Plessy v. Ferguson* lawsuit decided by the U.S. Supreme Court in 1896. The French heritage of much of Creole New Orleans provided the rationale for equal rights that sparked Creole protest up to 1896. Yet white Creoles were notably silent. Their silence merely continued an attitude that had originated with the Louisiana Purchase and was reinforced by the oppression of the Civil War. White Creoles accepted the American victory and recognized there was nothing to be gained from protesting the central tenant of American power—segregation of the races. White Creoles knew that the Americans could just as easily suppress French culture and language should they chose, an eventuality quickly reached in the twentieth century.

Statewide, the election of 1896 was crucial to the reformers. The fusion candidate of the farmers and the Republicans made a concerted effort. Yet, when the election was over, it turned out that many black votes had been counted for the Democratic Party, giving it a sweeping victory. Within days the legislature went to work changing the election laws. Through literacy and property requirements the voting rolls were chopped. The number of white voters was cut by more than half, from 164,000 to 74,000. The number of black voters was cut ninety percent, from 130,000 to 13,000. So Louisiana became a one-party state even before the Constitution of 1898 ratified these voting restrictions.

After Governor Murphy Foster's departure from office in 1900, the reformers stayed out of office for twenty years. With the cooperation of leaders of the political ring in New Orleans, notably Martin Behrman, many reforms were consolidated during that interval. Reformer John Parker flirted with Progressivism and third parties, but the insistence on a one-party state forced him back into the Democratic Party. There his charisma won him the governorship in 1920. It seemed to be another chance for reform. But times were different. In the 1890s Louisiana had started the only leprosarium (Carville) in America. In 1920 the state turned it over to the Federal Government. In 1912 the state had created a minimum severance tax. Parker had the opportunity to make it a real source of state income. He missed the opportunity. Yet business leaders in the twenties accomplished a number of long-range benefits for Louisiana. In Shreveport the business community led a

Above: Martin Behrman (1864-1926) served as mayor of New Orleans from 1904 until 1920, and again from 1925 until his death in 1926. He brought the great institutions created by the reformers to fruition—drainage, port facilities, a public belt road, and school reform. These institutions carried New Orleans throughout the twentieth century.

Below: Elmer Candy Factory in 1917. Notice the women workers and their sanitary clothing.

COURTESY OF THE LOUISIANA STATE MUSEUM.

✧

Joseph E. Ransdell (1858-1954) of Lake Providence in northeast Louisiana was one of the most remarkable and energetic individuals to live in Louisiana. Over the course of his life, he had three careers. Originally, he planted cotton and developed pecan groves. He went on to serve in Congress in 1899 and in the U.S. Senate in 1913. While in the Senate, he introduced legislation to nationalize the leprosarium in Carville, Louisiana. He also introduced legislation creating the National Institutes of Health and spearheaded flood control acts that put in place the levee and reservoir system in use today. After Huey Long took Ransdell's seat, Ransdell became a businessman and served on the board of supervisors of Louisiana State University.

COURTESY OF THE LOUISIANA STATE ARCHIVES.

campaign to raise $1.65 million to purchase 21,705 acres for what became the Barksdale Air Force Base, since then a major economic force in northwest Louisiana.

The reform impulse faltered in the 1920s, yielding to a renewed burst of populism sparked by the charismatic Huey P. Long. A number of Louisiana men had strode the national stage before Long. The one who held the highest office was Edward Douglass White, chief justice of the United States Supreme Court from 1910 to 1921. Senator John Slidell played the role of Presidential king maker during the 1850s. Remarkable Louisiana Senator Joseph E. Ransdell, who was born before the Civil War and lived survived the reign of Huey Long, pushed flood control legislation that benefited the Mississippi Valley, introduced the legislation to create the National Institute of Health, and brought Carville into the national government. Lawyer Edward Livingston of New York and New Orleans served as United States secretary of state under President Andrew Jackson. But Livingston was most widely admired in United States and Europe as creator of a model code of criminal law. But it was Huey Pierce Long who pounded the national stage the hardest.

Huey Long came from a prosperous family in one of the poorest parishes in the state. His older brother Julius supported him for one year in New Orleans to study law. He selected a number of law courses at Tulane University Law School, but principally studied on his own. In 1915 he was admitted to the bar. He returned to Winnfield, but then moved his practice to booming Shreveport. Huey was the original personal injury lawyer. He was also one of the first Louisiana politicians to campaign by automobile, employing an Overland 90 in 1918 to solicit votes for railroad commissioner. This successful campaign gave Long his most enduring and useful adversary—the Standard Oil Company. It operated, arguably, the largest oil refinery in the world at Baton Rouge, and it depended on a large coterie of pipelines for supplies. As a new member of the Louisiana Railroad Commission, soon to become the Louisiana Public Service Commission, he recognized that pipelines should be a public utility, transporting all oil at equal rates for all refiners. John Parker's gubernatorial election in 1920 brought a progressive, albeit a timid one, into the governor's chair.

Long was blessed in his opposition. Besides Standard Oil, the other major force was the Old Regular Party in New Orleans. Consisting of the seventeen ward leaders following the lead of Mayor Martin Behrman. It used every tactic available to ensure its vote and eliminate the opposition. This included the use of police intimidation. The Old

Regular organization persisted as a force in the city from the 1880s to the 1950s. It strongly opposed state regulation of utilities, remained satisfied with high electric rates, opposed cheap natural gas, and did nothing to oppose child labor.

Long made his first run for governor of Louisiana in 1923, standing for a stronger and more active state government. He introduced the issue of free textbooks for school children, an idea foreign to Louisiana but already in practice elsewhere in the South. He continued to use the automobile effectively, and he plunged forward into the new medium of the radio, speaking in New Orleans over radio station WCAG. His most important backers were still members of his family. One of the biggest issues in 1923 was the Ku Klux Klan. The other serious candidates, Henry L. Fuqua and Hewitt Bouanchaud, were both opponents of the Klan, so it was supposed that Huey was pro-Klan. Yet, Long ignored the issue, continuing to talk only about the secret power of Standard Oil. Though Huey ran third, the election was so close that his stature actually increased. The following year he was swept into a second term as public service commissioner. By then he was the odds-on favorite in the gubernatorial election of 1928.

Louisiana at the time held her accustomed spot near the bottom of the nation, not only geographically but in average income (39th of 48), farm property value (43rd), and literacy (47th). When he won the gubernatorial election on his second try in 1928, he embarked upon a series of changes that went beyond reform to outright rebellion against the ruling class. He raised severance taxes on natural resource industries to pay for schoolbooks for every child, regardless of whether they went to public or private school.

During his term as governor, the state built over 2,300 miles of paved roads, 111 bridges, and, in 1931, employed ten percent of the men involved in road building nationally. He moved to abolish the practices of straitjacketing and chaining and to introduce dental care at mental institutions (at one, he claimed, dentists extracted seventeen hundred diseased teeth from inmates). Long's appointee as head of Angola, still considered one of the toughest prisons in the country, instituted the state's first prisoner-rehabilitation program. Long implemented an adult literacy program in Louisiana that largely served African Americans.

In 1930, Long ran for the U.S. Senate and won. But a break with his Lieutenant-Governor Paul St. Cyr convinced Long not to take the seat until the end of his term as governor. It was not until 1932 that Long

Bonnie Parker and Clyde Barrow killed dozens of police officers in a six-year rampage across Middle America. Texas special agent Frank Hamer set up a trap near Plain Dealing, Louisiana. Their bodies were brought to the rear of a furniture store in Arcadia, Louisiana. In the car was a saxophone, 15 guns, and 3,000 rounds of ammunition.

COURTESY OF THE LOUISIANA STATE ARCHIVES COLLECTION.

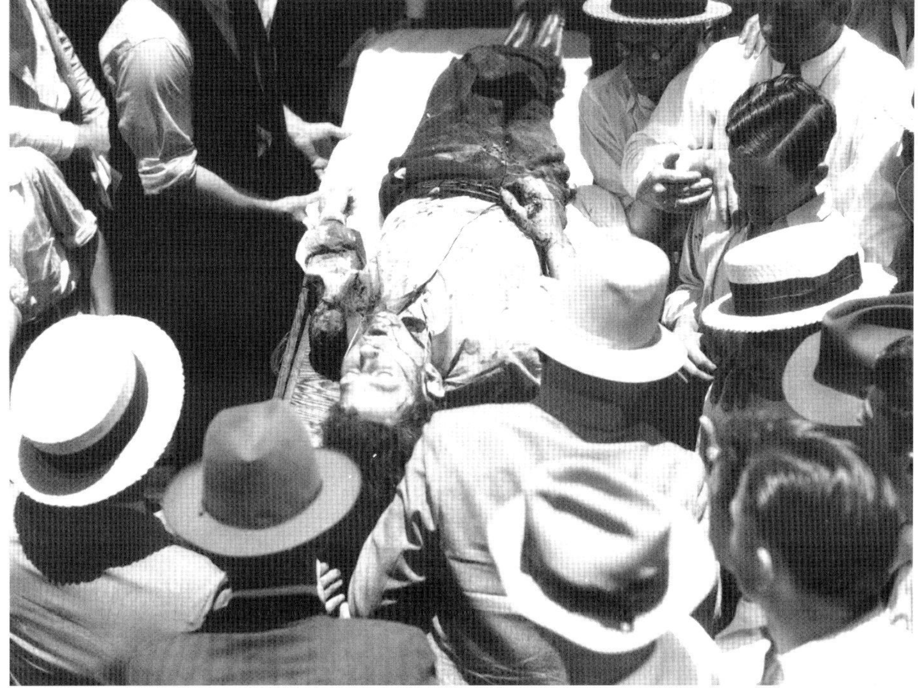

Right: *Huey Long with his son, Russell. Russell Long, along with Earl Long, Speedy Long, and Gillis Long, were the heirs to the Huey Long mystique. Russell Long served as a U.S. senator from Louisiana from his election at age thirty in 1948 until the middle of President Ronald Reagan's administration in 1985.*

COURTESY OF THE NEW ORLEANS PUBLIC LIBRARY.

Below: An early political cartoon by John Chase, characteristically combining Louisiana's ethnic history with satire of its current political figures at the time.

COURTESY OF SPECIAL COLLECTIONS, TULANE UNIVERSITY.

went to Washington. There, Long joined the progressive forces led by Senators Burton Wheeler and Bob Lafollette. But back in Louisiana, Long was crafting not progressive legislation, but tyranny. In 1934 he sent two thousand state troopers into New Orleans to overawe the mayoral election. He prevented a duly elected member of the legislature from taking his seat, and employed a subservient state supreme court to defend the outrage. Long gradually became more and more authoritarian as the need for his personal attention spread to an ever-wider stage.

There was no longer time for the democratic process. Long's agenda in Washington and Louisiana needed his personal attention; caveats of due process were merely tricks of the upper classes to prevent enactment of Long programs. When Long wanted something done, he did it. Duly elected officials were mere figureheads. Long sat in the chair of the speaker of the house and presided over the state legislature. In one four-day special legislative session presided over by Long, bills were enacted centralizing in the governor's hands all the police and prosecutorial power of the state. In two special sessions in 1935, he stripped the City of New Orleans of its powers to tax and to make appointments, centralizing everything in the office of the governor. The bills went through the legislature with no speeches and no opposition because none was brooked. It was tyranny out and out. By 1935, Long had accomplished a revolution. Representative government was now a sham. One party ran the state and one man ran the party. By 1935, Long had so suppressed the legislature that no one even bothered to speak for or against his bills. The bills were introduced, read, and passed. The Louisiana Supreme Court was in his pocket. Without examining Long's motives, his stated programs should be applauded. But it is clear that as his power grew, the quality of the programs he championed cheapened. His program came more and more to be anything that made his power more arbitrary.

But on September 8, 1935, it all came to an end. At 9:20 p.m. that evening, Dr. Carl Weiss approached Long in the capitol corridor outside of the governor's office and got off one shot with a .32-caliber automatic pistol. Long stumbled wounded, then ran to a stairwell. His bodyguards shot Weiss repeatedly. Though Long underwent surgery, his doctor missed closing a severed artery to the kidney. By the next day, when the omission was noticed, Long was too weak to be operated on again. He died on Tuesday, September 10, 1935.

Long's opposition to President Franklin Delano Roosevelt had forced the president to cut federal relief efforts to a trickle. With Long's removal from the stage, the federal spigot opened wide and numerous new projects began moving along, everything from building the new football stadium in City Park to rebuilding Tchoupitoulas Avenue. The Long henchmen led by Governor Richard Leche cooperated fully in return for control of the patronage in new projects. As Long himself had predicted, his hand-picked stooges could not keep the operation running smoothly. The Federal Government launched an investigation in 1938 that led to the arrest and eventual conviction of the governor and many others in 1939.

Another reform faction led by Governor Sam Jones took office in 1940. Among the many scandals that were not corrected from the 1930s was the lease of much of the state's oil and gas lands to the Texaco Corporation in return for a hidden percentage to the Win or

Lose Oil Company, controlled by Long interests. Within parishes like Plaquemines, local bosses created their own private oil holding companies. As government officials, they leased the vast marshlands of Louisiana to powerful northern oil companies in return for secret royalties.

Longism long survived Huey. Its immediate heir was his brother, Earl, who served as governor in 1939, 1948 to 1952, and again from 1956 to 1960. His most potent heir was his son, Russell, who served as United States senator from 1948 to 1985. Other Long relations served in the United States House of Representatives, notably Gillis Long and Speedy Long. They all strongly supported the national Democratic Party. Governor Robert Kennon (1952-1956) was the purest reformer in the twentieth century. He reinstalled state civil service, fought gambling, and at the same time tried to preserve segregation.

Governor John J. McKeithen (1964-1972) was the closest Louisiana came to melding the extremes. A close ally of the Longs and of the oil industry, he was an avowed reformer. He promoted code of ethics and state civil service. Remarkably, however, he was on the constructive side of the racial conflicts of the sixties. Governor Edwin Edwards began where McKeithen ended as a reformer and supporter of integration. He presided over the 1973 revision of the state constitution. But when the state had valuable franchises to distribute, whether hospital beds, bank charters, or riverboat gambling licenses, he felt that the payment should go to his friends, not to the state. But his federal conviction on corruption charges is perhaps more a tribute to the incredible complexity of the laws then to any intention by Edwards to violate them. Edwards is the public man who saw political office as an opportunity for private aggrandizement. He typifies the Louisiana political climate that oscillates between private corruption and public reform.

For all the misfortunes and burdens of the past century, Louisiana is a better place today for all its people. The suppression of slavery and segregation has broadened opportunities for the mass of its people.

A crowd gathers to listen to Earl Long give a speech in 1940.

COURTESY OF THE LOUISIANA STATE MUSEUM.

Chapter VI Endnotes

1 Howard, L. Vaughan. *Civil Service Development in Louisiana* (New Orleans, 1956). p. 9.

2 *The Daily States*, November 17, 1898.

3 Common Council of the City of New Orleans, Ordinance No. 15,391, C.S., June 22, 1899.

4 Official Proceedings of the City Council, May 1, 1900, in Dreyfous files.Official Proceedings of the City Council, May 1, 1900, in Dreyfous files.

This aerial view of New Orleans highlights the low-rise French Quarter against the high-rise American Quarter.

COURTESY OF THE LOUISIANA OFFICE OF TOURISM.

SHARING THE HERITAGE

historic profiles of businesses, organizations, and families that have contributed to the development and economic base of Louisiana

TEXACO, INC.

"First," "largest," and "most" are all words that appear frequently in any history of Texaco's petroleum production and refining operations in Louisiana. With its presence here dating back to the founding of The Texas Company in 1902, Texaco takes pride in the part it has played in the development and economy of the Pelican State over the past century.

In September 1902, the Company first qualified to do business as a marketer, producer and refiner of petroleum and its products in Louisiana. A pumping station and storage tanks were constructed at Amesville, across the river from New Orleans, that same year. This was followed in 1906 by construction of the Company's first Louisiana bulk plant, located in Lake Charles, and its first automobile gasoline filling station, which was opened in New Orleans in 1914.

Among The Texas Company's earliest customers were sugar planters along the Mississippi River, who bought crude oil to fuel the engines that ground their cane. Like the economy of Louisiana, the Company's markets have steadily diversified and expanded ever since that time.

New Orleans ranks as one of the busiest ports in the United States in terms of foreign trade and total tonnage of waterborne commerce. Texaco ships huge quantities of natural gas through a complex network of pipelines to hundreds of Southern Louisiana industries ranging from shipyards to petrochemical plants to aerospace-related manufacturers.

In the metropolitan New Orleans area, two manufacturing plants operate for every mile of the Mississippi River in St. Charles Parish.

Petroleum continues to be the backbone of business in Louisiana. Its importance has grown steadily through the years, and this industry continues to dominate the state's economy. Texaco has paced the industry throughout the past century, and that leadership continues today.

The Company's first pipeline facilities in Louisiana were constructed in 1906 in the Evangeline. Fifteen years later the Texas Pipe Line Company acquired facilities formerly owned by its parent company, The Texas Company, and obtained a license to operate in the state.

The pipeline company's first installation was a gathering system between Lafitte and Marrero in 1935, followed the next year by facilities in the Garden Island-Pilottown area; and in 1937 by those in the New Iberia-Avery Island area. In 1943 the first extensive main line facilities were built from the South Louisiana fields to Port Arthur, Texas.

In 1950 the Marrero Terminal opened as a waterfront terminal on the site of Texaco's first terminal at Amesville, with expansion in 1958

to handle bunker fuel. The Houma Terminal, a waterfront station designed to receive barge shipments, opened in 1949, with additions and improvements in 1952 to accommodate deliveries to marine customers.

The Company's oil and gas exploration and production activities in Louisiana began in 1904 through a subsidiary, Producers Oil Company in Acadia Parish, with the first production obtained in 1906, on the Latreille Lease in North Louisiana's Caddo Parish.

Entering the Vinton (or Ged) Field in Calcasieu Parish in July of 1910, production began on the Vincent property. This was followed by discovery of the Nabroton Field in De Soto Parish of North Louisiana, and purchase of the properties of Christine Oil & Gas Company with completion of its first commercial well in 1913. In North Louisiana in 1917 the Elm Grove Field was discovered in Bossier Parish. Its No. 1 Caplis, a gas well, was completed in October of that year. In the Homer Field in Claiborne Parish, discovered in 1919, the Company's first producing well, the Langston B-1, was completed on October 1, 1919.

Although Texaco operated consistently in South Louisiana throughout the period from 1907 to 1928, no new discoveries of importance were made until November 12, 1928. On that date the Company entered into an operating agreement with The Louisiana Land & Exploration Company covering properties along South Louisiana's coastal areas.

Among the projects Texaco took over was a drilling operation in the East Hackberry Field, which Texaco completed as a producing well on November 13, 1929. Texaco also discovered production on a large tract owned by Botany Bay Lumber Company in St. Landry Parish.

Production by the Company on properties covered by The Louisiana Land & Exploration Company contract accelerated, producing considerable quantities on six additional properties. These included the Dog Lake Field, Lake Pelto Field and Lake Barre Field, all in 1929; Four Isle Field and Bay St. Elaine Field, both in 1937.

In addition, the Company discovered three other prospects—Lafitte in Jefferson Parish, Golden Meadows in Lafourche Parish, and Paradis in St. Charles Parish.

As is the case in oil exploration on land, geophysical crews use seismic exploration to find promising geological trademarks in Louisiana's marshes and offshore. In these areas, oil and gas are usually found trapped in salt domes. The exploration crews detonate small explosive charges or use special trucks to tamp the ground to create subsurface sound waves that are recorded on seismographic equipment. From the scores of sound wave data produced, specialists estimate the chance of finding oil in a specific area.

Even the most advanced seismographic data can provide only a guide. The only way to be sure oil and gas lie thousands of feet below is to drill, and in Louisiana's coastal marshes, this involved some unusual challenges. Texaco, which was among the first oil companies to attempt drilling in water in South Louisiana, worked out practical methods of meeting these challenges.

Between 1928 and 1932, Texaco drilled in these areas by erecting derricks on foundations created by driving pilings into the lakes and swamps, a costly procedure. Records show that over twenty percent of the time spent on wells in the early days in South Louisiana was consumed in operations that were unrelated to drilling or completing the wells. This was the time required to construct foundations, move in equipment, set up and dismantle the rigs, and move out.

In the early 1930s, however, Texaco acquired patent rights to a new drilling method—the first submersible drilling barge, invented by Louis Giliasso, a retired sea captain. The design of this barge allowed it to be towed through water to the prospective well site. It could then be submerged during the drilling operation, eliminating the need for building a foundation. After the well was completed, the drilling barge would be re-floated and moved by water to the next drilling site.

Once these barges were successfully developed, the Company shared its patent rights with others in the petroleum industry. The process has been of inestimable value, not only to Texaco, but also to the entire oil industry. It has facilitated the production of oil, gas and sulphur on underwater sites and has made possible the opening of many fields on which production previously would have been impossible.

Submersible barges are essentially unaffected by tides, winds and waves, an important factor considering the need for adequate blow-out control. In addition, they remain vertical during all drilling operations and offer unusual stability.

As increasing numbers of barges came into use in South Louisiana, their designs varied as to size, shape, and arrangement of equipment, as well as the type of equipment. The earliest steam-powered models gave way to those powered by gasoline to a few diesel-electric barges. The trend today is to the use of gas, diesel and gas-diesel engines with superchargers.

The earliest drilling operations in South Louisiana were confined to marshy and shallow water areas, with water depths reaching a maximum of about eight feet. After World War II, however, there was more interest in drilling in greater water depths.

Today, as an outgrowth of the submersible drilling barge technology introduced by Texaco Inc. offshore drilling platforms—many times larger and stronger than the early models—have allowed the search for oil to move out to sea. One-fifth of the substantial petroleum production in Louisiana now comes from offshore rigs.

Throughout its century of operation in Louisiana, Texaco has continued to discover and develop new fields.

In addition to its ranking in crude oil production in the state, the Company is also a principal supplier of natural gas to the huge petrochemical plants along the Mississippi River. In fact, nearly every aspect of the oil business–from exploration to production to pipelining to both industrial and retail marketing–is found in Southern Louisiana.

Utilizing the technological, engineering, geological and operational expertise of its personnel, Texaco has been a leader throughout the twentieth century in Louisiana's petroleum industry in producing and refining this rich natural resource that is so vital to the state's and country's economy.

Frank's Casing Crew & Rental Tools, Inc.

Above: Frank Mosing, founder of Frank's Casing Crew & Rental Tools, Inc. (1904 - 1988).

Below: (left to right) Donald and Janice Mosing, Ray Todd, Louisiana Gulf Coast Oil Exposition representative, Frank and Jessie Mosing. Janice Mosing accepting First Place outside booth award at 1987 LAGCOE.

Frank's Casing Crew & Rental Tools, Inc., was started sixty-one years ago out of Frank Mosing's garage in Lafayette. Today it is one of the largest casing-crew supplier in the world and is still run by Frank's sons Donald and Larry. (Their late brother Billy had also been active in running the firm.) A third generation of Mosings is now involved in the organization Frank founded, and in the new company that handles international operations. Grandchildren head departments as diverse as aviation, marketing, and international, as well as acting as CEO of the international company. Companies in Frank's legacy employ over 2,000 people in 53 countries, with a presence on every continent except Antarctica.

Frank Mosing was born in 1904 on an Oklahoma farm and left to work in the Oklahoma oil fields on a casing crew. With his wife, Jessie Kiser, Frank followed the oil business to Louisiana. On a job in Raceland his paycheck bounced, so Frank took his casing crew with him and left the job. On October 15, 1938, with no orders, no equipment and $3,000 in savings, Frank opened his own company in Lafayette, working out of his garage with Jessie acting as dispatcher at home.

Frank's Casing would become known for persistence and dependability, along with a knack for finding new ways to do a better job. On a drilling site, casing crews are responsible for installing the conductor pipe that guides

initial drilling, install casing to maintain the integrity of the well, and then install the tubing pipe used to pump the oil and gas out of the well. Oil companies soon found that using crews from a specialty company like Frank's resulted in jobs that were done better, safer, faster and for less money.

Frank's Casing also began acquiring tools that companies could rent. Starting with one elevator and one spider, the company inventory grew. Besides keeping well-maintained tools on hand, Frank's began introducing innovations. The stabbing board is the platform on a rig from which new pipe is added to the existing pipe string already in the hole. Frank's new electric adjustable stabbing board was lightweight and belt-driven, so it could be safely moved up and down the rig.

Frank Mosing called the introduction of power tongs the most significant change in the casing business. With deeper holes, companies needed tighter casing connections than human muscles and a steam-powered rope could provide. The power tongs were the answer, and Frank's was one of the first companies to put them into service. By 1978 Frank's would be engineering and manufacturing its own power tongs, setting the standard for safety in the industry.

The next big technological change came in the early 1960s when the company entered the

diesel hammer business. In the old method, casing crews had drilled out the hole, installed casing pipe and then cemented the casing into the hole—often mixing concrete on the site and hauling ninety pound sacks of concrete for each job. With the diesel hammer, the casing crew just pounded the pipe into the hole—no drilling, no cementing, and a lot less mess. Plus, it took half the time. The diesel hammer transformed the casing industry and Frank's, which today is the largest hammer operator in the world with an inventory of over one hundred diesel and hydraulic hammers, profited. The company began a period of rapid growth, both in terms of services and employees.

Frank's sons became involved in the business. Billy joined the company after completing his term in the Air Force and concentrated on sales. He learned to fly and soon was making sales calls to outlying island barges in the Gulf in the company's amphibious plane.

Larry serves as secretary-treasurer, and believes that the two companies have achieved a good balance of domestic and international income. Donald, a mechanical engineer, was the first to insist on acquiring rental tools and then improving them. He was instrumental in setting up Frank's engineering department with impressive results.

After perfecting the power tongs, the first hydraulic thread-cleaning machine was designed and manufactured by Frank's. Frank's also has used computer technology to create its computer Connection Analyzed Makeup (CAM) department. Over the years the company has become a major research and development center. It holds over 19 U.S. patents and scores of international patents. Frank's currently carries more than 150 different products, many designed and manufactured in Lafayette. In addition to rental tools, Frank's also stocks pipe and is today the largest independently owned pipe distributor and pipe service company in the world.

Frank's opened its first branch office in Houma in 1968. The success of that office saw Frank's domestic operations expand dramatically with offices established in Alvin, Corpus Christi, Kilgore and Bryan, Texas, and in Laurel, Mississippi and Oklahoma City, Oklahoma. When the oil bubble burst in the late 1970's, Frank's was in better shape than most companies (thanks to Frank Mosing's natural conservatism) and was able to purchase equipment and occasionally entire companies for cents on the dollar. The equipment was brought to the Lafayette yard for reconditioning and was used to fuel Frank's overseas expansion.

✧

Top: Aerial photo of the Frank's Casing Crew & Rental Tools, Inc., facility in Lafayette which includes the corporate office building, casing, hammer, fill-uptool, and CAM shops, pipe yard and the manufacturing facility.

Below: Jessie Mosing and sons (clockwise from bottom left) Donald, Larry, and Billy Mosing.

✧

Frank's Casing Crew's riser manufacturing facility at the Port of Iberia.

While Frank's had done work in South America, its first permanent extension into overseas activity came with the founding of Frank's International and its Singapore operations in 1981. Donald's son Keith, as CEO of the International company, grew that company throughout the Orient and into the North Sea market. Now the company has sizeable operations in South America, Africa, and Asia.

Frank Mosing died at the age of eighty-four in November 1988. His oldest son, Donald, who had been serving as executive vice president, became president of Frank's Casing Crew. His son Larry still serves that company as secretary and treasurer. Brent Mosing has succeeded his late father Billy as a director and head of marketing of the company. Donald's oldest son Keith serves as chief operating officer of Frank's Casing Crew, and CEO of the international company.

The company would move heavily into the deepwater field, developing techniques and tools for the fabrication, packaging and installation of risers and other work for sub-sea completions. Frank's, ever innovative, pioneered the fabrication of risers for high-fatigue applications. A new facility at the Port of Iberia supports Frank's deepwater operations, with fivty-five hundred feet of waterfront property designed to service a fleet of barges.

Today Frank's manufactures a range of power units in both air-cooled and oil-cooled models to handle environments from the frozen Arctic to the deserts of Arabia. Other Frank's products include auto welders, a wide range of pipe connectors and cementing tools, fill-up and circulation tools, completion products and data-tracking systems, plus an array of items to allow drilling at angles and in failed wells. In all, the company offers more than 150 different products and, ever looking to the future, is perfecting new tools for automated rigs, checking them with state-of-the-art testing equipment.

A long-term workforce, good training, and technological innovation contribute to Frank's impressive safety record. Twenty and 30-year veterans and three-generation families are common among Frank's employees. This longevity in the workforce contributes to safety–new employees are matched with experienced crews and given extra attention. Frank's training includes lectures plus work experience on a drilling rig and test hole at the Lafayette location. Casing and tubing is tripped in and out of the hole giving new and experienced crews hands-on experience to insure that company procedures are always followed. Any safety issue is looked at carefully—and when innovation can solve the problem; Frank's is ready to find that solution.

A family company, Frank's Casing Crew & Rental Tools, Inc., is holding its own in the competitive atmosphere of today's oil and gas service business. With the third generation on board, Frank's looks forward to a future as interesting and profitable as the past has been.

Dominion Exploration & Production, Inc.

Dominion Exploration & Production, Inc.'s roots extend through Consolidated Natural Gas Company's (CNG) lengthy oil and gas history—back a century to John D. Rockefeller's Standard Oil Company and the earliest days of the natural gas business. For this leader of independent natural gas and oil exploration, it all started with the search for oil.

As a by-product of oil exploration, Standard Oil was quick to translate large discoveries of Appalachian gas in the 1800s into commercial opportunity. Over a thirty-year period, Standard formed, merged, and acquired companies to explore for gas throughout the Appalachian Basin and pipe it to growing industrial cities such as Pittsburgh, Cleveland and Akron. By 1911 an integrated network of gas production, transmission and distribution facilities had been assembled under Standard's umbrella. The final component was in place in 1930 when Standard organized a pipeline to supply non affiliated utilities in New York State. In 1943, to avoid being declared a public utility holding company, Standard chose to spin off five of its companies as a single and totally independent entity. Thus, Consolidated Natural Gas was born.

During the boom of the 1950s, CNG became one of the first utilities to join the move to the Gulf of Mexico, first as a partner in drilling ventures, then, in 1962, as a lease owner. CNG's successes in exploration and production in the Gulf led to the establishment of operations in New Orleans in 1966. Developing and maturing quickly, the E&P division began operating many of its leases, and in 1972, became a subsidiary of CNG—CNG Producing Company.

In 2000, Consolidated Natural Gas merged with Dominion Resources, Inc. CNG Producing Company properties were integrated with Dominion's existing oil and gas properties and the name was changed to Dominion Exploration & Production, Inc.

Today Dominion Exploration & Production, Inc. is one of the largest independent domestic natural gas and oil exploration and production companies in North America. With operations in most major basins in the U.S. and Canada, assets include more than six trillion cubic feet equivalent of natural gas and oil reserves and 450 billion cubic feet equivalent of annual production. The company has 1,110 employees nationwide and in Canada, with more than 300 located in New Orleans. Dominion has concentrated recently on onshore property growth, but when its two large deepwater discoveries, Devils Tower and Frontrunner, reach peak production capacity in 2004, Dominion E&P will be solidified as a leader among independent operators in the Gulf of Mexico.

Dominion Exploration & Production plays a significant civil and charitable role in New Orleans and Louisiana. The Dominion Learning Center and Intern program at the Audubon Zoo, the New Orleans Ballet Association, and Parkway Partners, and endowments in geology and petroleum engineering at the University of Louisiana, Lafayette are but a few of the beneficiaries of Dominion's philanthropy.

✧

Above: Ship Shoal 246 "A" and "E" Platforms. Ship Shoal 246 "A" (on left) was the first platform for the former CNG Producing Company. It was installed in 1973.

Bottom, left: Production foremen monitor operations on offshore platforms in the Gulf of Mexico.

Below: Neptune (Visoka Knoll 826) was the world's first production spar platform. Installed in 1995 in two thousand feet of water, it was CNGP's second deepwater venture. It has fourteen wells that are supported on their own buoyancy cans with dry trees at the surface.

FREEPORT McMoRAN COPPER & GOLD, INC. AND McMoRAN EXPLORATION COMPANY

To many Louisiana residents, the Freeport-McMoRan name may be best known not for mining and production activities, but rather for commitment to the community. The depth of the Freeport organization's commitment is rare, spreading Freeport-McMoRan companies' success into communities through millions of dollars of philanthropic programs, including:

- A $5-million commitment to the Audubon Institute in New Orleans to create the Freeport-McMoRan Audubon Species Survival Center.
- A commitment to building a $5 million endowment grant to the New Orleans area Metropolitan Arts Fund.
- Millions of dollars for education support programs across Louisiana.
- More than $1 million to rejuvenate inner-city playgrounds and sponsor youth programs in New Orleans and Austin, Texas.
- More than $1 million for research into cancer and AIDS.
- A commitment of one percent of gross revenues from Indonesian mining operations (averaging over $15 million per year since 1996) for community development programs in the province of Irian Jaya, Indonesia.
- Numerous other commitments wherever the Company operates.

Above: Port Sulphur.

Below: Grande Ecaille.

Although the Freeport-McMoRan name is synonymous with success, minerals, philanthropy and community, writing about the organization in the twenty-first century is no simple task. The companies represented in the landmark dark green building across New Orleans' Poydras Street from the Louisiana Superdome have undergone numerous changes during their rich history in Louisiana and across the world.

Their roots reach to a small sulphur company formed in 1912 and a small oil and gas exploration company formed in 1967. There is no longer a company called simply "Freeport-McMoRan." The name derives from a 1981 merger of Freeport Minerals Company and McMoRan Oil & Gas. A reference to "Freeport" now indicates two separately listed public companies based in New Orleans—Freeport McMoRan Copper & Gold, Inc. and McMoRan Exploration Company, which share some management.

Freeport-McMoRan Copper & Gold (NYSE: FCX) explores for, develops, mines and processes ore containing copper, gold and silver in Indonesia, and smelts and refines copper concentrates in Spain and Indonesia.

McMoRan Exploration Company (NYSE: MMR) is an independent public company that engages in developing, exploring and producing oil and natural gas offshore in the Gulf of Mexico and onshore in the Gulf Coast area; and in purchasing, transporting, terminaling, and marketing sulphur.

The "Freeport Organization" has a long, prosperous history in Louisiana. Even today, most long-time Gulf Coast residents associate "Freeport" with "sulphur." Founded to mine a deposit of the yellow element in Texas, the

Freeport Sulphur Company has been in the sulphur business longer than any other company. In 1933 it undertook a project then considered virtually impossible—developing a mine in the middle of the delta marshes near the mouth of the Mississippi River. Not only did the Freeport engineers succeed, they designed and constructed the mine and all support facilities in just twelve months. The Grande Ecaille mine produced more than 40 million long-tons of sulphur during its 40-plus years of operation, and transformed the economy of Plaquemines Parish, Louisiana.

Many important sulphur-mining projects followed, including the Garden Island Bay Project, also in Plaquemines Parish, and the offshoot Grand Isle, Caminada, and mammoth Main Pass 299 mines. The Main Pass reserve, discovered in 1988, remains the largest sulphur reserve in North America. McMoRan Exploration ceased sulphur-mining operations there in the year 2000, after sulphur mining became uneconomic amid low commodity prices. This marked the close of an important chapter in Louisiana's history, but enabled McMoRan to focus its operation on potential high returns from expanding oil and gas operations in the Gulf of Mexico. Today MMR is poised to capitalize on the vast opportunities in the region, through an aggressive exploration program on the Gulf of Mexico shelf. MMR has acquired large blocks of exploration lease areas in the region and is using "structural geology," augmented by 3-D mapping technology, to evaluate the hydrocarbon potential. Several discoveries were logged in 2000, and many drilling projects with significant promise are underway.

In the 1960's, when Freeport's sulphur business in Louisiana was in its heyday, the Company began diversifying into other minerals and metals. Freeport's chief geologist, Forbes Wilson, came across Dutch field notes describing untapped copper potentials in the mountains of New Guinea. He convinced directors and bankers to fund an expedition there, to confirm the initial reports that had been filed away since the 1930's. An arduous trek into virtually untouched mountainous terrain confirmed the discovery of the Ertsberg (Dutch for Ore Mountain). Freeport became the first foreign investor in the young Indonesian nation. Subsequent exploration yielded many additional ore strikes, including the massive Grasberg copper-gold discovery in 1988. Freeport-McMoRan Copper & Gold was spun off from Freeport-McMoRan Inc. in 1989 and became separately listed on the New York Stock Exchange.

Freeport-McMoRan Copper & Gold is the world's lowest cost copper producer and one of the world's largest producers of copper and gold. The company's Grasberg mine in Indonesia remains the world's largest single gold deposit, and one of the largest copper deposits. In 2001 alone, the Grasberg complex is expected to produce ores containing 1.6 billion pounds of copper and 3.1 million ounces of gold. The operation in the province of Papua, Indonesia employs more than 13,000 workers, nearly 25 percent of who are indigenous Papuans. Many of the engineering and planning activities associated with the Grasberg operations take place in New Orleans, providing a significant impact to the local economy.

✧

Above: Grande Isle, No. 3 Platform.

Below: Lake Pelto.

Trico Marine Services, Inc.

✧

Below: Trico's fleet of North Sea-class vessels is equipped to work in deepwater and extreme weather conditions.

Bottom: Supply boats transport oilfield products and supplies to offshore drilling and production facilities.

Trico Marine Services is a premier provider of marine support services to the energy industry worldwide. From its headquarters in Houma, Louisiana, Trico owns and operates a diverse fleet of nearly one hundred vessels used to transport drilling materials, supplies and crews and provides support for the construction, installation and maintenance of offshore oil and gas facilities.

Trico is the second largest provider of supply vessels in the Gulf of Mexico and is the fourth largest operator of anchor handling, towing supply (AHTS) vessels in the North Sea. Its fleet includes supply boats and North Sea-class platform supply vessels, used to transport oilfield products and supplies to offshore facilities; crew boats, which move people, food and supplies to production platforms and drilling rigs; AHTS vessels, which set anchors for drilling rigs and tow mobile drilling rigs and equipment from one location to another; and an advanced SWATH vessel, which transports up to 250 passengers between an operations base and production platforms offshore Brazil.

Trico focuses on providing customers with the most responsive and efficient service available in the marine industry. Its customers are major and large independent oil and gas companies as well as foreign government-owned or controlled companies involved in offshore oil and gas exploration and production.

The company also has offices in Houston, Texas; Fosnavag and Kristiansand, Norway; Aberdeen, Scotland; Lagos and Port Harcourt, Nigeria; and Macae and Rio de Janeiro, Brazil. Trico supports its operations in the Gulf from a 62.5-acre docking, maintenance and office headquarters facility in Houma. Located on the intra-coastal waterway, the facility provides direct access to the Gulf of Mexico.

Trico is managed and operated by people who are among the most experienced in the marine services industry. It is the successor to several companies formed in the early 1980s by Chairman of the Board Ronald O. Palmer and President and Chief Executive Officer Thomas E. Fairley. Fairley and Palmer have more than sixty years of combined industry experience. In 1993 they joined with Berkshire Partners to acquire vessels owned by Chrysler Capital Corporation to create this leading offshore marine support company.

Trico is a publicly owned company with its stock listed on the NASDAQ Stock Market under the symbol "TMAR." In mid-1996 the company completed an initial public offering of its common stock in order to facilitate continued growth. That same year, the company established operations in Brazil with the acquisition of eight vessels, which operate under long-term charters for Petrobras, the Brazilian national oil company. Then, in December 1997, Trico became a major player in the North Sea oil and gas industry when it completed the acquisition of Saevik Supply ASA of Norway, a leading operator of marine support vessels. The North Sea fleet is equipped to work in deepwater and under extreme weather conditions. In March 2002 Trico opened in offices in Lagos and Port Harcourt, Nigeria, to support the operations of four of its vessels operating on long-term charters off the western coast of Africa.

From fifty-one vessels at the time of the initial public offering, Trico's fleet has grown to nearly one hundred vessels. In addition to acquisitions, the company has also constructed some of the industry's most technologically advanced vessels. Among those vessels are two state-of-the-art, 275-foot, dynamically positioned, deepwater platform supply vessels, anchor handlers and the first advanced, high-speed crew boat using the SWATH (small water plane area, twin hull) design. The SWATH is used as a high-speed ferry in the Campos basin offshore Brazil.

In recent years, Trico has expanded its services in specialty niche markets by offering a wide range of marine based services. The company has completed several projects involving the laying of fiber optic cable and well stimulation in offshore fields.

With the growth in the company's fleet has been a commensurate growth in revenues. From $6.4 million in 1995, revenues reached $182.6 million in fiscal 2001. The company has approximately 1,200 employees.

Guiding Trico's activities around the globe are five core values. These values underlie the company's commitment to providing its customers with the highest level of responsive service available in the marine industry today.

- Environment: Trico strives to protect the ocean and coastal environments that are its work sites and homes.
- Ethics: Trico respects and values its employees, its clients, its shareholders and its vendors and will always deal fairly and honestly with them. It conducts its business to the highest ethical standards, and it respects the laws and cultures of the countries in which it does business.
- Growth: Trico believes in giving all employees the opportunity to develop to their full potential, and to that end, it supports the career growth and training of its people. By promoting this growth, Trico ensures that it will always provide not only the best vessels, but also safe, professional and experienced personnel to serve its clients.
- Quality: Trico's reputation is based on the quality of its assets, its people, and the services it delivers.
- Knowledge: Trico builds on its core competencies based on its knowledge of ships, new vessel construction management, operations, marine personnel training and vessel fleet management.

For the future, Trico is well positioned to benefit from improving markets and will continue to maintain a large, diversified fleet capable of providing a broad range of services in response to its customers' needs. The company plans to continue its growth both through the addition of large, technologically advanced vessels as well as through acquisition opportunities that allow it to selectively upgrade its fleet to meet market demand. It also plans to continue expanding its international presence and to add new services serving specialty niche markets.

Above: The technologically advanced SWATH vessel is used to transport personnel to production platforms in the Campos Basin offshore Brazil.

Below: Trico's anchor handling, towing and supply vessels are used to set anchors for drilling rigs and two mobile rigs and equipment between locations.

MMR Group

✧

Below: For the massive PEMEX EPC-I (Offshore Production Decks) MMR Group was responsible for electrical and instrumentation installation.

Bottom: This Royal Dutch Shell oil refinery in Thailand depended on MMR Group work.

MMR Group corporate headquarters are in Baton Rouge, but their workplace is worldwide! And, while 2001 revenue topped $102 million, this Louisiana-based electrical and instrumentation contractor covers the globe with a can-do attitude and rigid adherence to quality control and workplace safety standards.

With operating subsidiaries of MMR Construction Inc., MMR Technical Services Inc., MMR Offshore Services Inc., and MMR International Ltd., they can offer an incredible array of services, and, at the same time, take pride in completion of projects with a good safety record for the workforce and numerous satisfied clients. As an added plus, MMR Group offers several different contract types for clients: lump sum, unit price, cost-plus, time and material, and unit rate (on an hourly or weekly basis), with target man-hour and target cost also taken into account.

Domestic locations, besides Baton Rouge, are in Lafayette and Belle Chasse, and in Atlanta and Houston. Foreign affiliates include MMR-DTI (Nigeria) Ltd., in Lagos, Nigeria; MMR-Thailand LTD, in Bangkok, Thailand; MMR-Venezuela, S.A. in Barcelona and Maracaibo Venezuela and ZAMMR Co. Ltd. in Dammom, Saudi Arabia.

Regardless of the project location, size or type, total client satisfaction is always top priority. Among the services that MMR Group provides are electrical power distribution, electrical instrumentation, pneumatic instrument installation, calibration, loop check, high voltage testing, panel fabrication, detailed design, start-up assistance and maintenance. Markets served include air separation, chemical and petrochemical, food and beverage, manufacturing, marine, metals and minerals, oil and gas production and processing, pharmaceuticals, power generation, pulp, paper and forest products; refining, special projects, synthetic fuels, and waste and water treatment.

MMR Group instrumentation services cover air supply installation, control room equipment installation, instrument installation, process leads, panel fabrication and signal wiring. Electrical services include controls, electrical equipment setting, grounding, lighting, power distribution and special systems. Technical services include calibration, detail design, high voltage testing, instrument procurement, loop check, maintenance, start-up assistance, and commissioning.

Some of MMR Group's special projects have included work for client Lockheed Martin on the Venture Star launch facility at Edwards Air Force Base in Palmdale, California, and a climactic testing facility for the U.S. Air Force in Niceville, Florida.

Power generation projects by MMR Group include work on cogeneration for SMUD-Procter & Gamble in Sacramento, California; a power station for LCRA in La Grange, Texas; resource recovery for American Re-Fuels in Niagara Falls, New York; cogeneration for Gray's Ferry in Philadelphia, Pennsylvania; and a power station for Siemens-Westinghouse in Chonburi, Thailand.

MMR Group also worked with Duke Fluor Daniel on the Odessa Ector Natural Gas Fired Power Plant for Texas Independent Energy. Total plant output will be 1,000 megawatts on completion. At peak construction MMR has 180 employees on the project. Time on this job exceeded 200,000 hours.

In the realm of chemicals and petrochemicals, MMR Group can take credit for completed projects at oil refineries for Royal Dutch Shell in Map ta Phut, Thailand; Coastal Aruba in San Nicolas, Aruba; and PDVSA/Maraven in Punto Fijo, Venezuela. A gas processing project for Williams International in El Furrial, Venezuela, and air separation projects for Praxair in McIntosh, Alabama, and Air Liquide in Geismar, Louisiana, are also reasons for MMR Group to take pride.

In work for the pulp and paper industry, MMR Group completed work at a plywood plant for Martco in Chopin, Louisiana; a paper mill for Procter & Gamble in Cape Girardeau, Missouri; and a paper machine for Liberty Paper in Beckeer, Minnesota.

MMR Group work in oil and gas production and exploration included fabrication on production modules for Shell de Venezuela, S.A. on Lake Maracaibo, Venezuela; fabrication in New Iberia, Louisiana for a hook-up in Nigeria for Mobil USARI Development; and work on the Shell Spirit Platform in New Iberia, Louisiana, for hook-up in the Gulf of Mexico. MMR also performed the electrical and instrumentation work on ExxonMobil's record-breaking Deep Draft Caisson Vessel, *Hoover Diana*.

MMR Group was also responsible for the electrical and instrumentation installation on the mammoth Pemex EPC-1 project. With a deck covering five acres, and with both the world's largest offshore desalinization system and hydrocarbon and condensate plants, onshore work took one and half years to complete. The Pemex EPC-1 is currently installed offshore in the Bay of Campeche.

MMR Group projects for pharmaceuticals and clean room facilities were done for AmGen in Longmont, Colorado and for Merck in Albany, Georgia. Other projects included work at a food additives plant for Bio Products in St. Gabriel, Louisiana and a steel mill for Tuscaloosa Steel in Mobile, Alabama.

MMR Group helped complete the IPSCO (Alabama) steelworks in Mobile, Alabama, expected to produce 1.25 million tons of steel per year when running at top capacity.

MMR Group's commitment to workplace safety garnered the company a national award from the Business Roundtable, an association of chief executive officers of leading United States corporations. The Construction Industry Safety Excellence (CISE) award placed MMR Group in the top names in the Construction Specialties category.

CISE Award criteria included management commitment and accountability, staff qualifications, written and budgeted health and safety programs, use of proven safety practices, and proven results in lowered incident rates. Prior to granting the award, three client companies confirmed MMR Group's safety attitudes and practices.

Satisfying clients and operating with safety and efficiency are good reasons why MMR Group is a corporation of which Louisiana can be proud.

✧

Above: This Gas Compressor Station for WILPRO at Maturin, Venezuela, included MMR Group involvement.

Below: A Power Station for LCRA in La Grange, Texas, is one of MMR Group's power generation projects.

MOTIVA ENTERPRISES, LLC

Motiva Enterprises, LLC in Norco, Louisiana, converts light, sweet, low sulfur crude oil, seventy-five percent from Louisiana and the remainder from overseas oil or from other feedstock, into automotive gasoline and other oil products, supplying primarily the southeastern United States.

Approximately 38 to 55 percent of the volume of each crude barrel is separated directly into primary products. The remaining 45 to 62 percent of the volume must be converted into primary products by further processing. The maximum sulfur-in-crude weight is 0.70 percent.

The refinery processes 10.1 million gallons of crude oil daily and produces gasoline (7.1 million gallons daily premium and regular grades, unleaded); Jet-A aviation fuel (1.9 million gallons daily supplying New Orleans' Armstrong International Airport); low sulfur diesel (2.1 million gallons daily); furnace oil; liquefied petroleum gases (propane, propylene and isobutene); and anode grade coke (1,000 tons daily). Motiva products are transported on ships, via pipelines, and on barges, trucks, and railcars.

Motiva Enterprises is part of the largest gasoline production company in the United States, is headquartered in Houston, and operates four U.S. refineries, including the one in Norco (a town named for the New Orleans Refining Company, begun seventy-five years ago and long operated by Shell.)

In Norco, Motiva has undertaken a project, in collaboration with Shell Chemical, called the Good Neighbor Initiative. GNI represents a multi-million dollar investment and has three major components: Environmental and Operational Improvements, Community Health and Safety, and Quality of Life.

The Environmental and Operational Improvement component of the GNI focuses on Motiva Norco Refinery and Shell Chemical improving the operation of facilities and enhancing environmental performance. The plan calls for a reduction in Toxic Release Inventory (TRI) emissions by thirty percent through 2005 based on 1998 TRI emissions data. The initiative also focuses on improving operational performance by reducing episodic releases, such as flaring, by fifty percent for both Motiva and Shell. The final aspect of the Environmental and Operational Improvement component includes third party validation, which will be accomplished through ISO 14000, an international program for environmental standards or a similar program.

The Community Health and Safety component of the GNI includes the installation of an air monitoring system in the community that will provide air quality information to the Louisiana Department of Environmental Quality and Norco residents. The companies will also conduct a community healthcare review, as a means to identify the healthcare needs of the community. This effort is being done to determine the best ways to provide healthcare access to those in need. The final aspect of the Community Health and Safety component of the GNI focuses on emergency response. The purpose of this is to ensure that Norco residents know what to do in case of a chemical-related emergency.

Finally, the Quality of Life component of the GNI includes the establishment of a community betterment trust fund, which will be used for Norco-based community projects and programs that help to enhance the quality of life for all Norco residents. Motiva and Shell donated $1 million to get the fund started. The companies will work together with the community to manage the trust.

Motiva and Shell will also establish a greenbelt system along the east and west fence lines for the Norco community, which will create a park-like atmosphere while also providing a buffer zone between the community and the plant. In an effort to accelerate the creation of this greenbelt, property offers and incentives have been made to neighbors located along the fence lines as part of the Voluntary Property Purchase Program (VPPP), a strictly voluntary program in place for nearly thirty years. The last aspect of the quality of life component involves business and professional development. This program will provide Norco residents with the necessary information needed to obtain a job or conduct business effectively with local industry or related businesses.

Motiva continually strives to help its Norco neighbors and all of St. Charles Parish grow and thrive, and has participated in the Norco/New Sarpy Community Industry Meeting panel; Safe Harbor Program, blood drives, local fund-raising events for fire victims and the CORE team.

Motiva serves as the partner in education with Destrehan High School and New Sarpy Kindergarten Center. Other education ventures include the CHOICES program, the Employment Academy, Junior Achievement; Science Investigations Program; tutoring programs and Science and Social Studies Fair judging; La Branche Wetland Watchers; and the donation of more than two hundred surplus computers and monitors to area schools, nonprofit organizations and churches.

Motiva also contributes funds to local causes, including the Norco Community Trust Fund, United Way of St. Charles, Cystic Fibrosis Foundation, Renee Mauduit Scholarship Fund, Project READ, New Sarpy Kindergarten Center, Good Hope Youth Academy, Destrehan High School College Scholarship, Destrehan High School Vocational Scholarships (2), Boy Scouts of America, Louisiana Special Olympics, Angel's Place, Louisiana Sportsman's Invitational, Society of Women Engineers, St. Charles Business Association, Volunteers of America, Urban League, Associated Builders and Contractors, First Community Antioch Baptist Church, Belize Association of Louisiana and the Providence Christian Academy.

The people of Motiva take great pride in being good corporate citizens while serving their customers, and helping them get where they need to go. Whether it's by plane, train, boat or automobile, consider Motiva as your motor fuels source to travel the world!

Omni Royal Orleans

Above: *The charm of the French Quarter is right outside the elegant front entrance of the Omni Royal Orleans.*

Below: *The Omni Royal Orleans rooftop swimming pool and observation deck offer spectacular views.*

The Omni Royal Orleans upholds a long tradition of luxury and sophistication in one of the world's most spirited cities. Nestled in the heart of the French Quarter, the Omni Royal Orleans is just moments from the excitement of Bourbon Street, Jackson Square and "all that jazz." Richly deserving the honor of being chosen one of the world's best places to stay in 2002 by *Condé Nast Traveler*, the AAA Four-Diamond Omni Royal Orleans offers a multi-lingual staff and amenities including a year-round, heated swimming pool on its rooftop deck, where La Riviera offers frozen drinks and light lunches. The rooftop fitness center offers a variety of machines, bikes, treadmills and weights for cardiovascular or weight training.

The Rib Room Restaurant, winner of the prestigious Zagat Award, features prime rib, beef specialties, fowl and seafood prepared on giant French rotisseries and a mesquite grill. On the lobby level, with its sumptuous antiques, the Esplanade Lounge offers a live pianist, with a bar, coffee and desserts. Nearby, the Touché Bar serves the best mint juleps in town!

Conference and Banquet facilities include 17 magnificent function rooms on two floors, totaling more than 14,000 square feet, all with state-of-the-art audio/visual equipment. The Grand Salon area offers 5,284 square feet of function space and divides into three salons. On the lobby level, the Esplanade, Café Royale and Escoffier Salons can accommodate up to 200 people. Nine additional meeting and banquet rooms on the second floor open onto balconies or a lush tropical courtyard, perfect for romantic weddings or VIP meetings.

Guests at the Omni Royal Orleans can avail themselves of full service, on-site barber and beauty salons, voice mail messaging, a gift and sundries shop, newsstand, and a transportation and sightseeing desk. Covered, on-site parking is provided. All guest rooms offer computer modem hook-up and multi-line telephones, a hair dryer, iron and ironing board, umbrella, and complimentary *USA Today*.

The business center offers photocopying, facsimile transmission and Internet access. Our on-site audiovisual technicians provide state-of-the-art microphones, player/recorders, video data monitors, video-data projection equipment and overhead projectors. Everything that might be needed for an audio/visual presentation in a variety of formats is available.

The Omni Royal Orleans rests on the site of what was first called the City Exchange and soon became known as the St. Louis Hotel. From its 1838 beginning, when architect J.N.B. DePoilly signed the contract to design it, the St. Louis Hotel was meant to outshine any competitor,

including ones, such as the St. Charles, in the American sector of town on the other side of Canal Street. With a facade along St. Louis Street reminiscent of the Rue de Rivoli in Paris, the interior housed a huge rotunda, which served as the city's principal auction room or exchange. Real estate, furniture and possessions, even slaves went to the highest bidder. The bars and restaurants welcomed locals and visitors alike to marvel at the ceiling painted by artist Dominico Canova and to nibble on the complimentary hors d'oeuvres available at the bar. Thus began the tradition of offering free lunch to bar patrons. The St. Louis Hotel was popular, and also resilient. When a fire destroyed the building a few years after its opening, it was quickly rebuilt and was soon hosting Mardi Gras balls, even before that festival became the public event it is today.

When New Orleans fell to the Union Army in 1862 the St. Louis became a military hospital, and during the Reconstruction era following the Civil War the St. Louis figured in armed struggles as Federal forces finally left. Afterwards, the St. Louis Hotel fell upon hard times: the building was a desolate ruin when English author John Galsworthy visited in 1912 and described a horse wandering through the crumbling rooms. By the 1940s that hotel was gone, and a lumberyard occupied the property.

The visionary who foresaw the glorious future of a hotel on that spot was Edgar Stern, a New Orleans businessman who, with his wife Edith, a Sears Roebuck heiress, would leave New Orleans remarkably improved by personal involvement. Stern's executive assistant Lester Kabacoff, who would also leave his mark on the city, was the man who ably coordinated the hotel's construction and affiliation with the Hotel Corporation of America. In a graceful salute to its past, the hotel was constructed to echo the appearance of the old St. Louis Hotel. On the Chartres Street side today you will see part of the original walls, with faint sign painting remaining.

Opening in 1960, the Royal Orleans Hotel as designed by architects Arthur Q. Davis and Sam Wilson, was a success. Soon a mansard roof and rooms were added. So legendary did the hotel become that author Arthur Hailey was in residence there and plied the staff with questions while he wrote his novel "Hotel." When it became a movie, the cast was housed there.

Now known as the Omni Royal Orleans, this grande dame of the French Quarter still welcomes visitors with the same panache and grace as its remote ancestor the St. Louis. The past still lives in New Orleans!

✧

Below: The lobby of the Omni Royal Orleans presents an artful mélange of nineteenth century artifacts and the essence of Creole grace.

The Ernest N. Morial Convention Center

✧

Above: The Morial Convention Center-New Orleans is one of the five largest convention centers in the nation.

Below: With 1.1 million square feet of contiguous exhibit space, virtually every NFL team can play simultaneously in the Center's massive exhibit halls.

New Orleans is the heart of the booming meeting and exposition market attracted to the city.

Beginning with a crescendo in 1985, the Ernest N. Morial Convention Center gains momentum with each successive year. Its operations impact every segment of the local hospitality/tourism market—including hotel bookings, dining, transportation, shopping, entertainment, local tours and cruises.

The facility has evolved considerably since its beginning, but the mission remains the same: to attract and host conventions and tradeshows that fuel the financial fires of local, regional and state economies.

In fifteen years, the Convention Center's growth, in both status and scope, has produced over $1 billion dollars in new statewide tax revenues and provided $25.08 billion in overall economic impact.

The building, originally the New Orleans Convention Center, was renamed in honor of Ernest N. "Dutch" Morial, New Orleans' first African-American mayor and father of Mayor Marc Morial. Conceptual development of the facility began in 1978 when the New Orleans Exhibition Hall Authority, governing body of the planned convention center, was formed to spearhead construction. The first phase of construction was used for the 1984 World's Fair, a major factor in redevelopment of the city's warehouse waterfront area.

The locale today, on the Mississippi River and within walking distance of the French Quarter, the Aquarium of the Americas, downtown shopping and business districts, the arts district and major museums as well as thirty thousand hotel rooms, is unquestionably the center of New Orleans' tourist industry.

The Morial Convention Center holds 1.1 million square feet of contiguous exhibit space. Key marketing amenities include 12 separate/combinable exhibit halls, a 4,000-seat Conference Auditorium, two luxurious ballrooms as well as 140 separate meeting rooms. State-of-the-art in-house technical services are available, including live video teleconferencing, innovative video advertising, and a fiber optic system capable of transmitting the most sophisticated data, video, and voice phone signals anywhere in the world.

Due to marked growth and its rising stature as a leading convention destination, the future looks as promising as the past. In 2000 the facility was recognized as the third leading site for the largest 200 tradeshows in the nation. To meet the growing demands for meeting space, the facility's governing board, the Ernest N. Morial New Orleans Exhibition Hall Authority, is planning a Phase IV expansion that will include 500,000 to 600,000 square feet of exhibit space in a separate, adjacent facility. Targeted for a 2006 opening, Phase IV will attract 280,000 additional out-of-town visitors, create 7,200 new jobs and generate an estimated $576 million in new economic impact.

The Morial Convention Center maintains an interactive web site at www.mccno.com. You can take an interactive tour of the facility and explore the exhibit halls, meeting rooms, ballrooms and Conference Auditorium. And, you can find out how the Morial Convention Center can help plan your next event, meeting or convention!

Southern Comfort and M. W. Heron

From the start, Southern Comfort was destined to become an American icon like its founder—New Orleans bartender Martin Wilkes (M.W.) Heron. Now a multi-million case brand available in nearly sixty countries worldwide, Southern Comfort's story begins with an innovative young entrepreneur in the heart of New Orleans.

During the 1870s, Mississippi riverboats ruled the waterways, playing a critical role in developing communities along the river. New Orleans benefited from the flow of cargo and passengers in and out of the community, and was soon teeming with crowds wanting to see the great floating palaces. As the population grew, so did competition among local businesses. It also attracted young entrepreneurs like M. W. Heron.

Born in Ireland on July 4, 1850, Heron immigrated to the United States as an infant with his family. He spent much of his early adult life traveling the Mississippi River, selling his skills as a whisky rectifier and bartender. According to historians, Heron was working as a bartender at McCauley's Saloon in the French Quarter when he created a smooth inviting drink capturing the spirit of New Orleans. Dubbed "Cuff & Buttons," the unique spirit was a big success.

Heron recognized the 1885 World's Industrial and Cotton Exposition in New Orleans as a great marketing opportunity. He changed the name of his drink to "Southern Comfort" and gave it the slogan "The Grand Old Drink of the South."

To keep up with the demand for his creation, Heron began bottling Southern Comfort and obtained a copyright from the U.S. Patent Office. "The Grand Old Drink of the South" continued to grow in popularity until the advent of Prohibition. In April 1920, Heron passed away, just months after Prohibition was enacted.

Southern Comfort was reintroduced to the world in 1934 in its distinctive fluted bottle and the Currier & Ives illustration of Woodland Plantation on the label. Built in 1834, the plantation house is located in West Point à La Hache in Plaquemines Parish about thirty-four miles southwest of New Orleans. The property has been completely restored and now serves as a country inn. The original painting of Woodland Plantation was by artist Andrew Waud, called *A Home on the Mississippi*.

Today, Heron's unique drink lives on. Purchased by Brown-Forman in 1979, Southern Comfort continues to promote its New Orleans heritage as the forty-ninth largest inter-national spirits brand and the second largest liqueur brand in the world.

Top, left: Woodland Plantation has graced the label of Southern Comfort since 1934.

Below: Southern Comfort received its first gold medal for taste and quality at the 1900 World Exposition in Paris, France. Reflecting the honor, labels included M. W. Heron's trademark slogan, "None Genuine But Mine."

BEST WESTERN HOTEL ACADIANA

✧

Best Western Hotel Acadiana in Lafayette, Louisiana.

Visitors are invited to step into Old World Charm at Best Western Hotel Acadiana in the heart of Cajun culture in Lafayette, Louisiana. Originally built as the Lé Chateau Lafayette, a replica of a French mansion, Hotel Acadiana is truly Lafayette's "Hotel of Distinction," where Southern heritage and true hospitality are a tradition. The courtyard structure of this beautiful hotel represents the traditional culture of New Orleans, with 295 deluxe, oversized guest rooms offering up-to-the-minute amenities ranging from coffeemakers and refrigerators to hairdryers and ironing boards. For the ultimate experience, Hotel Acadiana offers their "Crown Service," Hotel Acadiana's concierge service, which includes complimentary breakfast, hors d'oeuvres and drinks, *USA Today* delivered daily to your room. Additionally, travelers can remain in touch with the world through dual phone lines and data ports on the Concierge floor.

Built in 1982, the hotel's structure qualified it for Sheraton standards when it was later acquired by that hotel chain, after the oil industry bottomed out, leading to the failure of many businesses in the Lafayette area. Samuel Huang and Lin of Huntington Beach, California, who operated several other properties, purchased the original Lé Chateau of Lafayette in 1992 and began extensive renovations and reconstruction. Because of the hotel's culture and class, they named it "The Best Western Hotel Acadiana," and chose a motto reflecting their recognition of its special character, "a unique Best Western."

Additional enhancements are underway at this time and will be incorporated during 2003, including additional staff and numerous renovations and continuing improvement of both facilities and services. A new seafood restaurant will open during 2003 with possible future additions to include a special dessert corner, possibly with the very traditional Southern custom of an afternoon teatime.

Best Western Hotel Acadiana is conveniently located in central Lafayette, only a step away from a variety of dining, including Bayou Bistro, featuring Cajun cuisine and classic favorites prepared by an award-winning chef. Guests will also enjoy the seasonal entertainment featured at Heymann Center, which is within a few blocks of the hotel. Banquet facilities, offering a variety of seating including schoolroom-, theatre-, and banquet-style arrangements, are available for groups from six to six hundred. Hotel Acadiana is also conveniently located near a large hospital to accommodate family members who wish to remain close by during the illness of a family member and the Lafayette Regional Airport.

Please join us, whether your stay is business, pleasure, or simply to dine in our Bistro, to experience the casual or elegant ambiance of Southern hospitality from a gracious era. Best Western Hotel Acadiana is located at 1801 West Pinhook Road, Lafayette, Louisiana 70508; or you may reach us by calling 337-233-8120 or toll free at 800-826-8386.

Sonesta Hotels of New Orleans

Above: Royal Sonesta Hotel located at 300 Bourbon Street in New Orleans.

Below: Chateau Sonesta at 800 Iberville Street in New Orleans' French Quarter.

The guest experience at New Orleans' Chateau Sonesta Hotel and Royal Sonesta Hotel is best captured by the company's slogan: "This is What You Came to Find." Located in the world-famous French Quarter, both of these Sonesta hotels offer the best of Old World tradition and the incomparable history and ambiance of New Orleans, seamlessly combined with the most modern comforts and amenities.

The Chateau Sonesta, a landmark building constructed in 1849, was occupied by the former D.H. Holmes Canal Street Department Store until its closing in 1989. Its transformation into a twentieth century hotel includes complete interior renovation, and skillful exterior restoration to retain the building's historic character.

Located at 800 Iberville Street, the Chateau Sonesta offers the French Quarter's most spacious guest rooms, featuring grand twelve-foot ceilings. Many offer balconies overlooking Bourbon Street, the French Quarter, or the hotel's lush garden courtyards or outdoor swimming pool.

Its location, just steps away from the Central Business District and one block from the Royal Sonesta Hotel, provides all the fun and convenience of the French Quarter and its historic landmarks, as well as renowned restaurants and nightclubs. Sightseeing and airport transfers are available, along with shuttle service to most major conventions. Its flexible meeting space includes well-appointed meeting rooms accommodate groups of up to 300 for meetings and 200 for banquets and receptions.

The Royal Sonesta at 300 Bourbon Street provides all the fun and excitement of the French Quarter, combined with the elegance of a European estate. Luxurious rooms and suites, lace balconies, a pool and a hidden patio terrace surrounded by lush greenery provide the historical atmosphere for which New Orleans is famous.

The Royal Sonesta's architecture and landscaping are reminiscent of the historical nature of its site, which has a history extending back more than two centuries. Early owners of the property have included the great-grandfather of French artist Edgar Degas, whose impressive Spanish Colonial home later housed several banks, including the local branch of Alexander Hamilton's Bank of the United States; as well as a gardener; army officers; surgeons; educators; the American Brewing Company; a historic bakery; and the three-story home of New Orleans' first postmaster, where American Shakespearean actor Edward Hugh Sothern (1859-1933) is said to have been born.

The Boston-based company operating these two fine New Orleans hotels has a long-standing reputation for offering uncompromising personal service reflecting the culture and history of each of its 21 upscale hotels and resorts and 3 Nile Cruise ships. For more information, call 1-800-SONESTA (1-800-766-3782) or visit Sonesta's website at www.sonesta.com.

Sewerage & Water Board of New Orleans

The French settled New Orleans in 1718 on the high ground adjacent to the Mississippi River—only fourteen feet above sea level. As a result of its unusual topography, the city was subject to periodic flooding from the Mississippi River and Lake Pontchartrain, as well as frequent inundation from high intensity rainfall.

Water for drinking or general use was either collected in cisterns that stored rainwater or taken from the river and allowed to settle in earthenware jars. There were no purification or sterilization procedures. Without a municipal water supply, the greater part of the city burned to the ground in 1788 and again in 1794.

A sewage collection and disposal system was also nonexistent. Human waste was disposed of in privies, while household waste went into open gutters. Such unsanitary conditions gave rise to typhoid, yellow fever, cholera and other diseases. These conditions no longer exist.

Today, New Orleans is provided with water, drainage and sewerage facilities 24 hours a day, 365 days a year, where and when they are needed. The Louisiana Engineering Society, in honor of its seventy-fifth anniversary in 1973, selected the water, drainage, and sewerage systems of New Orleans as among the ten most outstanding engineering achievements in the state. This is a great honor accorded to both our community and the Sewerage & Water Board.

By 1893 it became apparent to city leaders that accommodation of area growth would depend on their ability to keep New Orleans drained, dry, adequately supplied with water for drinking and fire protection, and provided with a sanitary sewerage system. Planning for the three systems began that year.

In 1896 the New Orleans Drainage Commission was organized to carry out a master drainage plan that had been developed for the city. Three years later, in 1899, the Sewerage and Water Board was established by the Louisiana Legislature to furnish, construct, operate, and maintain a water treatment and distribution system and a sanitary sewerage system for New Orleans. In 1903 the Drainage Commission was merged with the Sewerage and Water Board in order to consolidate drainage, water and sewerage programs under one agency for more efficient operations. This combined organization retained the title Sewerage and Water Board, and remains as such today.

The Sewerage and Water Board consists of the Mayor, the two at-large members of the City Council, one district councilman selected by the Council, two members of the board of Liquidation, City Debt, and seven citizen members appointed by the Mayor, in accordance with the law, for overlapping terms of nine years. The Board holds committee and regular meetings once each month, to which the public is invited.

Once formally organized, the Sewerage and Water Board set out to fulfill its goals. Between 1879 and 1915, $27.5 million was spent on the construction of water, sewerage, and drainage facilities. At that time, funds for construction came from either a special two-mill tax on all property or one-half of the

✧

Above: The original Wood screw pumps, installed in the early 1900s, are still in service today.

Below: Twenty-two drainage pumping stations serve the below-sea-level city twenty-four hours a day.

surplus from the one percent debt tax. Today, the drainage system is funded though property taxes, while the water and sewerage systems are funded through service charges and user fees.

At the time the water works system was developed, New Orleans was relying on ground absorption and open drainage canals for storm water disposal.

Because the river levees are higher than the lake levees, most rainwater is pumped into Lake Pontchartrain. Exceptions are the two West Bank pumping stations and two stations in Eastern New Orleans that pump rainwater into the Intracoastal Waterway or the Industrial Canal. The original pumps designed by A. Baldwin Wood are still in use, admired by experts who come from nations with similar flooding problems, such as the Netherlands, to investigate and replicate.

There are twenty-two Drainage Pumping Stations in New Orleans. Station personnel are on duty 24-hours a day, seven days a week. There are also thirteen underpass stations, each with two or three pumps that are automatically turned on by rising water. The system's pumping capacity is over 29 billion gallons a day, enough to empty a lake 10 square miles by 13.5 feet deep every 24 hours.

The S&WB's drainage network includes approximately 90 miles of open canals and 90 miles of subsurface canals. Many of the subsurface canals are large enough to drive a bus through.

✧

Above: New massive subsurface drainage canals are under construction throughout the city.

Below: The S&WB purifies approximately forty-seven billion gallons of water per year. The Mississippi River is the city's only source of water.

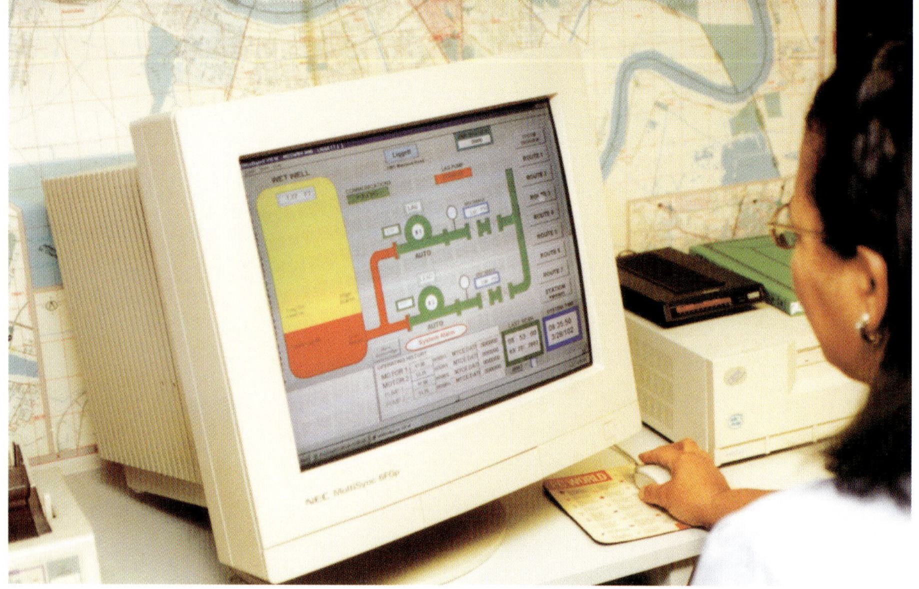

✧

Above: SCADA is a state-of-the-art system that constantly monitors the complex sewerage operations.

Below: The S&WB's sophisticated water treatment process and quality testing procedures help produce water that meets or exceeds all EPA standards.

Generators that provide much of the power for pumps throughout the city are located at the S&WB power plant.

Operations and Drainage Department crews watch the canal water level, monitor weather forecasts through a direct tie to the National Weather Service Radar System, communicate with other stations and senior management, and keep informed on weather activity around the city. They are accustomed to handling unexpected deluges.

If a hurricane should head towards the city, the S&WB would activate its emergency plan that calls for increased manpower, additional equipment and frequent strategy and update sessions.

The purpose of the Southeast Louisiana Urban Flood Control Project (SELA), a cooperative program between the U.S. Army Corps of Engineers and the Sewerage and Water Board of New Orleans, is to reduce flood damages in the City of New Orleans and surrounding parishes. This will be accomplished by constructing new pumping stations and new drainage canals throughout the city. The program was authorized in 1996 by the United States Congress and administered under a project cooperative agreement between the Sewerage and Water Board of New Orleans and the U.S. Army Corps of Engineers. Phase One Projects include:

- New Hollygrove Pump Station and Canals, Pump Station No. 1 Upgrade,
- Two New Napoleon Canals,
- New South Claiborne Manifold Canal (Nashville to Louisiana),
- New Dwyer Road Pump Station and Canals.

The cost for these projects is $140 million, seventy-five percent of which will be federally funded. The Sewerage and Water Board must pay the remaining twenty-five percent, or 40 million.

The sanitary sewerage system in New Orleans is a gravity collection system, consisting of 1,500 miles of lateral and trunk sewers, ranging in size from eight inches to seven feet in diameter and a force main system to transport the sewage to the treatment plants. Lifting and conveying the sewage (also called wastewater or effluent) by trunk sewers and force mains requires 82 electrically operated pumping and lift stations. Seventy-nine of those stations are automatically operated.

The S&WB system has two sewage treatment plants, one on the East Bank and one in Algiers. The combined treatment capacity of the two plants is 132 million gallons per day.

Both plants were built in the 1970s and have been upgraded to increase capacity and are in full compliance with EPA rules and regulations, discharging thoroughly treated wastewater into the Mississippi River.

The Sewer System Evaluation and Rehabilitation Program (SSERP) is a ten-year effort to study and repair the sewerage collection system throughout the city. The preliminary cost estimate for the improvements is between $500 and $600 million. Projects include rehabilitation of existing sewers, construction of new sewers and upgrading pumping stations.

To date, the S&WB has inspected 4.2 million feet of sanitary sewer lines,

rehabilitated 194,000 feet of sewer lines, inspected 15,400 sewer manholes, and repaired or renovated 2,320 manholes.

One modernization project already in operation is SCADA, (Supervisory Control and Data Acquisition) a sophisticated computer system which will provide online monitoring of the 83 sewer lift stations and pumping stations located throughout the city. Sewer Pumping Station A, located behind the Municipal Auditorium, houses the "heart and brain" of this state-of-the-art $1.7-million monitoring system.

The Sewerage & Water Board investigated all water sources and concluded by scientific testing that the Mississippi River was the best supplier.

Raw water from the Mississippi River is pumped to the Carrollton Water Purification Plant from both the Oak Street River Station and the Industrial Avenue River Station. The intricate purification process includes chemical treatment, flocculation and disinfections. Fluorosilicic acid is used to add fluoride to the drinking water to aid in the prevention of dental cavities.

The final step in the purification process is filtration through 44 rapid sand filters. After filtration, the purification process is complete, and drinking water is pumped out to customers.

The Sewerage and Water Board also operates a water treatment plant on the West Bank of the Mississippi River in Algiers. Combined, the two plants treat approximately 47 billion gallons of water per year.

The water is then pumped through more than 1,610 miles of mains to more than 164,000 service connections and delivered to approximately 440,000 people on the east bank of Orleans Parish and approximately 57,000 people on the West Bank.

The quality of finished water and river water is tested daily at the Water Quality Laboratory of the Sewerage and Water Board by a staff of highly trained chemists, microbiologists and technicians. Samples of drinking water from various points in the distribution system are also analyzed for chemical and microbial parameters at regularly scheduled times.

Samples of river water and finished water are analyzed daily for hundreds of compounds. In the years since this screening began, the running annual averages observed have always been found to be below the Maximum Contaminant Levels (MCLs) set by the EPA. In fact, since the inception of the Clean Water Act in the early '70s, the S&WB has never had an EPA violation.

The Sewerage and Water Board participates in two major multi-agency programs to protect the water supply for all consumers along the lower Mississippi River: the Lower Mississippi River Water Works Warning Network and the Early Warning Organic Compound Detection System.

From dependence on cisterns and jars for a water supply and trusting to shallow canals for drainage and privies for sewerage disposal, New Orleans has progressed. Through ingenuity, sophisticated engineering, an inventive spirit and the dedication of employees over more than a century, the New Orleans Sewerage and Water Board has created a model of an urban water infrastructure, engineering marvels and a safe home and workplace for its citizens. Thanks to the S&WB, the city can look forward to a healthy and prosperous future.

More information about the Sewerage and Water Board of New Orleans may be obtained on its website: www.swbnola.org.

✧

A complete rehabilitation of the sewage collection system is underway. Trenchless technology, like cured-in-place lining, is used whenever possible.

SLEMCO

Locally owned and operated since 1937, SLEMCO (Southwest Louisiana Electric Membership Corporation) is a multi-million dollar corporation and is the largest electrical company of its kind in the state. The company provides over 80,000 customers in eight Louisiana parishes along some 8,500 miles of line with quality electric service at rates among the lowest in Louisiana.

Formed because of the need to bring electricity to the rural areas of southwest Louisiana, the company owes much to its founding leaders. Among them were M.W. Scanlan of Church Point, Mrs. B.W. Spell of Ridge, Dr. E. Lafleur and H. F. Young of Opelousas, Lucius Leblanc of Arnaudville, A. F. Arceneaux of Lafayette, J. P. Gray of Iota, and Daniel Thibodeaux of St. Martinville.

The direction of the company has been steered straight and true by successive board members and management leaders that have included Harry Bowles, 1938-41; U. J. Gajan, 1941-79; Herman J. Kesel, 1979-85; Leon J. Mocek, 1985-96; and J. U. Gajan, 1996-present.

Today, SLEMCO has over $230 million in electric plant facilities with another $7 million in construction work in progress. Gross revenues exceed $103 million and some 265 employees receive nearly $16 million in wages and benefits. The overall contribution of the company to the economy exceeds $1 billion a year.

Once every home, farm or business in Acadiana had electricity, the quality of life here greatly improved. From lighting to food preservation to increased productivity on farms—families and businesses were able to truly meet and exceed their potential, setting ever-higher goals for themselves and their families. Many older customers still remember what life was like before electricity and gratefully remember when SLEMCO brought them power.

Because of this initial bond with its customers, the company naturally evolved into one deeply enmeshed in local communities and is well known by urban and rural citizens alike as a trusted community leader. Continually working to improve life for its customers, employees and area citizens while strengthening its core business of electric distribution, SLEMCO has become involved in many necessary community functions.

Improving the quality of and access to higher education has become one of the company's most important goals. SLEMCO has contributed endowed professorships to every college at the University of Louisiana at Lafayette. And, since 1992, two hundred college scholarships have been awarded to customers and their children in an effort to better educate and strengthen the workforce of the area.

Economic development is also an important part of SLEMCO's efforts to improve life in Acadiana. The Enterprise Center of Louisiana, a business incubator devoted to assisting and strengthening young and growing businesses, was created by the company and has resulted in new start-up companies employing local people. SLEMCO employees work with state economic development officials to attract new industry to the area to stimulate job growth and improve the economy.

The needy have not escaped notice, and together with contributing customers, SLEMCO, since 1995, has made over $1.4 million in grants to needy individuals through its Operation Round-Up program. Artificial limbs, life-saving medical equipment, eyeglasses, food and prescription drugs have been donated to those less fortunate with nowhere else to turn.

The terrorist assault on our nation on September 11, 2001, affected the employees

✧

SLEMCO CEO and General Manager J. U. Gajan.

and management of SLEMCO deeply. Located in the same building as 1st Rochdale Cooperative in New York City, the Hatzolah Ambulance Corps was one of the first rescue responders to the tragedy, and is headquartered less than a mile from ground zero. Two of their fully equipped ambulances were lost when the twin towers came crashing to the ground. Embracing fully the American spirit of cooperation that results after a natural disaster or tragedy, SLEMCO heard of the plight of the all-volunteer Hatzolah Ambulance Corps and was compelled to act. A brand new, state-of-the-art unit was donated by the cooperative to replace one of the destroyed ambulances.

Doing what is necessary is sometimes difficult and uncomfortable; the company has never retreated from doing what is right and good. From working through raging storms and hurricanes to restore power to fighting for the protection of fundamental rights, SLEMCO readily steps forward to meet adversity head on, working with its customers and the citizens of Acadiana whenever and wherever needed.

Recently, when a local government body attempted to pass ordinances that would infringe on constitutionally protected property rights, SLEMCO joined forces with its customers to fight and defeat their passage. A swift and concerted grassroots effort was initiated, leaving local political leaders stunned at the overwhelmingly unified and powerful effort of SLEMCO and its customers.

Because SLEMCO is locally owned and operated and is not a part of some large conglomerate with faceless shareholders or out of state directors and management, the company is more like a large family working together for the good of all. While excelling in the core business of providing retail electricity to its customers, its efforts in the community are ever changing to meet the needs of its customers and the people of southwest Louisiana. Its history and future are both rooted deeply in the concept of being able to help out when needed and a willingness to meet any challenge head-on.

NORTHEAST LOUISIANA TELEPHONE COMPANY

✧

Above: Corporate office of Northeast Louisiana Telephone Company located in Collinston.

Below: Stromberg-Carlson Cord Switchboard, circa 1930.

It's the early fifties. In an older home in a room near the kitchen, the old cord switchboard sits temporarily silent and unattended, the operator probably taking care of some household chore. Even though the system probably had less than 100 subscribers, only eight to ten calls seem to be in progress. Possibly all of these calls were local. Due to the expense, few persons made long distance calls and only then because of necessity. As few as two long distant circuits connected the exchange with the outside world. In small rural communities all across the United States the operation of the local telephone system was often a family affair, with the Villages of Collinston and Bonita being no exception. Since one person could not handle the exchange 24 hours a day, other family members or persons pitched in to help. Usually, after eight o'clock at night, unless an emergency situation occurred, subscribers would graciously wait until the next day to place their calls. They knew that the operator would have to get out of bed to answer the switchboard.

The owner of the small system would usually provide lines to residences close to the center of the village or maybe to the city limits. Beyond that the customer was responsible for building the lines to his home. Some of these "open wire" circuits were literally tacked to fence posts or sweet gum saplings.

The first telephone system in Collinston was developed around 1913 by Guy M. Boyd and served approximately fifteen people. In time, Boyd sold the telephone equipment to J. M. Rabb. The John Vaden family ran the switchboard for Rabb. In the 1930's, W. Clarke Williams bought the Collinston exchange from Rabb and it became the Oak Ridge-Collinston Telephone Company. The Vaden family continued to operate the switchboard for Williams.

The "Gum Swamp" area around Collinston was difficult to serve. This area was the last large section of Morehouse Parish to be settled, was heavily covered with timber, swamps, and canebrakes, and was a renowned place to hunt bear. During long periods of wet weather, the dirt road from Oak Ridge became impassable and Williams had to resort to the use of a boat and bicycle to reach the Collinston exchange. The system was then sold to E .N. Gibbs who in turn sold it to a Collinston resident, Tom Linzay. Linzay operated under the name Collinston Telephone Company.

In late 1946, Ben W. "Hop" Hopgood purchased the small exchange. Forty-one telephones were in service at that time on five miles of pole line. The fifty-line magneto switchboard remained at the Linzay residence for several years. In the early 1950s the switchboard was moved to the Hopgood home. Soon after the switchboard was moved, Hop learned that the Bonita telephone exchange was for sale.

Records show that the Southeast Arkansas Telephone and Power Company, based in West Memphis, Arkansas, owned the telephone company in Bonita in the early thirties. In 1936, Lawrence M. Lavender, a resident of Wilmot, Arkansas, purchased the Bonita telephone exchange for $350.00. He paid $35.00 down and $10.00 a month plus interest for thirty-two months.

Mrs. Montene Copeland said that she worked for Lavender and there were less than twenty telephones in Bonita at that time. Her salary was $5.00 a month. Over the next several years the ownership of the telephone company changed hands several times, passing to F. M. Lavender, to Fred Petty, back to the original Lavender, to Mrs. Beatrice Humphrey, and finally to Victor Watts in 1944. Victor's wife Doris served as the switchboard operator. The Watts family ran the company until December 1952, when Alton Norsworthy joined Ben Hopgood in partnership and the Bonita Exchange was purchased and became part of the new

Northeast Louisiana Telephone Company, Inc. Fifty-two customers were being served on twelve miles of pole line

Northeast management operated on a "shoestring budget" for many years and used every penny made from the telephone company to purchase materials to upgrade and expand the system.

In 1953 Northeast Louisiana Telephone applied for a loan through the Rural Electrification Administration to replace all lines and equipment and to provide dial telephone service to all subscribers in the Collinston, Bonita-Jones service areas. This loan was granted in 1955. By late 1956 the old manual switchboards were replaced with Stromberg-Carlson X-Y dial switching equipment. These improvements were just the beginning

In 1968 the company tried diversification by adding IMTS mobile telephone service. This proved to be quite popular with area farmers as this was the only mobile service available in the parish at the time.

Also in 1968-69 all open wire circuits were replaced with buried telephone cable

In 1982 the company answered a demand for voice paging service in its area by launching their first subsidiary: Northeast Telepage. It currently maintains towers in Bonita, Collinston, and Monroe. The little hometown company was well on it's way to becoming a true telecommunications provider.

Things continued to happen. In 1987, with no cable provider in the area, TV Northeast was formed. Today, it services the communities of Collinston and Bonita with 29 basic channels and two pay channels (HBO and Cinemax). There are plans to double offering in the near future.

In 1992 the Collinston and Bonita exchanges were connected via fiber optic cable and joined with the South Central Bell network in Mer Rouge. This provided quality digital long distance to all subscribers. Also, in 1994, the company replaced the old step-by-step dial offices originally installed in 1956, with new state-of-the-art digital switching systems manufactured by Seimens-Stromberg Carlson. The REA once again provided loan funds for this replacement to help hold down costs to rural subscribers.

Beginning in 1996 all buried cable was replaced. This prepared the way for the higher speeds of the upcoming Internet revolution.

With the explosion of the information age and the fast paced growth of the Internet, NortheastNet was born. It provides convenient access to the "Information Super Highway" with local dialup numbers in Bastrop, Monroe, West Monroe, Ruston and Swartz. Northeast Long Distance was launched in 2000 to answer a growing need for a local long distance carrier.

NortheastNet Wireless Internet was introduced in 2001 to serve Monroe and West Monroe immediately. Soon, our wireless service will be available in Bastrop and Ruston.

With all this growth, the company soon found itself "bursting at the seams" for want of more space. The small business office they were in at the time had served faithfully since 1956 but they had simply outgrown it. So they started a modern office complex across the street. June of 2000 saw the completion of the Northeast Louisiana Telephone Company Home Office.

"The officers and staff of Northeast Louisiana Telephone Company, Inc. are dedicated to improving the quality of life for our customers and subscribers. We recognize the vital role that telecommunications plays in the continued growth of our communities and are firmly committed to leadership in the areas we serve." The officers of Northeast Louisiana Telephone Company, Incorporated are President Rector Hopgood; Vice President William A. Norsworthy; Secretary Dorothy Anne Norsworthy George; and Treasurer Mike George.

✧

Above: Wireless Internet Parabolic Antennae located in Ouachita Parish.

Below: Stromberg-Carlson Switchboard from the 1930s and a state-of-the-art Siemens Stromberg Carlson Digital Telephone Switch serving Collinson and Bonita.

LATTER & BLUM, INC./REALTORS

✧

LATTER & BLUM was already twenty years old when this photo was taken in the new office in April 1936.

A tradition of quality service provided since 1916 has led LATTER & BLUM Inc./Realtors to the forefront of the real estate business in New Orleans and the Gulf South covering Louisiana and Mississippi. Throughout the firm's history, it has helped shape the city's dynamic economy while respecting its rich heritage, a balanced approach that has made LATTER & BLUM itself a part of the city's past, present, and dynamic future.

The year was 1916 and two young entrepreneurs, Harry Latter and Joseph Blum, formed a partnership that has flourished to become the largest and most successful real estate company in the Gulf South. Latter arrived in New Orleans in 1908, bearing a brief letter of reference: "H. Latter is a bright and willing lad and is sure to give satisfaction. He is leaving London." His natural gifts for the real estate business, enhanced by his love and enthusiasm for his adopted city, were a perfect complement to the attributes of Joseph Blum, a quiet, thoughtful man, who had never experienced the slightest doubt about the future of New Orleans.

In the earliest years, agents who served both commercial and residential clients handled all real estate transactions from a single, central location. Because the city's suburbs had not yet been developed, a large part of the business took place in the city, and the company handled primarily commercial real estate.

During this period the name LATTER & BLUM Realtors became synonymous with the incredible historical growth and development of the New Orleans region.

LATTER & BLUM's leadership responded to the growth and development of the city and the corresponding needs of its people for more specialized service by adapting and expanding the company's operations. This expansion led to LATTER & BLUM's position as market leader in the real estate industry, including services to clients needing homes, commercial and industrial properties, leasing, shopping centers, high-rise buildings, insurance, mortgages, and more. With its unequaled background and expertise, LATTER & BLUM is positioned to handle both individual and large corporate clients.

In the early 1980s, as regional industries began to experience a slump in production resulting from decreased oil production, LATTER & BLUM decided for the first time to attain leadership outside of the founders' families.

Robert W. Merrick, a nationally respected appraiser and community leader, assumed ownership of LATTER & BLUM in 1986 and within a few short years grew the firm to its current regional presence as the dominant real estate firm in the Gulf South. LATTER & BLUM grew from internal growth as well as numerous large and small strategic acquisitions of quality real estate firms in the region.

Growth has been constant in the years since, including the acquisition of over fourteen companies, development of a large property management division in 1988, formation of LATTER & BLUM insurance in 1991 and Essential Mortgage in 1999.

LATTER & BLUM has grown its nationally recognized Relocation Division to its current status as the largest organized relocation service in the Gulf South, handling more incoming corporate transferees than any other firm in the region. In 2001 LATTER & BLUM was recognized by RELO, the premier relocation network in the nation, as the top Relocation Broker in its category, nationwide.

Latter and Blum expanded the company's operation into Baton Rouge, with two offices

opened there in 1991, and bought C. J. BROWN Realtors when owners of that well-established company, founded in 1917, decided to sell. The firm also expanded into the newly energized economy of the Mississippi Gulf Coast area, where three offices were opened in 1994. With these acquisitions and expansions, LATTER & BLUM became one of the nation's largest independent real estate companies. The company now encompasses over twenty-three offices and is ranked as the twenty-first largest independent real estate company in America.

With its own dynamic growth paralleling that of the New Orleans region, LATTER & BLUM continues to lead the way in business and community success in the Crescent City. The company's contributions extend far beyond the realm of business, to its role as a good neighbor to the New Orleans area, where it has played a major role in many projects and programs to improve the quality of life for all.

The company's leaders have continued to support community endeavors of all types, including donation to the city of the Latter family home for use as a public library, support of local schools, college scholarships offered to children of LATTER & BLUM employees, and continual support of such charitable organizations as United Way. Current Chairman and CEO of the company, Robert Merrick, recently donated funds to the University of New Orleans College of Business to establish the Merrick Chair in Real Estate Finance.

"At LATTER & BLUM Inc. and C. J. BROWN Realtors, we are interested in being good neighbors, as well as in serving your real estate, property management, commercial appraisal, and home insurance needs," Merrick said. "We take pride in our community and in the eighty-five year family tradition which helped lay the groundwork that allowed our companies to flourish into the largest and most successful real estate company in the Gulf South."

✧

Above: Robert W. Merrick, chairman and CEO, LATTER & BLUM Companies.

Left: The Milton H. Latter Memorial Library was donated to the city of New Orleans by the Latter family.

Tulane University Hospital & Clinic

Above: *Patients, faculty, residents and students come from around the world to Tulane University Hospital & Clinic in downtown New Orleans. The 353-bed hospital has established centers of excellence in the fields of transplantation, cancer care, mental health, pediatrics, sports medicine, women's medicine, and cardiovascular health.*

Below: *Tulane's commitment to providing outstanding research, diagnosis and treatment is unsurpassed. The hospital is a site for numerous post-graduate medical education programs and specialized applied research projects.*

In the face of catastrophic death and disease sweeping New Orleans, seven physicians united in 1834 to form the Medical College of Louisiana. They envisioned a place to study and combat epidemic diseases brought from around the globe via hundreds of ships to this international port. They envisioned a place where the public at large could receive better health care. At that time only fourteen medical schools existed in the United States, and none west of the Allegheny Mountains. Within just a few years, the medical college was viewed as the best in the Southwest, and had achieved a national reputation of excellence.

The sense of forging ahead—of fulfilling a need—has always been central to the institution that evolved over the next 167 years into one of the nation's leading medical schools, Tulane University Health Sciences Center. From a faculty of seven to a full teaching and research medical center, Tulane has grown with our country and our world.

Pioneers in medicine saw the need for Tulane to build its own hospital as early as the 1940s. In October 1976 vision became reality when Tulane University Hospital & Clinic registered its first patient. At that time, we became the first university-based teaching hospital in the Gulf South. Then in April 1995, Tulane again made history when it became the first teaching hospital in the United States to partner with a health care management company.

Today Tulane University Hospital & Clinic, a partnership of Tulane University Health Sciences Center and HCA, marries best practices with capital resources and expert management. Our patients benefit from the highest quality care and customer service.

Tulane's seven Centers of Excellence provide patients access to leading-edge research in a comforting environment.

Tulane Cancer Center, opened in 1997, provides a multidisciplinary approach that coordinates the entire range of cancer care disciplines into one convenient location, eliminating the need for patients to travel from specialist to specialist. It provides state-of-the-art radiation therapy, a minor surgery suite, infusion suite, laboratory, pharmacy, patient resource library, counseling services, and almost two hundred research protocols.

DePaul • Tulane Behavioral Health Center, founded in 1861 merged to become part of our facility in 1997. This teaching facility, which serves patients of all ages, specializes in eating disorders, addictions and residential treatment.

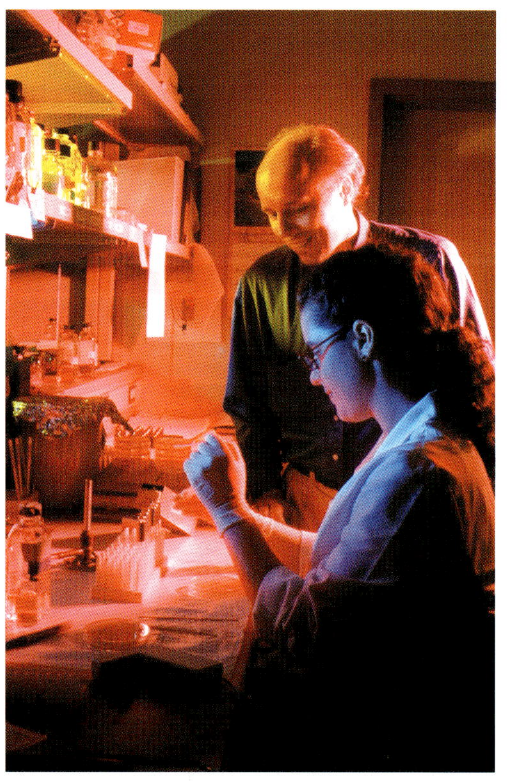

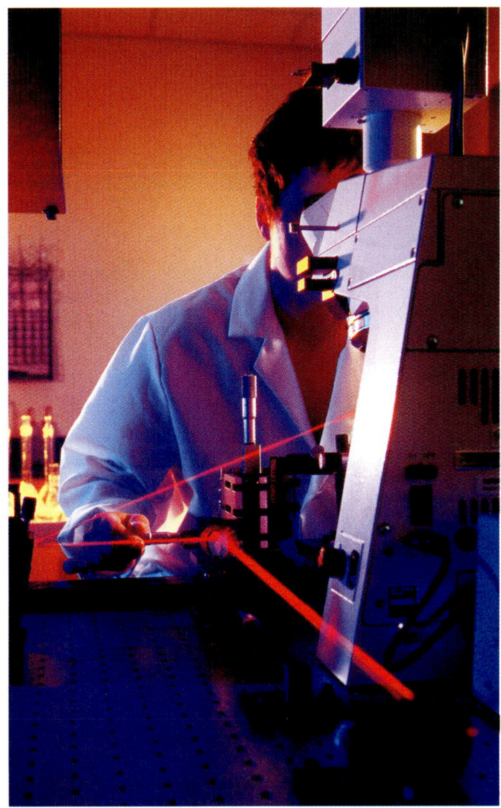

Tulane Hospital for Children addresses the unique needs of children. It was the first infant heart transplant facility, and is noted for research in pediatric kidney transplantation, cystic fibrosis, sickle cell anemia, hemophilia and genetics. It is a principal center in the region for research in pediatric kidney transplantation, cystic fibrosis, sickle cell anemia, hemophilia and genetics.

Tulane Institute for Sports Medicine, the premier sports medicine facility in the nation, provides unique programs for the athlete, including diagnosis, treatment and effective management of sports-related injury, overall fitness programs, a performance laboratory, nutritional consultation, competitive conditioning, performance enhancement, and injury prevention and management.

Tulane Xavier National Center of Excellence in Woman's Health offers a wide range of services and health education for women in all stages of their lives. Created through a national initiative by the Department of Health & Human Services, it joins seventeen other such centers across the country.

Tulane Center for Abdominal Transplant is dedicated to providing quality care to patients with end-stage organ failure who seek transplantation as a treatment option. It provides a comprehensive team approach across scientific and clinical disciplines, to produce optimum treatment outcomes. Tulane's kidney transplant program has been chosen as Louisiana's exclusive participant in the nation's leading transplant system, United Resource Networks.

Tulane Cardiovascular Center of Excellence is the first hospital in the Gulf Coast to offer many new diagnostic breakthroughs. Its newest tool, the EBT (electron beam tomography) scanner, provides the quickest and most accurate method available for early detection of calcification in the coronary arteries, a precursor to atherosclerosis and a major risk factor for sudden cardiac death.

Tulane's hospital and physician practice clinics are conveniently located in the heart of downtown New Orleans. Physicians also provide care in outpatient offices across southwest Louisiana, the Mississippi Gulf Coast, and the Florida panhandle. Patient and international relations department staffs are available to coordinate arrangements for patients and their families who travel to Tulane from across the country and around the world.

Patients can receive care at Tulane by calling one convenient telephone number: 504-588-5800, and pressing the star key (*).

✧

Above: The medical and diagnostic services offered by Tulane's hospital and clinics are extensive, encompassing a wide range of specialty departments working to provide the highest level of health care available.

Below: This photograph shows the work in progress as Tulane University Hospital & Clinic was built. Its twenty-fifth anniversary was celebrated in 2001.

DePaul • Tulane Behavioral Health Center

As the Civil War raged across the United States in 1861, a small group of nuns began treating mental illness in New Orleans. Although little could be done for many mental illnesses at that time, the Daughters of Charity of St. Vincent de Paul lovingly persevered.

By 1874 the Daughters had outgrown their original building, and moved to a site then considered a country retreat, located a day's buggy ride from downtown New Orleans. This spacious thirteen-acre campus, which the Daughters called DePaul Hospital, has become an integral part of uptown New Orleans.

Psychiatry has changed dramatically since 1861. In the 140 years since, the Daughters, and now the Hospital Corporation of America (HCA) have worked to bring a new age of enlightenment to mental health issues.

DePaul Hospital merged with Tulane University Hospital & Clinic in 1997. The facility was re-named DePaul • Tulane Behavioral Health Center, and continued to offer programs for children, adolescents and adults. Now, in addition to the cornerstones of love and care that have always been in place at DePaul, patients have access to the most modern of therapies, the latest advances in psychopharmacology and hundreds of other new therapeutic tools.

DePaul • Tulane Behavioral Health Care Center is well known for successfully treating difficult cases and accepting referrals from other facilities and therapists across the nation. The hospital specializes in eating disorders, chemical dependency, and residential treatment.

Offering a wider range of services than any other psychiatric facility in New Orleans, DePaul runs a full spectrum of programming from residential, outpatient and day patient programs to acute inpatient programs. Specialty units include:

- New Life Center—New Orleans' first facility for treating alcohol and drug problems, the center's experienced staff works with all addictions and dependencies on an inpatient, outpatient or day patient basis.
- Adult Care Units—Separated into two floors, this program offers one unit for gravely disabled patients and a separate unit for mood and anxiety disorder patients.
- Child and Adolescent Program–This highly acclaimed program is among the largest and most comprehensive in the United States, treating children and adolescents ages 5 to 17. In a child-appropriate environment, residential, inpatient and outpatient settings are used to explore issues including sexual trauma, depression, suicide attempts and chronic problems at school.

Below: By the 1950s, DePaul Hospital had begun to spread out over its 13-acre campus in uptown New Orleans. Then, as now, trees and gardens accent its beauty.

Bottom, right: A Daughter of Charity directs the filling of Christmas baskets for the poor.

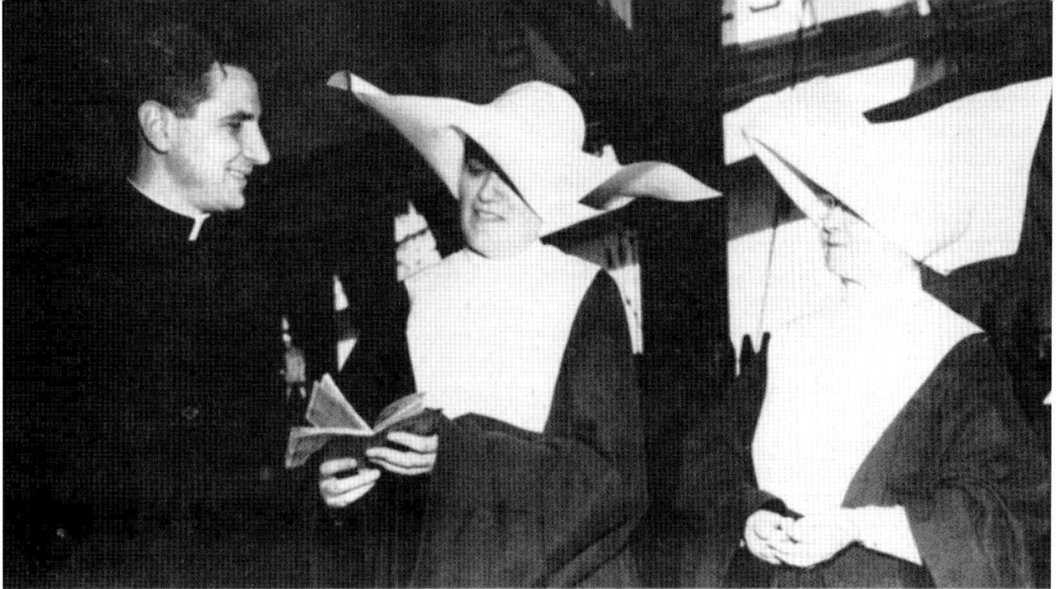

DePaul is a place to grow in body and spirit. Spacious courtyards and red-bricked grounds accentuate an "Old World" feeling. Patient treatment includes art therapy; ceramics; movement and dance; and recreational, leisure, and vocational therapies. Patients can also take advantage of an indoor gym, Olympic-size swimming pool and other outdoor facilities.

Treatment teams consist of nurses, psychiatric technicians, teachers, physicians, psychologists, social workers, creative art therapists, all of whom rely on a host of other support personnel. Realizing how difficult it can be to ask for help, the staff works consistently to be courteous and sensitive. The admission and assessment center makes calling for help as stress-free as possible for those who need assistance. Admissions can be made by adult or child psychiatrists, or through referrals by family physicians, psychologists, social workers, school counselors, EAP specialists, ministers, agencies or caring individuals.

Dedicated to training the mental health professionals of tomorrow, hundreds of internships, residencies or practicums are served in DePaul units each year. Tulane Child Psychiatry Fellows and Adult Psychiatry Residents take rotations at DePaul, as do nursing students from several universities and programs, such as LSU, Charity, Dillard and William Carey College. Social work interns rotate from other universities, including Loyola, Holy Cross College, UNO, Xavier, and Southern.

Workshops, community breakfasts, and school lectures show the responsibility DePaul has always shown to educate the public about mental health.

DePaul is fully accredited by the Joint Commission of Accreditation of Health Care Organizations, and has received accreditation under both AMH and Consolidated standards. DePaul is also licensed by the State of Louisiana, is approved to care for CHAMPUS and Medicare patients, and is the only CHAMPUS-approved residential facility in Louisiana and Mississippi. HCA is a modern pioneer in American health care. DePaul is proud to be a part of HCA and shares its commitment to a quality of care unparalleled in medicine. Treatment cost is covered by most health care insurances.

DePaul's staff has witnessed the rebirth of thousands of patients. Although this process does not occur overnight, the staff of DePaul • Tulane Behavioral Health Center strives to bring lasting success to the lives of patients and their families.

For more than 140 years, DePaul has been making tomorrows better for those who seek help.

✧

Above: A Daughter of Charity of St. Vincent de Paul is celebrated for her war relief work.

Below: A large group of sisters from around the U.S. and Latin America join Sister Anne, DePaul Hospital's administrator, for a sightseeing trip of the New Orleans harbor.

Morris & Dickson Co., Ltd.

With a history dating back over 160 years, Morris & Dickson Co., the oldest family-owned drug wholesaler in the United States, combines traditional customer service with cutting-edge technology to continue as a leader in the field.

In the spring of 1838, John W. Morris and Thomas Henry Morris, brothers from Wales, received degrees in pharmacy and chemistry and immigrated to the United States. With a letter of recommendation from the Church of England, they met with Bishop Leonidas Polk. Bishop Polk told them, "Shreveport is destined to be one of the most considerable towns of the upper Red River." In 1841 they opened J.W. Morris & Co., an apothecary shop, in Shreveport, Louisiana.

Despite the adverse effects of the Civil War, Reconstruction, and an 1873 yellow fever epidemic, the community, with its financial base including timber, cotton, and retail commerce, prospered, and the business grew along with it. After John Morris' death in 1854, his brother Thomas changed the business' name to T.H. Morris & Co.

A dozen miles upstream from Shreveport, the Dickson family operated Rush Point Plantation. Two of the family's sons, W. L. and Samuel A. Dickson, studied medicine at Tulane and eventually set up practice in Shreveport as doctors and social leaders. In 1885, Dr. Samuel Dickson purchased an interest in the Morris Company, the name of which had been changed to Iler, Morris & Hibbett. After Thomas Morris' death, his son, Allen Morris, continued working in the business.

Above: Morris & Dickson's warehouse from 1905 to 1984 on Travis Street is now a downtown hotel.

Below: Even in its early years, Morris & Dickson took great care to provide the best pharmaceuticals.

In 1896, the company was incorporated in the name Morris & Dickson Co., LTD., and with Allen Morris' departure to Fort Smith, Arkansas, W.L. Dickson bought his interest. That left the company under the management of the Dickson family where it continues into its third century.

In addition to leading the company's growth and prosperity, S.A. Dickson was active in civic affairs, serving as city councilman and for two terms as mayor. He also was the head of the levee board, of vital importance to a river community, and was influential in state politics. After the deaths of W.L. Dickson in 1912 and S.A. Dickson in 1916, the company's presidents have been Mrs. W.L. Dickson, 1916-1920; S.A.'s son, Allen Dickson, 1920-1924; Claudius Markham Dickson, 1924-1946; Markham Allen Dickson, 1952-1995; and Markham Allen Dickson, Jr., 1995 to present. Markham

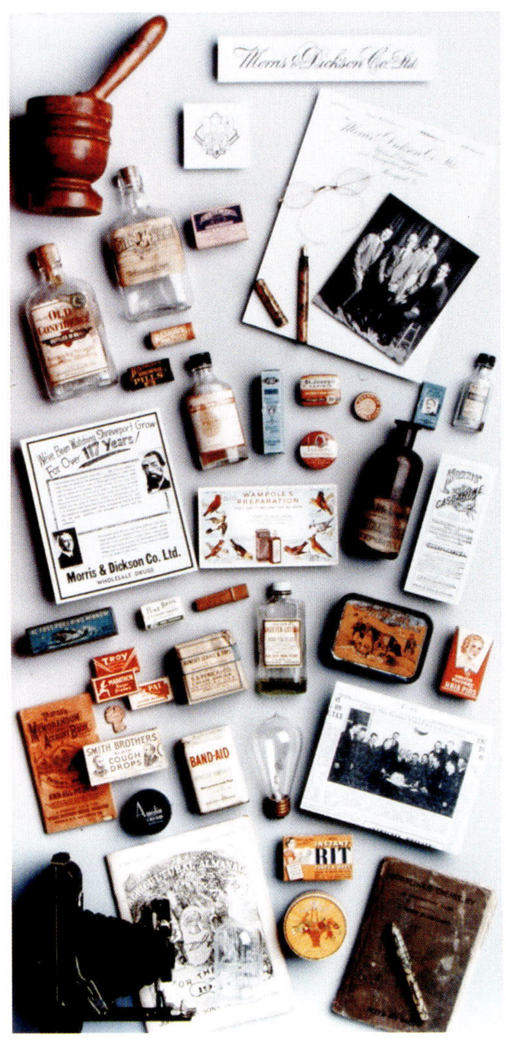

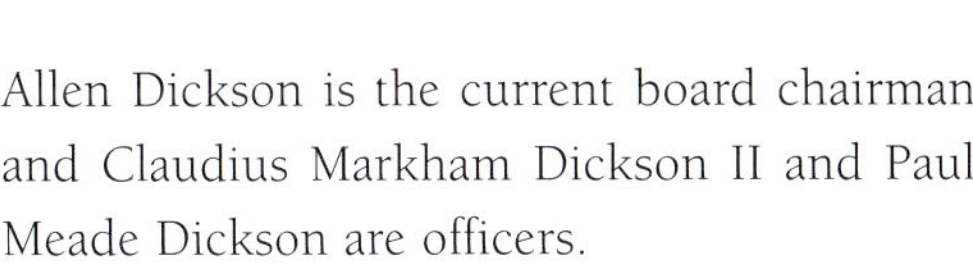

Allen Dickson is the current board chairman and Claudius Markham Dickson II and Paul Meade Dickson are officers.

Utilizing an innovative physical plant and embracing technology and automation to enhance its efficiency and to provide value-added services to its customers, the company continues to maintain its competitive edge and is a recognized industry leader in these areas.

In 1985 the headquarters moved from a downtown warehouse to a site just south of Shreveport. With two hundred thousand square feet of uniquely designed architecture, the setting is both effective and pastoral with a relaxed atmosphere reflecting the corporate personality.

With an unusually large trading area extending from New Mexico, north to Oklahoma, Kansas, and Missouri, east to Alabama, and south to the Gulf of Mexico, the distribution facility is the largest in the South. The company operates its own trucking fleet, which they feel makes a more personal relationship with their customers while maintaining a higher level of service.

A key to the company's recent growth has been the Dicksons' recognition that their automation technology expertise can be directed toward modifying the operations of their customers, both retail and hospital. By enhancing the operations of those they serve, the company has become not just a distributor, but also a provider of cutting-edge technology to the benefit of its customers, and moreover to the industry as a whole.

Skipper Dickson says, "Morris & Dickson's continued success is based on continuity of management under family ownership and operation, through which today's leaders 'grew up in the business,' creating personal relationships with both employees and customers, who know they can always talk to a Dickson."

✧

Left: Products from the early days of Morris & Dickson.

Right: The Dickson family management team (from left to right): Allen Dickson, Paul Dickson, Mark Dickson, and Skipper Dickson.

THE ADVOCATE

For Baton Rouge residents, reading *The Advocate* is as regular a morning custom as sipping a cup of rich Louisiana coffee. The journalistic excellence found in this family-owned newspaper is also a long-standing tradition.

"It is our intention to print a newspaper whose editorials are not for sale, and whose news items cannot be suppressed, a newspaper commensurate with the hopes and plans of Baton Rouge..." wrote Charles P. Manship in his first 1909 editorial as manager of the Baton Rouge paper in which he had just invested. Since that time the Manship family has lived up to his promise, and to his additional pledge to support no political party, but only those candidates and issues which a consensus of the editors feel are worthwhile for Baton Rouge.

With a circulation today of 93,360 daily and 124,848 Sunday, *The Advocate* is a major presence in Louisiana media markets, and its coverage of the state–including Louisiana's always interesting politics—has garnered the paper and its journalists numerous awards. *The Advocate* is still very much a family enterprise in Louisiana's capital city with Douglas Manship, Jr., grandson of the founder, being named publisher in 1999.

The history of Baton Rouge's newspapers is a turbulent one, dating back to a journal published in both French and English in the early nineteenth century. When the state capital located there in the 1840s, Baton Rouge was already accustomed to partisan politics in the local press and flamboyant editors at the helm—one unfortunate such journalist being fatally shot in a duel. It was in those heady days in 1842 that an ancestor of today's newspaper began publication as the Democratic Advocate (with the agenda of defeating all candidates of the rival Whig party).

During the remaining ninteenth century the Baton Rouge newspaper scene was an exciting one—even when two editors left town to join the Confederate Army in the Civil War. *The Capitolian* came on the scene in 1868 with the flamboyant Leon Jastremski at the helm (alone, after his partner succumbed to a well-aimed shot by an irate reader.) This paper soon merged with *The Weekly Advocate*. By 1889 the *Weekly* was being published daily, except Mondays. In 1904 a new owner, William Hamilton, renamed it *The Baton Rouge Times*. *The Daily State* newspaper, founded in 1904, bought The Times and the paper was again renamed the State-Times. However, by 1909 this newspaper venture was floundering and yet another Advocate had come into print.

At this point a new player joined the journalistic game. Charles P. Manship and James Edmonds created Capital City Press in 1909 and bought the *State-Times*, an afternoon paper.

✧

Above: A 1941 photo portrait of Charles P. Manship Sr., founder of Capital City Press.

Below: This handsome brick building was the home of the State-Times *newspaper in 1909 when Charles P. Manship Sr. entered the newspaper field. The building was at the corner of Lafayette and Florida streets. The style of architecture resembles buildings constructed before the Civil War.*

The following year the fledgling *Advocate* was absorbed. Manship managed the resulting single newspaper, and two years later, in 1912, he bought Edmonds' interests. A newspaper dynasty had begun. Charles P. Manship, who had come to Baton Rouge from his hometown of Jackson, Mississippi as a correspondent for *The Daily Picayune* of New Orleans, was now editor, publisher, and sole owner of the *State-Times* of Baton Rouge.

Only in 1925 would the *Morning Advocate* be created, giving Capital City Press both morning and afternoon papers. The two would have different personalities, with the *State-Times* focusing more on city coverage and the *Morning Advocate* and its *Sunday Advocate* providing a newspaper serving regional needs as the dominant voice in a number of nearby parishes.

As a newspaper editor in Baton Rouge, Manship had his share of problems with Louisiana Governor Huey P. Long. Long's regard for the press can be summed up in the word he coined and often used: "lyingnewspapers." In 1934, Manship established WJBO-AM radio station in Baton Rouge, the first of media ventures that would include a television and FM station.

In 1947, on his father's death, Charles P. Manship, Jr., became editor and publisher of the two Baton Rouge papers. Under his guidance the company grew, and the newspaper building at 525 Lafayette Street was built. In 1970 his brother, Douglas Manship, Sr., became editor and publisher, while Charles retired and assumed the presidency of Capital City Press.

Douglas Manship, Sr., oversaw modernization of production, with the old hot-lead presses and typewriters phased out and a new computerized production center located on Bluebonnet Road. In 1989, David C. Manship, one of Douglas Manship, Sr.'s sons, was named associate publisher.

In 1991 the afternoon newspaper the *State-Times*, ceased publication, and Douglas Manship, Sr., became president of Capital City Press while David Manship was named publisher. Charles Manship died in 1994. In December 1995 *The Advocate* went live with *The Advocate Online*, the Internet version of the newspaper. In 1996, Douglas Manship, Jr., who had worked as a Washington correspondent, news features editor and editorial writer, and had overseen the development of The Advocate Online, was named director of new media, the online operations of Capital City Press.

In 1999, Douglas Manship, Sr., died and in that year Douglas Manship, Jr. became publisher of *The Advocate*. Today the newspaper and its parent company, Capital City Press, continue to flourish.

Capital City Press, besides the newspaper, operates a successful offset printing business serving Baton Rouge and the Gulf South. From its beginnings with one newspaper in 1909, the media company has grown and indeed, is up-to-the-minute in communications systems with an interactive website, www.theadvocate.com, welcoming avid Advocate readers to the twenty-first century.

✧

Above: This photograph of the Manship family was taken in 1992 in front of The Advocate *building at 525 Lafayette Street. From the left are David Manship, Richard Manship, the late Charles Manship Jr., the late Douglas Manship, Douglas Manship Jr. and Dina Manship Planche.*

Below: This three-story brick structure designed by the architectural firm of Bodman and Murrell has been home to The Advocate *since March 1953. Located at 525 Lafayette Street, the building is near Louisiana's capitol, and one block from the Mississippi River.* The Advocate *is two blocks north of the site of Charles Manship Sr.'s first newspaper, the* State-Times.

Piccadilly Cafeterias

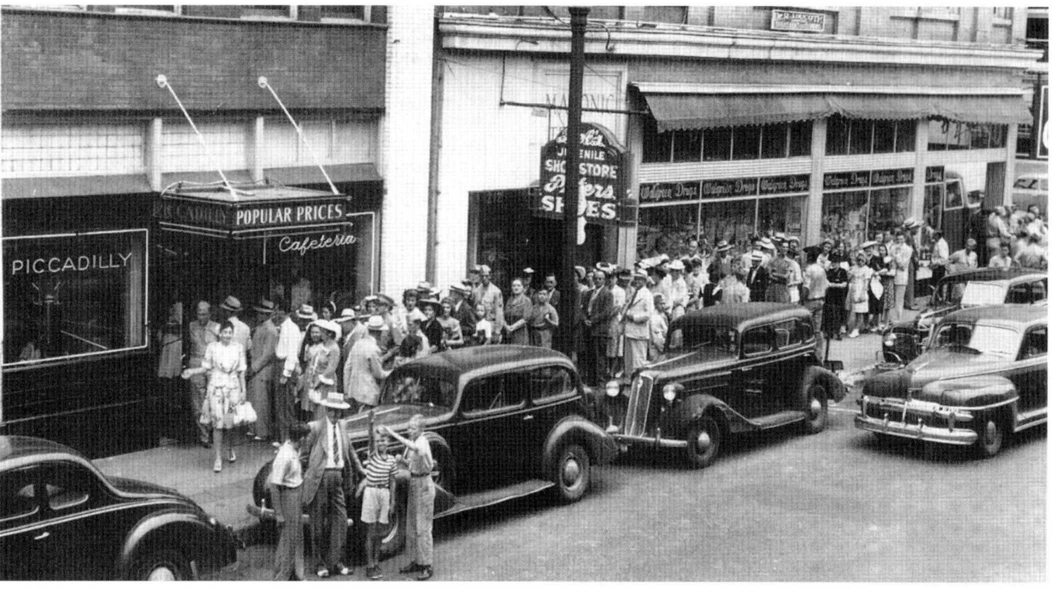

✧

Above: The first Piccadilly Cafeteria opened in 1941 in downtown Baton Rouge.

Below: Tandy Hamilton's original plan of owning 40 restaurants became 200.

The Piccadilly Cafeteria motto, "Liberal Portions, Highest Quality, Fair Prices," is as important today as it was when T. H. (Tandy) Hamilton founded the cafeteria chain in 1944 with a single small café and cafeteria. By the time he retired in 1972, he had exceeded his goal of owning a chain of 40 cafeterias. Tandy's legacy to the company is now enjoyed daily by thousands of customers in over 200 cafeterias in 16 states.

One of the nation's largest cafeteria chains, Piccadilly was voted the number one cafeteria in the country and awarded the Choice in Chains Platinum Award by *Restaurants and Institutions Magazine* in 2001.

This award, based on a national consumer survey, gave Piccadilly the highest rankings in the cafeteria/buffet restaurant category with regard to food quality, service, convenience, cleanliness, value, atmosphere and menu variety.

Ronnie LaBorde, Piccadilly CEO, said this award is a tribute to Piccadilly employees, who make sure customers receive the highest quality service, and who guarantee that customers' needs are met and concerns are heard.

"We take pride in listening to our customers and appreciate them for making this honor possible," LaBorde said.

Piccadilly offers a wide variety of home-style and regional dishes in a casual, family-friendly atmosphere. Headquartered in Baton Rouge, Louisiana, Piccadilly operates primarily in the southeast and mid-Atlantic regions. With nearly 200 cafeterias Piccadilly registers annual sales of nearly $400 million and employs more than 9,000 people.

The size of the company is astounding in light of Tandy Hamilton's background and the chain's modest beginnings. Born in the Indian Territories of Oklahoma in 1897, Tandy was eight years old when his father, a federal marshal, was shot and killed by an outlaw as he and Tandy attended a baseball game.

The family was large, including two brothers and a sister at home, and a half-brother and half-sister reared by their mother's relatives in the Choctaw Nation. After his father's death, Tandy's mother remarried, and he had another half-brother.

Tandy and his brothers picked the family's

cotton field for 50 to 75 cents a day. When he was 15, Tandy packed his clothes, took his $5 in savings and rode away on a bicycle with a suitcase balanced on the handlebars. He and his Indian half-brother rounded up loose horses and cattle in the city limits of McAlester, Oklahoma. After a while he hoboed, then moved on to Wichita, Kansas, where he began his first restaurant job. He was only 16 years old.

He started by peeling potatoes, working 11 hours a day, seven days a week for $5 per week. Fascinated with restaurant work, he decided he wanted to become a cook and immediately began spending his spare money on cookbooks and culinary equipment.

He progressed from potato peeler to second cook, then worked as a waiter at an upscale restaurant before returning to the kitchen to take up baking, salad making and line cooking, gaining confidence along the way. He eventually became chef at one of Wichita's better restaurants.

When the country went to war in 1918, Tandy joined the Army and was sent to a training school where he was taught by a "capable French chef" before being sent to France for additional training under "the finest chefs of Europe." Tandy considered this the chance of a lifetime.

After the war, he met and married Tela Meier in Oklahoma. They moved to Wichita Falls, Texas, where in 1920 he was hired as a sous chef at the luxurious Kemp Hotel. From the head chef he learned the importance of a stockpot in making stews and gravies, literally taking notes about the kitchen's operation, and later creating his own recipes using the homemade stock.

The family now including a daughter Julie, moved several times, eventually taking root in Kansas City, Missouri where in 1923 Tandy took a job with The Forum, a midwestern cafeteria chain. He credited his work there with having introduced him to the importance of organization in the food business. Rapidly promoted through the ranks and into management, he eventually was named general manager of the chain, working from the headquarters in Kansas City. In his "spare" time Tandy studied courses as varied as law and violin, psychology and public speaking.

By early 1941 Tandy realized he wanted to build his own chain that would eventually grow to include 40 cafeterias, but the opportunity did not present itself until 1944, when he was 47 years old. By this time Tandy had worked in the cafeteria business for 21 years.

Learning that a small cafeteria and café in Baton Rouge was for sale, Hamilton visited the city and was impressed with its potential. The place looked promising, and he even liked the name, "Piccadilly," indicating you could "go through the line and pick a dilly of a meal." On February 1, 1944, he and his wife, daughter and son-in-law purchased the business for $65,000. He had considered potential employees while awaiting the opportunity to purchase the right property and immediately enlisted several of them.

Tandy and Tela moved to Baton Rouge and he took over the operation without losing a day of business. Changes were immediate–a better variety of food, acquiring meats and vegetables from local farmers, improvements to the food display, and adaptation of several recipes to compensate for wartime shortages of commodities like sugar.

Within a few months, Tandy was ready to expand and located a small restaurant in

Above: Piccadilly offers home-style meals every day.

Below: Whole meat entree's are served by chefs on carving night.

Beaumont, Texas. Like the first Piccadilly it was chosen as a "100 percent location"–defined as a street with heavy downtown traffic. Other early expansions were in Memphis, Tennessee and Waco, Texas.

Described by a colleague as "the Walt Disney of the food business," Tandy's training and management styles are still incorporated in Piccadilly operations. He insisted that Piccadilly could "season and cook our food as tasty as in any home, and we can serve it, too, just as fresh and attractive." He instituted a custom line check before opening, with the manager inspecting the appearance and presentation of each food item, and the appearance and attitude of the serving staff.

His ability to instruct and motivate was legendary, whether it was a matter of teaching the proper mixing of pie dough–so the result is "tender, but crisp and has a long flake"–or the mixing of cornbread dressing–"if it didn't fluff up while baking, it wasn't made right."

When it comes to choosing recipes, flavor has always been the guide at Piccadilly. If it is on the food line at Piccadilly, it is going to be properly prepared. From scrumptious homemade rolls to tangy three-bean salad, and from broiled fish that's done to a turn, to creamy cheesecake, customers vote Piccadilly's dishes the best they've ever eaten.

Part of the secret of this accomplishment is the uncompromising insistence on using only the very best ingredients and checking con-

Above: Variety, value, courteous service, and home-style cooking have made Piccadilly an American favorite.

Below: Piccadilly is famous for fresh-baked pies and cakes.

stantly for quality. Customers' taste buds can tell that Piccadilly's chefs prepare tried-and-true recipes made with only the highest quality ingredients. The result is juicy roast beef, flavorful chicken and dumplings, crunchy carrot and raisin salad, creamy French-style squash, and all the other luscious dishes on the menu.

New items are added to the line constantly, to suit the changing tastes of Piccadilly's guests. These include boneless, skinless grilled chicken breast and sugar-free pies for those who want to reduce the fat and sugar in their diets. And Piccadilly continues to insist on exceptional variety to ensure that guests can choose items that suit both their diets and palates. Tuesday is carving day at Piccadilly, where whole meat is special cut by chefs; and Wednesday features 79-cent desserts.

Over the years, families large and small have gathered together at Piccadilly to share great times and great food. These have included a fair share of celebrities. Among them was the legendary Elvis Presley, who would slip away from his mansion and the limelight to enjoy home-style meals at the Piccadilly in Memphis–once forgetting his wallet and having to sign a counter check.

The future looks promising for this great American institution, thanks to modern leaders who share Tandy's values and vision of a great restaurant organization.

McIlhenny Company

Since 1868 the McIlhenny family has been committed to premium products that enliven the flavor of food. "Our mission is to assure that our Tabasco® diamond provides uncompromising quality," the family pledges.

McIlhenny Company founder Edmund McIlhenny was born in Maryland. McIlhenny arrived in New Orleans in 1841 and became a banker. He married Mary Eliza Avery in 1859, and they had eight children. During the Civil War, the McIlhennys moved to the Avery Plantation on Petite Anse Island (now Avery Island) near New Iberia. When conflict neared, the family moved to Texas and afterwards returned.

It's said McIlhenny obtained his special Capsicum frutescens peppers "after the Civil War from a traveler recently returned from Mexico or Central America." McIlhenny mashed the peppers with Avery Island salt, fermented them for thirty days, added French white wine vinegar, and let them age at least another month. McIlhenny then strained the sauce into narrow-necked cologne-type bottles.

McIlhenny was urged to sell his sauce commercially. He named it Tabasco®, a word of Mexican Indian origin, began marketing it in 1868, and patented it in 1870.

During McIlhenny's entire career (1868-1890) he produced about 350,000 bottles of Tabasco® Sauce. Today, 550,000 bottles are produced daily.

Tabasco® Sauce was sent to soldiers in Vietnam and in Operation Desert Storm. The sauce was included in troops' MRE (Meals Ready to Eat) packages. Walter McIlhenny, retired Marine Corps general, even had a special camouflage holster designed for the bottles.

President and CEO Paul C. P. McIlhenny notes "Tabasco® Sauce remains the leader and the standard in its condiment category." New sauces include milder Tabasco® green pepper sauce, zesty Tabasco® garlic pepper sauce, super-hot Tabasco® habanero pepper sauce and Tabasco® chipotle pepper sauce.

Tabasco® Country Stores, stocked with apparel and gift items, are located on Avery Island and New Orleans, Louisiana; San Antonio and Kemah, Texas. Heinz Ketchup and other food products are now spiced with Tabasco® Sauce.

McIlhenny Company sponsors African-American marketing internships and an African-American "Real Men Cook" program, as well as the Food Bank in Los Angeles, California. The New Orleans House of Blues Foundation, the "Scottish Treasures" exhibit at the New Orleans Museum of Art, and the Pacific exhibit planned for the National D-Day Museum all have McIlhenny Company support.

Aim your computer to www.TABASCO.com and experience PepperFest® or visit the McIlhenny Company Visitors Center on Avery Island, with bottling plant and museum, Jungle Gardens and Bird City, the sanctuary begun by Edward Avery McIlhenny, who created a garden paradise with native and exotic plants.

Rest assured. McIlhenny Company's future is secure! It always stores some of its specially selected pepper seeds in a fireproof, walk-in vault on Avery Island as a hedge against any crop failure.

Top, left: An 1857 portrait of Tabasco® brand pepper sauce inventor Edmund McIlhenny.

Below: A global cultural icon from Louisiana: The modern Tabasco® brand pepper sauce bottle.

Community Trust Bank

✧

Below: The Bank of Choudrant in Choudrant, Louisiana, 1926. It served as original Community Trust Bank) building..

Bottom: Community Trust Bank Financial Center, West Monroe, Louisiana, 1998.

Choudrant, Louisiana, was far from a banking Mecca in 1912. Yet it was the birthplace, and remains the headquarters, of one of Louisiana's most successful and respected financial institutions. Community Trust Bank had its origins as the Bank of Choudrant, founded in November 1912, with a capitalization of $10,000.

Providing a unique brand of personalized, "relationship" banking and financial services to an ever-expanding list of customers and communities over the past ninety years, Community Trust Bank has excelled in its mission of placing as much emphasis on creating opportunity and growth for their communities, customers and employees, as they do for their shareholders. Employees are involved in every worthwhile endeavor within the communities served, while placing the customer first as they go about their daily business of banking. Walk into any office of Community Trust Bank and happy, smiling employees will be found who are knowledgeable and eager to meet the customer's needs.

The original bank building, constructed in 1912, faced the Vicksburg, Shreveport and Pacific Railroad, which had been completed through Choudrant nine years before. The Bank occupied this location until 1959, when it relocated near U.S. Highway 80, formerly known as the Dixie Overland Highway, a highway that eventually spanned the continent. As the banking environment began changing through mergers and regional bank competition, Community Trust Bank determined that to be able to compete, it must provide greater convenience to its existing customers while expanding its trade area.

The first step toward this goal was the opening of an office in Ruston in 1983. Then, in 1987, an expansion was made into Union Parish with the acquisition of the Bank of Bernice and its branch in Farmerville. The name of the merged institutions was changed to Community Trust Bank. With this merger, the bank almost doubled in size, resulting in total assets of $39 million.

In 1990 the Rock Island Depot/Freight House in Ruston was acquired and converted to the Bank's fifth office.

Another Ruston office, the Community Trust Bank Financial Center, was opened for business in 1996, providing a twenty-three-thousand-square-foot facility that offers the latest in financial products along with Community Trust Bank's legendary attention to personal service. In addition to retail banking, the Financial Center offers commercial lending, home mortgage lending, and trust and equity services. A unique feature of this office is a Community Room available to civic and charitable organizations and various youth groups as a meeting place. This room is provided as a community service free of charge.

In 1998 the Bank expanded into Ouachita Parish by constructing a three-story, 30,000-square-foot facility in West Monroe. At the end of 1998, two additional offices were opened in Ouachita Parish, with a branch in Calhoun and an in-store location within the K-Mart in West Monroe. Also in 1998, Community Trust Bank acquired a former office of a regional bank in Ruston, adjacent to Louisiana Tech University.

The Bank crossed the Ouachita River into Monroe in 2001 by adding a beautiful, freestanding location on Highway 165, close to the University of Louisiana–Monroe. In addition to providing local convenience for existing customers, this new facility gave the Bank many opportunities in the Monroe area within commercial and consumer markets, thus increasing market share and sustaining growth.

In March 2003, the bank will open a three-story 35,000-square-foot facility at the corner of North Eighteenth Street and Hudson Lane in Monroe, Louisiana, which is an area that has become the hub of commerce. This new office will be the bank's flagship in Ouachita Parish.

As of December 31, 2001, the Bank's financial network consisted of eleven full service branch offices, sixteen ATM's, and an affiliate insurance agency. Total assets were $295,183,000, with capital of $23,290,000.

While infrastructure is very important, leadership is crucial to an organization for success. Over the years, Community Trust Bank has been most fortunate to have outstanding citizens serve on its board and in the management of the bank.

During the first five years of the Bank's existence, there were three different presidents. The position was mostly honorary, as the title passed to various board members. This changed in 1917, with the election of T. J. Norris, who served as president until 1929. Howard H. Smith became associated with the bank in 1927, was elected president in 1929, and served until his death in 1981—a total of fifty-four years.

W. Grady Kelly was named cashier of the Bank in 1929, and served in various capacities for sixty years until his retirement as chairman of the board in 1989. His wife, Virginia, joined him as assistant cashier in 1933 and retired thirty-seven years later in 1979.

John F. Emory, through an affiliate, became associated with the Bank in 1955, was elected to the Board in 1973, named CEO in 1981, and continues to serve as chairman of the board and CEO.

Drake D. Mills, joined the bank in 1983, working his way through the ranks, and was promoted to president in 1997. A position he holds today.

The long terms and overlap of management have insured an enduring focus on the Bank's goals and objectives, and have been a major factor in the Bank's success. The culture and values passed from one generation to the next, along with the Corporate Mission Statement—to preserve our status as a profitable, independent, community owned and operated financial institution by providing superior products and services to all customers while balancing technology and relationship banking—and an ever-expanding delivery system, have all contributed to positioning Community Trust Bank well for the future.

✧

Above: Community Trust Bank, Highway 165 North, Monroe, Louisiana, 2001.

Below: Community Trust Bank, 1511 North Trenton, Ruston, Louisiana, 1996.

New Orleans Firemen's Federal Credit Union

The New Orleans Firemen's Federal Credit Union began in 1934, in a small room behind the New Orleans Fire Department's Central Station. Today it is a successful, stable and growing financial institution with over $65 million in assets and more than two hundred Select Employee Groups in addition to the New Orleans Fire Department. The corporate office is located at 4401 West Napoleon Avenue in Metairie, Louisiana.

The New Orleans Firemen's Federal Credit Union proudly holds the sixth charter issued to a federal credit union in the United States and will celebrate its seventieth year of operation in October 2004. "The key to our success is that we have never forgotten that our mission is to serve our members. Our members' financial needs are our primary concern, and we take pride in the fact that we listen when our members, our owners, talk." said NOFFCU President Donald Bock.

"In 1934, when the credit union was organized for New Orleans firemen," Bock added, "firemen had it twice as difficult. Starting wages were only $85 per month for a 72-hour week. Being in a high-risk job made lenders shy even further away."

"Six or seven people put up a few dollars each to start the credit union," Bock reports. "For years, the credit union operated out of a room in New Orleans Central Fire Station with one full-time person and three or four part-time people."

In 1980, when Bock became the president of NOFFCU, it had $3 million in assets. In the twenty years since, it has grown to over $65 million in assets and serves 17,000 members, with 5 full-service centers, located in Orleans, Jefferson, St. James, and St. Tammany Parishes.

"Over the years, our membership has expanded to include several Select Employee Groups and has become a full service financial institution with twenty-four hour access," says Chief Executive Officer Judy DeLucca. "As a full service institution we help our members by giving them an option to the banking industry. With a multitude of products to offer, our goal is to become the primary financial institution to all of our members. We want them to think of us as family—the entity they turn to when they need help."

In President Lyndon Johnson's words, "We labor to increase the total abundance of all… by pursuing the growth of all, we advance the welfare of each."

Above: The New Orleans Firemen's Federal Credit Union serves the New Orleans Fire Department plus over two hundred other select employee groups.

Below: The corporate headquarters for the New Orleans Firemen's Federal Credit Union is located at 4401 West Napoleon Avenue in Metairie, Louisiana.

Whitney National Bank

When people say the Whitney National Bank "feels like family," it's not surprising, since it was founded by a family, the Whitneys, and has been meeting the financial needs of families and businesses since 1883. The oldest continuously operating bank in New Orleans and a banking industry leader in the Gulf South, the Whitney offers the expert combination of old-fashioned, personalized service and lasting relationships, along with state-of-the-art banking products and convenience. At the Whitney, bankers still know the customers well enough to call them by name.

With over 120 branches and more than 200 ATMs available in five Gulf South States—Alabama, Florida, Louisiana, Mississippi, and Texas—the Whitney emphasizes the convenience that is so important to customers. A mobile ATM, "Whitney on Wheels," provides customers on-site convenience at festivals and other special events. Banking services can also be accessed 24/7 through the Whitney Information Line, which handles over four million calls annually. Over fifty thousand customers utilize the Whitney's online service, including such features as balance reporting and fund transfers, as well as loan applications and bill payment.

Founded on the tenets of sound ethical values, solid business experience, strong capital and outstanding customer service, the Whitney continues to adhere to those principles. As its franchise is expanded geographically throughout the Gulf South, the benefit of having a trusted Whitney banker is becoming ever more widely recognized.

Hard work and constant communication, enthusiasm, knowledge and availability, as well as active community service are all key factors in reinforcing the trust clients have in their Whitney banker. This philosophy has traditionally provided solid business returns, and is clearly reflected by the steady increase in the Whitney's deposits, loans and non-interest income over the past five years.

Throughout its lengthy history, Whitney's commitment to community service has extended far beyond banking relationships, to include volunteer work and civic endeavors. Whitney employees provide both financial and personal involvement as volunteers for a wide range of organizations in the communities served by every branch. Whether the need is United Way, Big Brothers/Big Sisters, the Crescent City Classic (as seen in the photo below), the Audubon Zoo, March of Dimes, Junior Achievement, Public Television or many others, the Whitney is represented, continuing its personal relationships to aid the community as a whole.

Louisiana Federal Credit Union

"It's about people helping people," insists Ronald E. Thomas, Sr., who in 1935 helped found and was the first manager of what is now Louisiana Federal Credit Union. It began as the Norco Refinery Employees Federal Credit Union, and in the 1990s was renamed Louisiana Federal Credit Union and added other Select Employer Groups.

Thomas, a Kansas City native who was transferred to Norco by Shell in 1929 and retired after fifty-nine years with the company, recalls that a credit union representative visited and made a presentation, and "before we got our charter we had 107 people signed up."

Originally the credit union office was at the main gate of the refinery, and it was a popular spot. Having a credit union and payroll deductions meant that workers could save their money and handle debts and health crises more easily. Annual meetings could be fun, too. "One year the meeting was in the gym and people were able to dance," Thomas added.

Thomas's wife of sixty-eight years, Helen Marie Muller Thomas, also worked actively for the credit union. "I think our first loan was $25," Mrs. Thomas said. She remembers families who were able to educate their children and buy homes with the credit union's help. Some families have had members for four generations.

As Rhonda Hotard, now president of Louisiana Federal Credit Union, explained, "Mr. and Mrs. Thomas are such an important part of our credit union. They help us remember where we started."

Above: Ronald E. Thomas, Sr. helped found and was the first manager of what is now Louisiana Federal Credit Union.

Below: Louisiana Federal Credit Union's new LaPlace Branch, located at 350 Belle Terre Boulevard, opened January 7, 2002.

COURTESY OF PORTRAITS BY SUSIE.

Today, with nearly nineteen thousand members, Louisiana Federal Credit Union still exists for the same good reason it was founded: to serve the financial needs of members with a personal touch. Credit unions are "not-for-profit" financial institutions where profits are returned to members in the form of lower loan rates, higher savings rates, and other free or affordable services.

Louisiana Federal Credit Union has three branches: at 1001 Third Street in Norco; 350 Belle Terre Boulevard in LaPlace, and at 42162 Veterans Avenue in Hammond, Louisiana. All three locations offer drive up services. As participating members of the Credit Union Service Center Network, Louisiana Federal Credit Union members can use facilities at 7018 Siegen Lane in Baton Rouge, 5500 Veterans Memorial Boulevard in Metairie and at 5848 Line Avenue in Shreveport, as well as in one hundred cities nationwide.

Louisiana Federal Credit Union can be found on the Internet at www.lafed.org. Future plans include expedited loan services, with a goal of 15-minute turn-around during working hours, and home banking over the Internet. At whatever hour, members can always dial the CALL24 automated response unit at 1-888-888-0024 to complete a wide variety of transactions.

"We're still about people helping people," Rhonda Hotard explained.

THE LOUISIANA HISTORICAL SOCIETY

The Louisiana Historical Society was founded in 1835, and is the oldest organization of its kind in our State. Among the presidents of the Society were such prominent men as Supreme Court Judges Henry A. Bullard and Francois Xavier Martin and historians Charles Gayarre and Alcée Fortier. Historical writers, educators or notables in every cultural field in Louisiana have belonged to the Society. Beginning in 1895 the Society published forty-eight annual volumes of the *Louisiana Historical Quarterly*, over thirty thousand printed pages. This journal constitutes the finest single collection of published historical source material in existence relating to Louisiana.

For a century the Society has presented monthly public lectures on subjects relevant to Louisiana history. Today it meets eight times a year in September, October, November, March, April, and May on the second Tuesday at 7:30 p.m. Since 1836 the Society has taken the lead in observing the important anniversaries of Louisiana's historic past notably the victory at the Battle of New Orleans on January 8 and the Louisiana Purchase on or about December 20 of each year. An important lecture on an aspect of its history accompanies each anniversary.

The Society conducts annual tours to important sites in Louisiana history, frequently visiting seldom-opened homes. Tours are available to members at a nominal cost. It also sponsors symposia on topics in Louisiana history. Current information on the Society is on its website located at www.louisianahistoricalsociety.org. The entire *Louisiana Historical Quarterly* series and other publications are available at the website to members of the Society.

You are cordially invited to join The Louisiana Historical Society, the statewide organization devoted to the exploration and dissemination of Louisiana history.

Left: The Cabildo served the Spanish government, city courts, and the Louisiana Supreme Court. In 1912, The Louisiana Historical Society founded the Louisiana State Museum to preserve the many documents and paintings owned by The Louisiana Historical Society.

Below: The Louisiana Purchase Transfer Ceremony, 1803. Oil on canvas, 1903, by Brur Thure Thustrup. The transfer ceremony took place on December 20, 1803. This painting is in The Louisiana Historical Society collection.

The Officers of
The Louisiana Historical Society

Sally K. Reeves, President

G. Howard Hunter, First Vice President

Edward O. Gros, Jr., Second Vice President

H. J. Bosworth, Jr., Third Vice President

William D. Reeves, Treasurer

Mary Moore, Corresponding Secretary

Harold J. Gorman, Recording Secretary

Doris Ann Gorman, Archivist

Executive Council Members-At-Large

Edward F. Martin
Dr. William J. Perret
Cheryl Thompson
Button Parham

Grambling State University

Grambling State University emerged from the desire of African-American farmers in rural north Louisiana who wanted to educate other African Americans in the northern and western parts of the state. In 1896 the North Louisiana Colored Agriculture Relief Association was formed to organize and operate a school.

After opening a small school west of what is now the town of Grambling, the Association requested assistance from Booker T. Washington of Tuskegee Institute in Alabama. Charles P. Adams, who was sent to aid the group in organizing an industrial school, became its founder and first president.

Under Adams' leadership, the Colored Industrial and Agricultural School opened on November 1, 1901. Four years later, the school moved to its present location and was renamed the North Louisiana Agricultural and Industrial School. By 1928 the school was able to offer two-year professional certificates and diplomas after becoming a state junior college. The school was renamed Louisiana Negro Normal and Industrial Institute.

In 1936, Ralph Waldo Emerson Jones became the second president. The program was reorganized to emphasize rural education. It became internationally known as "The Louisiana Plan" or "A Venture in Rural Teacher Education." Professional teaching certificates were awarded when a third year was added in 1936, and the first baccalaureate degree was awarded in 1944 in elementary education.

The institution's name was changed to Grambling College in 1946. Thereafter, the college prepared secondary teachers and added curricula in sciences, liberal arts and business. With these programs in effect, the school was transformed from a single purpose institution of teacher education into a multipurpose college. During the 1950s, the college obtained full membership in the Southern Association of Colleges and Schools (SACS). Later, the addition of graduate programs in early childhood and elementary education gave the school a new status and a new name—Grambling State University—in 1974.

From 1977 to 2000, the University moved and prospered. Several new academic programs were incorporated and new facilities—including a business and computer science building, school of nursing, student services building, stadium, stadium support facility, and an intramural sports center—were added to the 384-acre campus.

Five presidents served during this period: Dr. Joseph Benjamin Johnson, Dr. Harold W. Lundy, Dr. Raymond Hicks, Dr. Leonard Haynes III, and Dr. Steve A. Favors.

The advent of a new millennium and the beginning of a second century of service ushered in Grambling State University's first female president, Dr. Neari Francois Warner.

A constituent member of the University of Louisiana System (ULS) with continued full membership in SACS, Grambling State

Above: The main entrance to Grambling State University.

Below: The presidents of Grambling State University from the twentieth century.

University's instructional programs are delivered through the colleges of Business, Education, Liberal Arts, and Science and Technology; the professional schools of Nursing and Social Work; and the Division of Graduate Studies.

Within this structure, the University offers sixty-six academic programs, leading to certification, associate, baccalaureate, masters and doctorate degrees.

The two Reserved Officers' Training Corps (ROTC) units of Army and Air Force provide students with another dimension for intellectual growth, service, and leadership development.

For incoming students, the University's College of Basic and Special Services offers hands-on assistance; the Earl Lester Cole Honors College offers advanced opportunities for academically talented students, and the Division of Continuing Education and Special Programs is designed to enhance the learning opportunities of non-traditional students.

In addition to its Distance Learning Program—the first in the state to offer a bachelor's degree—GSU operates two Mobile Automated Learning Labs (MALLs) that provide community and worksite access to individualized and computerized instruction and learning.

Located in the center of the campus is A. C. Lewis Memorial Library, a technology-rich facility with outstanding resource materials and research tools for its nearly six thousand students.

Through the years, the University has acquired the prestige and academic strength noted only among much larger institutions. From its distinction of being one of the country's top producers of African-American graduates, to being the home of legendary football coach Eddie Robinson, Sr., and its inter-nationally renowned Tiger Marching Band, Grambling State University has become a household name in this country and abroad.

During Robinson's stellar fifty-seven-year coaching career, the University gained a national reputation as being "the cradle of the pros" because of the large number of student-athletes who joined the professional ranks in football, basketball and baseball.

After Robinson's retirement in 1997, former GSU standout and NFL Super Bowl XXII MVP Doug Williams took over the reins of the University's football program. He has led the team to national and regional championships.

Additionally, the University holds the distinction of being the only Louisiana institution to bring a sitting U.S. president to its campus. The Honorable William "Bill" Jefferson Clinton was the featured speaker during commencement exercises held in May 1999. Nearly two years later, the Tiger Marching Band was the only Louisiana entity included in the inaugural parade for U.S. President George W. Bush.

Steeped in history and a tradition of excellence, Grambling State University continues to emphasize the value and importance of each student, exemplifying its motto: "The Place Where Everybody Is Somebody."

Above: Coaches Eddie Robinson (left) and Doug Williams.

Below: A computer lab on the campus of Grambling State University.

SOUTHEASTERN LOUISIANA UNIVERSITY

Above: With more than fourteen thousand students, Southeastern has become Louisiana's primary university for the north shore and the Florida Parishes. The University offers sixty-three degree programs in a wide range of areas.

Below: Following World War II, veterans–armed with the G.I. Bill for financial assistance–flooded Southeastern's campus. The G.I. Bill provided for tuition, educational expenses, and a monthly stipend for living expenses. For many of the veterans who had grown up during the Depression, the monthly stipend was more money than they had ever had.

The dream of a junior college, conceived in the early 1920s by prominent citizens led by Dr. Lucius McGehee and Linus A. Sims, evolved to become today's Southeastern Louisiana University, a high-tech center for higher education.

Voters in southern Tangipahoa Parish approved a one-mill tax to establish the institution. The school opened September 14, 1925, on the second floor of Hammond High School, to 40 students and 6 faculty members. Enrollment grew rapidly, and voters approved more bonds to buy fifteen acres with existing buildings that could be adapted to living and classroom space.

As the renamed Southeastern Louisiana College continued to grow, new facilities replaced those in which a student's foot went through the science lab ceiling and the football team dressed in a barn and showered with a garden hose. By 1935, Southeastern had 20 teachers and 340 students, a 71-acre campus, and modern buildings. WPA funding, matching money from the state, and continued support from taxpayers financed nine new buildings from 1938-40, prompting the student newspaper to comment that "The era of progress is upon us."

An all-time-high enrollment of 612 in 1940 plunged to 250 as the boys went to war, with 29 of them sacrificing their lives for their country. The end of the war brought veterans back to Southeastern on the G.I. Bill, and many government surplus buildings from Camp Claiborne were rebuilt on the campus to provide needed space.

During the 1950s integration was peacefully achieved, and Southeastern's first African American graduate received her degree. Another enrollment boom, a new graduate program, a School of Nursing, and the addition of twenty new buildings marked the 1960s, along with the era of "Roomie," Southeastern's live lion mascot.

Although long hair and peace signs were part of the scene in the 1970s, Southeastern saw few of the campus protests and violence that made headlines elsewhere. On July 16, 1970, Southeastern found a new identity, becoming Southeastern Louisiana University. Enrollment spiraled from 1985-95, when Southeastern became "the fastest growing university" in the country, with enrollment reaching over fifteen thousand. Higher education had gone high-tech, as the university used the Internet, satellite locations, and other tools to meet students' needs and lifestyles. Admission standards were implemented, and school/business partnerships, diversity, community service, and international partnerships for student and faculty study abroad all increased.

With its growth and change, Southeastern has become Louisiana's university for the Florida Parishes and the north shore.

Orleans Materials & Equipment Company, Inc.

Orleans Materials and Equipment Company, Inc., one of the Gulf South's oldest steel fabricators, has satisfied customers from power plants in Taiwan, to an observatory in Chile, to the Honolulu airport, and including bridges in Chicago, National Aeronautics and Space Administration buildings at Cape Canaveral, and structures throughout the Southeast. However, OMECO's humble beginnings date to 1930 when founder Nelson Hawkins borrowed $600 to open his new enterprise, concentrating on buying, selling and renting steel sheet pile products.

During World War II, OMECO fabricated 125-pound bombs and small military barges. At war's end, the company resumed fabrication of commercial and industrial steel structures, and entered the steel distribution market and began fabricating steel bridges.

By 1970 OMECO had expanded its service to the oil industry in steel distribution and steel processing. When that market declined, OMECO concentrated on filling needs for bridge building and ship construction.

Today, OMECO is certified by the American Institute of Steel Construction to fabricate major steel bridges and is also a member of the National Steel Bridge Alliance.

Located on the Industrial Canal in New Orleans, OMECO's plant includes computerized plate burning and punching equipment, plate rolls, 1000-ton press brakes, submerged arc welding, wheelabrator blasting machines and painting facilities. But, OMECO's greatest asset has always been the skill and dedication of its many loyal employees through the years.

Customers appreciate the quality with which orders are processed and delivered, because of OMECO's quality control at every step. From processing steel to assembly, welding, and shipment by truck, rail or barge, OMECO takes pride in efficiency and fast turn-around on orders.

✧

Above: OMECO can take pride in work on the ramps of the Crescent City Connection Bridge over the Mississippi River.

Below: The OMECO plant site on the Industrial Canal in New Orleans.

OMECO experience includes welded plate girders for bridges and offshore structure, structural steel for commercial buildings and industrial plants; and miscellaneous specialty items for water purification and treatment plants.

OMECO's trade secret is combining quality product with service, at a competitive price. With old-fashioned standards of hard work and dependability, OMECO meets customers' needs and completes every job with attention to detail. Whether it's providing a simple pipe column or a custom-made 120-foot-long bridge girder, OMECO maintains a commitment to excellence in product and efficiency in service.

Village of Collinston

✧

Above: Morehouse Parish Library - Collinston Branch and Business Complex.

Below: Reily Memorial United Methodist Church with white steeple and well-manicured lawn.

There was a lawless wilderness in Morehouse Parish's Ward Eight in the early 1800s. Back then it was called Gum Swamp. It was a vast expanse of bogs and bayous, thickly timbered, cluttered with heavy cane breaks and completely devoid of roads of any sort. A forbidding and treacherous place it was, not only for the difficult terrain but also for the constant danger from outlaws. People were left to provide for their own defense and the wise wayfarer carried his gun ready to use at a moments notice. Be that as it may, it was quite renown in its day for its excellent bear hunting opportunities.

The first to brave a settlement in this forbidding swamp were intrepid pioneers from East Feliciana Parish. They trekked into the bogs in 1850 and began to scratch out a living, shaping the land into rustic farms. Hope of relief from this hard life came in the late 1880s. A determined gentleman, Samuel P. Collins arrived to begin construction of the railroad. At that time it was known as Keller's Station. Travel in and out of the area was unpredictable at best. Often, in the winter months, the roads were simply impassable. Collins, undaunted by the difficult terrain, completed his task in the year 1890. To honor him, Keller's Station took his name and became Collins. The railroad was a boon to the inhabitants, allowing easier access to the area, opening it up to expansion. At last, it began to prosper and in 1894, Collins updated its name to Collinston. The Village of Collinston was officially incorporated on March 17, 1904.

Today, Collinston is a fine "picture-postcard" town replete with well-manicured lawns and churches with white steeples. High pine ridges bound her to the northwest and lush, productive fields of cotton, rice, soybeans and corn line the main road into town. And with a population of three hundred and sixty-five, everyone is truly everyone else's neighbor. And it shows! There is a real spirit of belonging here, perhaps inherited from her early inhabitants, those hardy pioneers that found they had to rely on one another for survival. This spirit manifests itself in most delightful ways. For instance, Collinston entered the Cleanest City Contest in 1982. The entire community turned out en masse, pitched in, and took first place in District and then went on to take State. Since that time, Collinston has entered some eighteen times, winning District sixteen times and State eleven. Wouldn't those hardy pioneers of yesterday be proud to see what their children have made of old 'Gum Swamp'?

Village of Bonita

✧

Top, left: Awaiting the ribbon cutting for the opening of the Village Museum, Saturday, May 25, 2002 are Eloise Means, town clerk for twenty-two years; Patsy Woodard; Mayor Mike Lytle; and Irma Coleman.

Above: David Hill Jr. is in his seventies and still working as maintenance supervisor for the Village of Bonita. In this picture, he is explaining how horses and mules were used to till the land.

Below: Billie Owens sits next to pictures of her parents, Dr. Melvin Williams Owens and Letha Ellen Marshall Owens during dedication of the Bonita Museum. The building was originally Dr. Owen's office, c. 1920.

It was a clear, cool fall day in the year 1890. The trees were just starting to lose their leaves to the approach of old man winter as the first of the people began to arrive. Some came by horse-drawn cart. Some arrived mounted on horseback. However they came, before long the cotton field of Fayette Causey was soon reverberating with their excitedly chattering voices. They were, for the most part, settlers of a nearby farm community known as Lind Grove. The occasion was nothing less than the opening up of their little corner of Northeast Louisiana to travel by railroad!

The boundary of what would one day be called Bonita is basically defined by a north bend in the scenic Bayou Bonne Idée. Settlement of this corner of Morehouse Parish began in 1857 with the completion of the Boyd Smith House. The high-arched roofline of this Victorian-style residence enclosed a spacious thirteen-room interior and was built by the Dawson Family.

More settlers followed, dotting the landscape with their farms so that there was a considerable number available to watch as the first train arrived on that crisp autumn day. It must have been indeed exciting to watch as it plied toward them, belching out a thick column of smoke, its whistle knifing through the still, quiet country air. There would have been much to talk about for it was rumored that the railroad tycoon, Jay Gould rode in his private car at the rear of the train. They wanted to get a glimpse of that. He was not the real VIP, though. They didn't realize it but it was actually the conductor who was about to decide what the name of their future town would be.

With its audience anxiously watching, the sleek iron horse screeched to a stop. Out popped the conductor who gazed across the lush, green countryside with frank appreciation of its beauty. On that day, the name was born, for the conductor had been given the task of christening all the stops along the rail. And, though the town would not be officially incorporated until December 1903, she still retains the name given her on that auspicious day by a simple conductor: Bonita, which is Spanish for "Beautiful."

Today Bonita continues to live up to her name. The verdant green fields and majestic stands of hardwood and pine adorn the banks of a beautiful Louisiana bayou, making it a highly desirable place to live. The friendly, hometown attitude of its inhabitants harks back to those simple, honest farmers that gathered in that cotton field so long ago to watch the first train arrive.

Looking to the future, Bonita is striving to diversify its economic base beyond agriculture. Recent efforts have included moving a historic cypress building next to City Hall. The building, which was the office of an early doctor in the area, will serve as the Village Museum.

The Village Museum will be one of the attractions to entice travelers to stop in Bonita. Another is the transformation underway to turn City Hall into a visitor's welcome center. Being the first incorporated municipality south of Arkansas, Bonita already serves as an unofficial welcome center.

Also underway is a feasibility study on a man-made lake in the Bonita area. The Village has secured the blessings of the Morehouse Parish, Police Jury, the Morehouse Economic Development Corporation (MEDCO), the Morehouse Tourism Commission, the Chamber of Commerce, the Federal Emergency Management Agency (FEMA), and private citizens in pursuing a mixed use lake.

Other development ideas that have been floated include a doll museum, a candy kitchen, a business incubator and a gourmet coffee shop.

Harold Callais

Although Harold Callais was born in the extreme southern part of Louisiana, his contributions will have a lasting influence on the entire state.

Recognizing the value of education early in his life, Callais worked his way through high school as a janitor, and college by tutoring athletes and working on a chicken farm. He wanted others to experience the opportunities a good education afforded him by becoming an important force in the public higher education system.

As a businessman with a degree in electrical engineering from then-Southwestern Louisiana Institute in Lafayette (now ULL), he expressed his sentiments in an interview in 1999: "It (education) did so much for me," he said. "I am the generation who went to college. My parents were not able to finish high school, but they had five children—Doris, Clara, Ronald, David, and myself—and we all went to college. It was a dramatic change for our family. I saw how much college did for me and how important it was for my life. I want to give the people of Louisiana those same opportunities."

Appointed in 1993 to the Louisiana State Board of Regents for Higher Education, the policy-making board for Louisiana's colleges and universities, Callais served a six-year term, two years as chairman.

"During his tenure he helped guide public higher education in Louisiana through major reforms that will benefit the people of Louisiana for generations," said Joseph Savoie, Louisiana's commissioner of higher education.

Dr. Donald Ayo, president of Nicholls State University in Thibodaux, said Callais had a positive impact on the school. He credited Callais with assisting the university with approval of many of its initiatives, including several building projects. And Callais was a driving force in helping to create new master's degree programs at NSU, Dr. Ayo said. He was also instrumental in the establishment of the John Folse Culinary Institute and the drive to bring the New Orleans Saints training camp to Nicholls. Over the years, Callais' contributions have been recognized with some of the school's highest honors and awards, including the NSU Alumni Corporate Mark of Honor in 1999.

Callais was serving his second term on the Board of Regents when he died in 2000 at the age of sixty-four.

Bayou Lafourche has been blessed with many gutsy men and women who for reasons of adventure, fortune or service defied the odds with their own vision and determination. It was apparent early on that Callais was destined to be one of the region's pioneers.

His humble beginnings in Golden Meadow mirrored the times: His hardworking parents, Abdon and Ada, trawled during the warm

✧

Above: A portrait of Harold Callais as Chairman of the Louisiana Board of Regents hangs in the lobby of the main office of Community Bank in Raceland.

Bottom: A Callais family wedding 1999.

months and trapped when it was cold to support their growing family. While helping to support the family when he was not in school, Harold also developed an interest in scouting.

Typical of the drive within him, Callais set his goals on achieving Eagle Scout, the highest level in the organization. He earned the honor, becoming the first in the area to do so. His achievement so impressed national leaders that he was invited to Valley Forge, Pennsylvania, to represent the best in scouting.

While his parents imparted the value of education to their children, financial reality limited the number of children who could attend college at one time. Callais worked with his father on the family trawl boat for 18 months after his high school graduation.

Upon graduation from SLI in 1959, he took a job with Chevron Oil Company in Leeville, working with electronics. Callais was intrigued by the electrical engineers he worked with, and decided that was the career path he would follow. He soon ventured into a business of his own, Mike Electronics, selling, installing and repairing radio equipment on the fishing vessels, which worked the nearby waters.

Callais never stopped learning. When he was not working, he was researching the newest trends. It was through engineering publications that he first learned of the birth of the cable television industry. Cable TV was so new that Ted Turner had not yet become a part of it and the city of New Orleans had yet to be exposed to extended channel viewing. (Callais later was in attendance at a cable meeting in Atlanta in 1975 when Turner announced his intentions to begin the Turner Broadcasting Station.)

"We put our first customers on in April 1969," Callais said in the 1999 interview. "That was before satellites."

With less than 200 customers, Callais Cablevision was born. He built in phases, eventually offering the service to residents in the southern and central part of Lafourche Parish and Grand Isle in Jefferson Parish. In 2002 over 12,000 digital-ready customers are offered up to 200 channels.

With the New Orleans and Baton Rouge broadcast channels available to customers clearer than what home antennas or 'rabbit ears' could receive, Callais developed another incentive for residents to sign up: a local channel where he could showcase local talent and draw viewers in with audience participation. He partnered with a local supermarket owner to host a weekly bingo game. He encouraged adults and teens to show up at the studio for a weekly dance session, with music provided by local artists who eventually went on to prominence.

A weekly phone-in auction promoted local merchants, showcasing their products and services. Throughout his life, Callais encouraged community support of locally owned

Above: Harold Callais was one of the first in the region to achieve Eagle Scout status.

Below: Harold Callais opened Harold's Appliance and Hardware in 1961, followed by Mike Electronics, which led to the establishment of Callais Cablevision in 1968.

businesses. Local nonprofit groups continue to use the station, at no charge, to promote their events and fundraisers. Callais' local origination cable station also provides services to local residents, offering election coverage, hurricane information and cable override for emergency warnings. CCTV-5 airs the annual Cerebral Palsy Telethon, which has raised over $1 million for the cause through the years.

Near and dear to Callais' heart was the preservation of his Cajun heritage and the local channel, CCTV-5, offered an opportunity to further that cause. He brought in Cajun French-speaking locals to do the programs. Cajun French was the only language Callais knew until he was taught a second language, English, in grade school.

He bought the Cajun music-centered KLEB radio station in Golden Meadow for the same reason and maintained the local format. He later bought 94.3 FM, now WTIX in New Orleans.

The local chamber of commerce honored him with a "Pioneer of the Year" award in 1986, and he was recognized as the top "Small Business Person for Congressional District Three" in 1987. In 1996 the National Cable TV Cooperative, Inc named Callais "Cablevision Member of the Year." Callais also served as president of the Louisiana Cable Operators Association in the 1970s and also held other offices.

Callais' father, Abdon, was a local pioneer who converted his shrimp-trawling vessel to one, which could service the burgeoning oil and gas industry. Slowly, from 1945 on, his participation in the exploration for energy resources increased, building and buying boats. Abdon Callais Boat Rentals (now Abdon Callais Offshore) weathered the cyclical nature of the business, particularly in the late 1950s when oil was discovered in the Middle East and it seemed that the activity in the Gulf of Mexico would never rebound.

Abdon built the Lady Ada in 1962 when oil and gas exploration activity resumed, a tribute to his wife who not only raised their children while he was gone for weeks at a time, but who also worked as the company's bookkeeper in their home. Callais learned the business along side his father, and eventually became the sole owner.

Callais, too, had to weather the up and down nature of the boat business. The company reached its lowest point in the late 1980s, with only three boats in the fleet. It was a gamble to invest any further money into a business, which seemed to offer little future hope. Callais studied the industry and decided to build and purchase state-of-the-art boats, a risky move in uncertain times. His decision to move aggressively in the mid-1990s resulted in a fleet ready to service the upturn in exploration and the company was poised to react to increased activity. ACO today offers a fleet of over 30 diverse vessels, able to meet the needs of the industry today and tomorrow.

✧

Above: Recipient of the Congressional District VI SBA Award in 1987-Harold Callais and Callais Cablevision. Presented by Govenor Edwin Edwards.

Below: One of the lucky bingo winners on CCTV5. Check presentation by Dudley Bernard and Harold Callais. Bernard, a Cajun music legend, also performed live for the weekly dances, which aired on the cable channel.

✧

Harold Callais on a pilgrimage in Jerusaleum in 1991.

The same perseverance and dedication to his goals opened other doors for Callais. When a contractor defaulted on a solid waste disposal contract in Lafourche, the parish was divided into four segments, and Callais bid on servicing the southern portion. The successful bid enabled him to purchase three trucks and hire 11 employees to provide the service, and Solid Waste Disposal, Inc. was born in 1978. Today, the company has grown to over 185 employees servicing 75,000 residents in Lafourche and Terrebonne Parish, the City of Thibodaux and the Town of Grand Isle in Jefferson Parish. The company also provides disposal service in seven parishes to over 1500 commercial customers, ranging from Fortune 500 companies to small, mom-and- pop operations.

SWDI, that SweeDIee Company, is now the largest independent solid waste contractor in Louisiana, with a 69 ranking on Waste Age magazine's Top 100 companies in the world.

On March 7, 1979, Callais purchased four percent of the outstanding shares of Community Bank and became a director of the two-office bank. He eventually became chairman of the board and majority stockholder. Under his leadership and guidance, new offices were opened in Larose, Lockport, Golden Meadow, Napoleonville and Laplace, and additional branches opened in Thibodaux and Raceland. He was also instrumental in revitalizing and fostering the growth of banks in Welsh, Columbia and Gonzales, retaining the local identity of each institution.

Callais' business acumen and success has resulted in regional and national recognition for his companies through the years, including the Congressional District VI SBA award for Small Business in 1987 for Callais Cablevision; the same award for SWDI in 1999; Inc. 500's award to ACO in 1997, 1998, 1999, and 2001 for the nation's fastest growing businesses; and the Ernst and Young Entrepreneur Regional (Louisiana and Mississippi) Award to ACO in 1999, among many others.

The extent of Callais' philanthropy is known by only a chosen few, but he left his mark on the community he so loved with major contributions to agencies which could help the less fortunate. Religious organizations and civic and social groups also benefitted from his generosity. While he donated his time to advancing higher education in the state, he contributed financially to its success as well.

Harold Callais was a quiet, unassuming man, who used his God-given talent to anticipate the future, weigh the risks and invest wisely. His business acumen will be remembered for years to come in the community, which greatly benefited from his involvement and contributions.

Callais' life would have been incomplete without his beloved wife, Gloria Bienvenu Callais, his four sons, Michael, Corey, Peter and Paul, and his grandchildren, whom he loved to entertain with trips in his motor home to Disney World, skiing, and other exciting places.

Callais loved to travel; yet for all of his travels, for all of his pilgrimages, he remained rooted in Golden Meadow, near his family and among the people to whom he was so devoted.

In his later years, he discovered diving, a sport and a pastime which he shared with his sons.

"It's a wonderful feeling and a different world," Callais said of scuba diving. "God made a lot of beautiful things, and most of them are underwater." That's where Harold Callais died.

AMDG

The Castagnos Family

✧

Above: Castagnos Cane Loaders being shipped down Bayou Lafourche near Donaldsonville.

COURTESY OF ARTHUR LEMANN.

Below: Castagnos Cane Loader in early stage of production.

COURTESY OF PAUL MILANO.

Joseph Benjamin Castagnos came to Louisiana from France in 1889. He was a small man by today's standards and stood only five feet four inches in height. But Castagnos was a man with big dreams, and his invention of a cane loader would bring great changes to sugarcane growers.

Born in Mirande Defarment, France, on October 16, 1864, he emigrated from Lyon aboard the vessel *Marseilles* in December of 1889. He moved to Port Barrow, near Donaldsonville, with his father Dr. Pierre Jacques Castagnos, a veterinarian and a blacksmith, and his mother, Jeanne Couloumet. Other family members from France joined them in the area.

Castagnos married a native of Smoke Bend, Louisiana, Laura Martha Richard. They raised a family of four: Blanche, Edmund, Leonce, and Lee. Descendants of Leonce still live in Donaldsonville.

While today's Louisiana sugarcane industry continues to provide meaningful economic contributions, it was "the Industry" in the early 1900's. In those early years, sugarcane was loaded by field hands onto wagons, which then transported it to sugar refineries. It was slow, heavy, dirty work. Joseph, a man full of ideas, decided that there had to be a better way to harvest the area's labor-intensive crop. On July 22, 1908, he applied for a patent for a "new and useful improvement in automatic grab or grapple." With this grab, and a cart of lightweight design that didn't bog down in muddy fields, the cane loader became a sweet success. While other attempts at mechanical devices were made, in the end, they were too heavy and of no use in the mud.

Joseph's loaders were soon equipped with Fairbanks-Morse engines, a large, slow turning eight-horsepower engine with big flywheels. This was coupled by a chain drive to a draw-works mechanism, which would lift the load, hold it in place, and open and close the grab. Old-timers today still talk about the barking sound the engine made when lifting the load of cane.

Joseph had no money to manufacture his "dream machine" himself, but he soon found a financial backer in New Orleans. In October of 1908, he assigned the patent rights to Castagnos Cane Loader Company Limited for the sum of $5. He retained forty-nine percent of the company.

Joseph traveled widely, marketing his invention. Sales extended to South America, Cuba, and other sugar growing regions. Through the years many improvements were made and today, a Louisiana company, Cameco Industries, manufactures a loader that stands nearly two stories high, sits on four wheels that are over six feet high, and has an air-conditioned cab for the operator.

All of his descendants are proud of the contribution this invention made to the economy and lifestyle of South Louisiana.

Kalorama Nature Preserve

"The purpose of Kalorama is to conserve and preserve our natural heritage and to provide a protected area for all who come to enjoy, study, and learn." This is the mission statement of Kalorama.

Kalorama's unique geographical features and a long history of benevolent landowners dedicated to preserving its special qualities have helped create an outstanding example for gardeners who wish to garden lightly upon the land in this new millennium. Mr. and Mrs. William B. Reily bought the thirty-eight acres on the Bastrop Ridge above Collinston in 1927. They had searched extensively across the south for a location to build a country summer home as a retreat from their New Orleans home. William Reily wrote enthusiastically in his journal at that time of the beauty of the property, the large trees, and wide variety of plants and songbirds.

In the early 1950s, Mr. and Mrs. Nathan Bolton purchased the property as a permanent home. Nathan Bolton was an enthusiastic gardener and plant collector. He worked with daylilies extensively, creating new varieties and using them in the landscape, and lecturing on his work, as well. He also had a keen interest in bulbs of all sorts, hollies, and camellias. Visitors enjoy the fruits of his labors as each season passes.

In 1992 the William B. Reily Foundation purchased the property from Mr. and Mrs. A. Earl Ingram, Sr., to create a nature preserve in memory of Mr. and Mrs. Reily. The property is now owned and managed by the Kalorama Foundation, and is now available for public viewing.

Visitors to Kalorama enjoy the wildlife and the landscape as it changes throughout the seasons. Many of the plant species and varieties that were common in landscapes of previous generations are present. There are old species-type narcissus blooming in early spring, and the show of flowers in their various habitats continues until the season ends with a glorious explosion of color in late fall. The abundance of birds and butterflies that are present only enhances the experience.

Touring Kalorama offers a glimpse into the past. A walk through the peaceful ancient forest reminds us how important our actions are in our allotted time. The abundance of insect, bird, and animal life offers strong evidence of the importance of preserving habitat, and gardening with, not against, nature.

Located at 7197 Collinston Road–Louisiana Highway 593 in Collinston, Louisiana between Bastrop and Collinston: Kalorama is open to the public for tours on spring weekends between February 15 and May 15 and fall weekends between October 1 and November 15. It is open on any date of the year by appointment for tours or other nature study. All tours are guided and vary in length. To learn more about Kalorama, please contact Beth Erwin, curator, at 318-874-7777 or email to kalorama@kalorama.org. Hours are 9 to 5 Saturdays, 1:30 to 5 Sundays, weather permitting. Admission is $5 per person. Friends Group members are admitted at no charge.

The flora and fauna of Kalorama Nature Preserve (clockwise from top, left): a Yellow-breasted Chat, Prairie Coneflower, Indian Pink, and a Zebra Swallowtail.

INDEX